Unwrapping Japan

Edited by Eyal Ben-Ari, Brian Moeran and James Valentine

Unwrapping Japan

Society and culture in anthropological perspective

UNIVERSITY OF HAWAII PRESS
HONOLULU

© 1990 Manchester University Press

Published in North America by
University of Hawaii Press
2840 Kolowalu Street
Honolulu, Hawaii 96822

Published in the United Kingdom by
Manchester University Press
Oxford Road
Manchester, M13 9PL
England

Printed in England on long-life paper

Library of Congress Cataloging-in-Publication Data
Unwrapping Japan/edited by Eyal Ben-Ari, Brian Moeran, James Valentine.
   p.   cm.
Includes bibliographies and index.
Contents: Introduction: rapt discourses: anthropology, Japanism, and
Japan/Brian Moeran — Humidity, hygiene, or ritual care: some thoughts
on wrapping as a social phenomenon/Joy Hendry — On the borderlines:
the significance of marginality in Japanese society/James Valentine — The
feminine in Japanese folk religion/Teigo Yoshida — Intelligent elegance:
women in Japanese advertising/Keiko Tanaka — Tourism and the ama: the
search for a real Japan/Lola Martinez — Making an exhibition of oneself:
the anthropologist as potter in Japan/Brian Moeran — Many voices,
partial worlds: on some conventions and innovations in the ethnographic
portrayal of Japan/Eyal Ben-Ari — Deconstructing an anthropological
text: a moving account of returnee schoolchildren in contemporary
Japan/Roger Goodman — Sea tenure and the Japanese experience: resource
management in coastal fisheries/Arne Kalland — Festival management and
the corporate analysis of Japanese society/Michael Ashkenazi — Wrapping-
up: some general implications suggested by the essays/Eyal Ben-Ari.
ISBN-8248-1050-3 : $34.00
1. National characteristics, Japanese, 2. Ethnology—Methodology.
3. Ethnology—Japan. 4. Japan—Study and teaching—Japan. I. Ben-Ari,
Eyal, 1953- II. Moeran, Brian. III. Valentine, James, 1948-.
DS830.U58   1990
952—dc20
89-35666
CIP

Contents

Contents

Acknowledgements

This volume owes its origin to the third meeting of the Japan Anthropology Workshop (or JAWS as it has affectionately come to be called) which was held during April 1987 in Jerusalem. Financial aid for the JAWS meeting was given by a number of institutions: The Harry S. Truman Research Institute for the Advancement of Peace, The Hebrew University, The Israel Academy of Sciences and Humanities, and the Japan Foundation, (the last of which helped one of our Japanese participants to wing his way to Israel). The Truman Institute – through the good offices of its chairman Professor Ben-Ami Shillony – also extended financial help during the preparation of the book.

Of no less importance was the excellent organisational help that was warmly extended both during and after the conference. In this respect the following people are owed a special word of thanks: Nechama Cohen, Miriam Frank, Annette Mishali, Jenny Nelson and Dalia Shemer.

The editors would like to thank all participants in the Jerusalem conference for their patience and forbearance during the two years and more that it has taken to get this book to print. They wish also to extend their gratitude to John Banks of Manchester University Press for his interest and support, to Joy Hendry, secretary of JAWS, for constant encouragement, and to an anonymous reviewer for her or his careful reading of the papers and excellent advice about how to improve them and the volume as a whole.

Contributors

Dr *Michael Ashkenazi*
  Department of Behavioral Sciences
  Ben Gurion University
  P.O. Box 653
  Beersheva 84105
  Israel

Dr *Eyal Ben-Ari*
  The Truman Institute
  The Hebrew University
  Mt Scopus
  Jerusalem 91905
  Israel

Dr *Roger Goodman*
  Contemporary Japan Centre
  University of Essex
  Wivenhoe Park
  Colchester CO4 3SQ, UK

Dr *Joy Hendry*
  Scottish Centre for Japanese Studies
  University of Stirling
  Stirling FK9 4LA, UK

Dr *Arne Kalland*
  Nordic Institute of Asian Studies
  84 Njalsgade
  DK-2300 Copenhagen S
  Denmark

Dr *D. P. Martinez*
  Department of Anthropology
  School of Oriental and African Studies
  University of London
  Thornhaugh Street, Russell Square
  London WC1H 0XG, UK

Professor *Brian Moeran*
  Department of the Far East
  School of Oriental and African Studies
  University of London
  Thornhaugh Street, Russell Square
  London WC1H 0XG, UK

Dr *Keiko Tanaka*
  Centre for Japanese Studies
  University of Wales College of Cardiff
  10 North Road
  Cardiff CF1 3DY, UK

Dr *James Valentine*
  Department of Sociology
  University of Stirling
  Stirling FK9 4LA, UK

Professor *Teigo Yoshida*
  University of the Sacred Heart
  Hiro 4-chome 3–1
  Shibuya-ku
  Tokyo, Japan

Brian Moeran

Introduction: Rapt discourses: anthropology, Japanism and Japan

> Experience across cultures, like communication across languages, is neither unique nor universal. Its advantage lies rather in the sense of exaggeration it ensures.
>
> (Boon 1982:26)

Japanism as discourse

Given the characteristic Western attitude that Japan is a land of mystery, veiled as the cherry-blossomed slopes of Yoshino in spring,[1] the title of this book is somewhat optimistic. Is it really possible to *unwrap* Japan? Already, one hears the cynic thump down on the table of history the voluminous tomes that have been written over the past century, purporting to do precisely this. From Norman's *The Real Japan* (1892) to Buruma's *Behind the Mask* (1984), we have been bombarded with a succession of metaphors, of which *wrapping* would appear to be but one more. What, anyway, do we mean by *Japan*? It seems that the more that is written about this culture, society, country, people, the more orientalised and exoticised they all become. In short, we find ourselves entangled in pure *Japanism*.

And what is 'Japanism'? Here I shall borrow Said's definition of Orientalism (1979:1), and speak of Japanism as a way of coming to terms with Japan that is based on Japan's place in Western European and American experience. Japanism is a mode of discourse, a body of knowledge, a political vision of reality that represents an integral part of Western *material* civilisation both culturally and ideologically, with supporting institutions, vocabulary, scholarship, imagery and doctrines. Thus, in talking of Japanism in this century, we are referring to a Western academic tradition, a style of thought, and a corporate institution designed to dominate, restructure and have authority over Japan (*ibid.*, pp. 2–3). What is interesting is that this tradition has now been taken over by the Japanese themselves as they, for their part, attempt to set themselves apart from, restructure, and thus gain authority over, 'the West' through what is known as *nihonjinron* ('discussions of the Japanese'). In other words, Japanism exerts a three-way force – on Japan itself, on Japanists (or 'Japanologists'), and on Western consumers of Japanism. The process of *Japanisation* 'not only marks Japan as the province of the Japanist but also forces the uninitiated Western reader to accept Japanist codifications ... as the *true* Japan. Truth, in short, becomes a function of learned judgement, not of the material itself, which in time seems to owe even its existence to the Japanist' (*cf.* Said 1979:67).

The essays presented here are no more than what this word implies: *attempts* by a group of young, mainly European, anthropologists (with a little help from a couple of Japanese scholars) to divest Japan of some of the multiple layers of wrapping in which Japanism has over the years encased it. The basic premiss is that wrapping is 'an important and pervasive ordering principle' (Hendry, Chap. 2)) among the Japanese, whether they are wrapping their bodies in twelve layers of clothing, their conversation with politeness formulae, their priceless pots with wooden boxes, or even five eggs with straw.

Given that the Japanese themselves are sometimes confused by this wrapping, it may be that in some of these essays, we, too, have mistaken yet another layer of exquisitely decorated wrapping for the 'real Japan'. After all, we share with the Japanese an economic system in which not only does 'the beautifully designed surface of the commodity become its package', but that surface becomes detached from the commodity which 'develops and changes its countenance, like the fairytale princess who is transformed through her feathered costume' (Haug 1986:50). Thus, in the study of Japanese society and culture, the wrapping itself, or the *form* in which something is wrapped, very often takes on greater outward significance than the *content* thereof – witness the pottery critic or collector who pays more attention to the value of the box as *provenance* than to the work of art itself (Moeran, Chap. 7). By focusing on the *processes* rather than the forms of wrapping, these essays exemplify in various ways the problems involved in the procedures of unwrapping Japanese society. In short, they attempt to deal with Japanism itself – a point made by Ben-Ari when he 'wraps up' this book in an essay which some readers may find it useful to read at once.

Wrapped discourse

It is our contention that the notion of 'wrapping' is a discourse on and by the Japanese. As such, it becomes a pun on those forms of talk – the dozens, signifying, joning, or woofing – practised by Black Americans in the streets of New York, Chicago, Washington, or Philadelphia respectively (Labov 1972). 'Wrapping', in short, is no more than 'rapping', whereby the Japanese indulge in 'national mythmaking', creating and defining their concept of what it means to be 'Japanese', in the same way that men in a Washington ghetto, with their 'streetcorner mythmaking', create and define their concept of masculinity. In both cases, those concerned are careful not to state the principle, simply to imply it (Hannerz 1969: 115), although they may well create a multi-layered set of implications that then invite careful disentangling.

Clearly, by participating in this discourse, we have entered a game of persuasion: that our view of Japan is sufficiently different to warrant the attention of those who patrol the ghettos of both Japanism (or 'Japanology') and anthropology. What justification is there for such rhetoric? In the first place, there is a widespread feeling within this second generation of Japan's anthropologists that our masters were not always as perfect as their scholarly wrapping suggests. Some of them, of course, never bothered to learn Japanese properly. Others revealed remarkable lapses of concentration, or theoretical blindness (as Kalland's study of sea tenure delicately implies about a 'classic' work on a Japanese fishing village, Norbeck 1954). Most failed to consider Japan in comparative light. We have, as a result, suffered from a seeming obsession for detail and a curiously myopic view of general anthropological theories.

Boon is probably right when he suggests that 'perhaps anthropology in any society necessarily produces only what that society's internal conditions require it to conceptualize as *other than* itself' (1982: 6). In this instance, the 'very nature' of Japanese society (as created by both Westerners and Japanese) has invited those studying it to form their own 'unique' closed-in social cliques, and the result of most Japanists' refusal to see beyond the Inland Sea has been to make their work apparently irrelevant to anthropology in general. It is probably a sense of exasper-

3

Brian Moeran

ation rather than anything else, then, which has encouraged some anthropologists – whose ethnographic specialisation is anywhere but Japan, and whose knowledge of Japanese is, to say the least, limited – to enter what is clearly a rich and rewarding field for anthropologists and their ilk. Such forays, when conducted in the comparative safety of a Parisian library (Levi-Strauss 1985), can be worthy indeed. Others, involving the processing of observations made during a brief stay in Japan (Barthes 1982), tend to evince occasional flashes of welcome illumination, but more generally pangs of regret.

The problem that both groups face, then, is an old one: should Japanists be 'particularists' who wrap themselves up in Japanese society and culture until only their faces are left to reveal that they are, in fact, occidentals in disguise? Or can anthropologists be 'generalists', brazenly applying the same (Western-biased) set of theoretical concepts to different cultural situations (a problem bravely faced by Ashkenazi, Chap. 11)? In this context it is interesting to note that it is the historians and sociologists, rather than anthropologists, who have so far used Japan as a case for comparative generalisations (for example, Moore 1966; Bendix 1969; Dore 1973). It may be that anthropologists have in fact implied a comparison underneath an apparent lack thereof, but when they have made explicit comparisons, they have generally done so at 'the margins' of their monographs (for example, Rohlen 1974, 1983). Yet, nowadays, most 'post-modern' practitioners of anthropology – to use the fashionable parlance – appear to be shifting towards the 'particularist' pole of the continuum of intellectual fashion. It is perhaps ironic, therefore, that at the same time those whose work is presented in this volume should finally be emerging from their Japanist shells and be calling for general comparison.

It is, however, a comparison with a difference. The demand that is being made is not so much: what do Western anthropological theories tell us about Japan? But, what contribution can theories derived from the study of Japanese society make towards anthropology as a whole?[2]

One of these, it is claimed, is the principle of 'wrapping' itself. This metaphor is not new. Indeed, it is dangerously close to classical forms of Japanism:

In every gesture of daily life, in the style of conversation, in the proper form of giving a present, the main concern, it seems, is how to wrap up things, ideas, feelings. Wherever Japanese life is not governed by this law of laws behaviour it is in constant danger of becoming arbitrary and uncouth, crude and repulsive. It is as if the Japanese, not content

4

with living in a mountainous archipelago all too often visited by mists and clouds and rainstorms, had attempted, from the very beginnings of their civilisation, to reproduce in their social and cultural life an intensified image of their natural surroundings – an interior scenery veiled in vapour, divided into small compartments by mountain ranges, bays, and seas. Wherever they go they make a network of walls and fences behind which to retire: unwritten rules, ceremonies and taboos.   (Singer 1973: 45)

Although Hendry takes up some of the ideas originally put forward by Singer (architecture, ceremony, language), she attempts to eschew the kind of Japanist view he epitomises by arguing that 'wrapping' can be applied both to the theory of 'self-presentation' put forward by Goffman (1971), and to transactional analysis, as well as to sociolinguistic theories of code switching. At the same time she suggests that it might offer 'scope for an all-encompassing theoretical framework'. One might add here, perhaps, that such a framework would include the variety of mechanisms which any society uses to wrap itself attractively for presentation to other societies.[3]

The 'wrapping' theme lies at the heart of a number of other papers in this volume, and gives rise to a second theoretical premiss that is not new to anthropology, but which, in its present state of 'deconstruction', needs to be taken seriously to heart. This premiss concerns the nature of theoretical or cultural 'absolutism'. Goodman shows how, during the course of writing up his fieldwork, he found himself developing a number of different intellectual approaches in order to explain to his satisfaction the significance of Japan's returnee schoolchildren. As he went through his data, he first adopted the viewpoint of mainstream society, then that of the returnees themselves, before finally realising that there was a variety of role models and positions for returnee schoolchildren who constituted an important element in Japan's internal cultural debate.

This demand for multiple approaches is also echoed by Ben-Ari in his discussion of ethnographic writing as a 'literary' genre (Chap. 8). Yoshida (Chap. 4), for his part, conducts a detailed examination of the way in which Japanese women are seen as ritually polluted or sacred priestesses, depending on which part of the mainland, Shikoku, Kyushu, or the south-western archipelago they inhabit. He then concludes – *contra* Douglas (1970) – that notions of purity and pollution are blurred, since they depend upon context. Yet even the proposition of cultural particularism may not be accepted as an absolute: thus Valentine (Chap. 3), while recognising the general situational relativism propounded by those explaining Japanese culture, argues that certain marginals and outsiders are 'absolutely defined as below the mainstream, and excluded from its particular hierarchies'.

The rejection of theoretical absolutism, and of a single model of Japanese society, recognises that any characterisation of Japan will inevitably be partial, requiring supplementation from other angles. This call for what is almost a 'cubist' approach to Japanese anthropology is not entirely new. Almost all recent theoretically inclined works in the social sciences dealing with Japan have been arguing against the old image of Japanese society as 'group-oriented', 'harmonious', 'homogeneous', 'unique', and so on. Rightly judging the old interpretations to be ruled by ideology, they have posited alternative visions that focus on 'individual' rather than 'group' (e.g. Befu 1980), or 'conflict' rather than 'harmony' (Krauss et al. 1984), in an attempt to come to grips with Japan as it 'really' is. Yet the proponents of these alternative visions have been careful to point out that the old models cannot be ignored and must be taken in conjunction with the new (see also Ashkenazi). The contributors to this volume, therefore, by moving from a Western preference for dichotomies to a more Japanese-like pluralism, merely reinforce an already existing trend in Japanese anthropology. One has to admit, however – and it is a point to which we shall later return – that the new paradigms may well be merely mirrored reflections of the Japanist image, and hence determined by it.

Three further general theoretical issues that have arisen from other contributors' studies of Japan include, first, indigenous concepts of fishing rights and resource management in a highly regulated 'closed sea'. As Kalland (Chap. 10) points out, the Japanese experience is highly relevant to the construction of theories and models of sea tenure systems by maritime anthropologists. By suggesting the need for a more holistic approach to such systems in order to understand how both Western and indigenous elements may conserve a given sector of society, Kalland adopts a similar theoretical position to that taken by Lock (1980) and Reynolds (1980). Each of these works is an example of 'applied anthropology', designed to bring about a reconceptualisation of the general theoretical approaches to sea tenure, medicine and psycho-therapy respectively. That applied anthropology thus has both ethical and moral implications is to be seen in Goodman's personal account of writing up his fieldwork data (Chap. 9). 'Facts' are never innocent.

Secondly, on the basis of his own experience as a potter holding a one-man exhibition in a Fukuoka department store, Moeran takes issue with the Marxist approach to art. By adopting the tripartite distinction between aesthetic, commodity, and social values made by participants in the Japanese art world, he is able to extend the simplistic dichotomy between 'use' and 'exchange' values frequently adopted by Marxist scholars, and show how 'art' comes to be defined by a complex amalgam of critical ideals, marketing techniques and personal connections.

Finally, Ben-Ari – 'rapping' on a paper originally delivered at the JAWS Jerusalem conference (Moeran 1989a) – analyses the use of indigenous literary genres, styles and forms in ethnographic writing from Japan, and shows how three authors have made use of Japanese literary aesthetics to construct their monographs. The recent attempt by Geertz (1988) to place anthropology in the realm of literature is thus given a nudge in a new and intriguing direction, whose possibility is only vaguely hinted at by Clifford (1986: 19) and others in their work on 'writing culture'. Anthropologists are asked – where appropriate – at least to consider, and preferably to incorporate, indigenous literary genres in their writing as a means towards furthering their understanding of the cultures they study.

The discourse of language

The game of persuasion outlined above has been one in which we, mere *maegashira*, lower-ranking *sumō* wrestlers, have dared to pit ourselves against formidable *yokozuna*, grand champions – Japanists and anthropologists. This bout is refereed by the most venerable *gyōji* (umpire) of all, Japan, clad in silken robes with tassels, ceremonial cap, and open fan (which some might innocently mistake for a ping-pong bat). Shouting encouragement all the while, Japan observes our struggle and – ever ready to pronounce its verdict – judges whether we deserve applauded victory, or the humiliating sands of defeat.

We participate, then, in a second round of persuasive discourse held in the hall of Japanism – this time with Japan itself. Here the wrestling is primarily with language. As several works testify – sometimes testily (Miller 1982; Dale 1986) – language in Japanese society plays a major role in the definition of what it means to be 'Japanese'.[4] Take Hendry's discussion of honorifics, for example. One major question raised is the extent to which the use of honorific language may be breaking down in contemporary Japanese society, thereby signalling – to some – a corresponding 'breakdown' of traditional social mores. Is this true? Seemingly so. It is clear that young people in Japan these days do have trouble getting their usage correct, and that young girls entering companies as receptionists or telephone operators are obliged to spend some time training in order to perfect their honorific language to their employers' satisfaction. But it is also clear that complaints made by the older generation (or employers) about young people's (or employees') use of honorifics is by no means new. One suspects that this kind of linguistic niggling has been going on for *decades* – even *centuries*, if Sei Shōnagon (b.AD 965) is anything to go by. After all, under her list of 'hateful things', we find:

> Sometimes I am quite disgusted at noting how little decorum people observe when talking to each other. It is particularly unpleasant to hear some foolish man or woman omit the proper marks of respect when addressing a person of quality; and, when servants fail to use the honorific forms of speech in referring to their masters, it is very bad indeed. No less odious, however, are those masters who, in addressing their servants, use such phrases as 'When you were good enough to do such-and-such' or 'As you so kindly remarked'. No doubt there are some masters who, in describing their own actions to a servant, say 'I presumed to do so-and-so'! (Morris 1970: 47–8)

In other words, just as the search on the part of English writers and critics for a sense of 'organic community' appears to be never-ending back through time (Williams 1961: 252–3), so the 'proper' use of honorifics in Japan would appear never to have existed at all.[5]

This search, like that for such lost causes as 'community', may well be intensified by, if not result from, the characteristically industrialist, or urban, nostalgia that pervades much of contemporary Japan (Martinez, Chap. 6; see also Moeran 1984a: 223–30). But it is also very much part of an ongoing discourse in which the old do their utmost to maintain their authority over a younger generation, by 'wrapping' them with complicated forms of language. This power game might also be phrased in terms of a conflict between (capitalist) employers and (worker) employees, but it also affects women who tend – except, perhaps, on the tennis court (Hendry) – to be enveloped in politeness forms (Trudgill 1971). The fact that in Japan the old are generally both men and managers, if not employers, tends to reinforce this particular form of language use as one of single Power, rather than plural *powers* (*cf.* Hobart 1986: 19, fn 25).[6]

Of course honorifics, like pronouns, as Hendry points out, may imply solidarity as well as power (Brown and Gilman 1960), which is why we need to be careful about the view that they express *only* hierarchical relations.[7] It is clear that in reference, as opposed to address, they assert the solidarity of the in-group *vis-à-vis* an outsider (Martin 1964), rather than seniority within the group. This is just one example of the various means by which the Japanese divide the everyday world into covert and overt groups of 'we' and 'none-we', male and female, high social status and low (Miller 1971; see also Hendry 1985, 1988).

Eventually, however, such dichotomising ends up with an opposition between 'Japanese' and 'non-Japanese'. And that, of course, brings us back to the initial problem of Japanism. Like Orientalism, Japanism as a profession has grown out of such opposites, establishing sets of attributes which are often applied not only to Japan, but to the Orient in general. Homogeneity, irrationality, mystery, fatalism, harmony, an organic society – all serve to set Japan and the Japanese apart. What is interesting is that the Japanese themselves not only actively participate in this general 'topsy turvydom' (Singer 1973: 90); they practise it on the West.[8] The Japanese perceive 'the West' in large collective terms or in abstract generalities, in just the same way that Orientalists refuse to conceive of humanity as consisting of individuals (Said 1979: 154–5). They now see an absolute and systematic difference between Japan, which has its own rationality, morality, systems of democracy, economy and art, all of them superior, and the West, which is over-rational, amoral, too individualistic for the good of society, and hence inferior. They prefer abstractions about the West to direct evidence, and ignore particular details that would contradict such abstractions. They see the West as at bottom something to be feared (*yabanjin*, barbarians; *ketō*, 'red-haired devils') or to be dominated (by the arts, trade, the establishment of factories that occupy and convert foreign workers to the 'Japanese way'). Thus, they practise in reverse most of the principal dogmas of Orientalism (Said 1979: 300–1), and show that they *can* indeed imitate the Japanist. This reverse Orientalism is now a force so strong that it can persuade its own citizens, for example, to regard *ama* divers as epitomising the same fecundity, sexual promise, untiring sensuality and unlimited desire (Martinez) that is seen by Westerners to characterise the Orient as a whole (Said 1979: 188).

Of course, in order to establish a discourse of what it means to be 'Japanese' within Japan, people need to create an effective vocabulary. The question here is: who is responsible for the articulation of that vocabulary? All kinds of people are, of course, involved. Travel brochures, for example, draw up a neat distinction between urban and rural

Brian Moeran

societies (Moeran 1983), and entice tens of thousands of people to visit small communities that thrive on nostalgia (Martinez; see also Kelly 1985). In the meantime, back in the modern urban localities of Japan from which such tourists come, traditions are invented (Bestor 1985) and new terms like *komyuniti* are debated (Nussbaum 1985; Ben-Ari 1986). The language of advertising, discussed by Tanaka (Chap. 5), is another good example of the way in which a particular vocabulary (centring on such words as 'feminist', 'intelligent' and 'individualism') keeps one group of people – in this case, women – firmly in its place. At the same time, in that 'stupidity' is often linked with country people and 'intelligence' with city culture, it could be argued that advertising here serves merely to maintain the rural/urban dichotomy (Moeran 1989b: 138–40).

This 'internal cultural debate' (Parkin 1978; Moeran 1984b) is extended by Goodman is his discussion of returnee schoolchildren and the demand, from both within and outside, for Japan to 'internationalise'. The discourse now focuses on the difference between 'traditional' Japanese values of conformity, loyalty, harmony and homogeneity, on the one hand, and 'modern' Western values of individuality, creativity and heterogeneity, on the other. Once again we are brought full circle back to Japanist oppositions and to the suspicion that perhaps the Japanese can only define themselves in opposition to Western ideals about themselves (in the same way that the people of Kuzaki seem frozen in the mirror of urban society – Martinez). Indeed, the regeneration of the West that they envisage through management techniques, the martial arts, and concepts of 'personhood' may well turn out to be no more than the Romantic Orientalist idea in disguise (Said 1979: 115).

Nevertheless, even though Japanism may have ultimate control, a number of different groups within Japan are creating a common debate in which, publicly, the politicians and, privately, the advertisers are acting as Japan's 'captains of consciousness' (Ewen 1976). So far, they have tried to ensure that, in their 'writing', one single code of language *does* remain privileged and that there are, as far as possible, *no* 'fluctuating hierarchies' (Barthes 1986: 8–9). This is not to suggest that there are not in fact other voices, representing partial worlds (Ben-Ari). The question is, how long will these sounds of 'plural delectation' continue to constitute the all-encompassing 'rustle' of the Japanese language – from *pachinko* parlours to advertising agencies (Barthes 1986: 77)? Will they ever be able to articulate their own distinct discourses, and thereby escape the Japanist view first imposed upon them by Westerners and now actively practised by their captains of consciousness?

The discourse of anthropology

What, then, is this 'real' Japan, sought after by city tourists visiting the *ama* divers of Kuzaki (Maritinez), on the one hand, and by other 'pilgrims' (Said, 1979: 168), anthropologists writing up their fieldwork experience (Ben-Ari, Goodman), on the other? Here we move from a discourse on the discourse with Japan to a discourse on and with anthropology. Like the divers who pose as hostesses to entertain visiting tourists at night, anthropologists play a double game – first with their informants, then with their fellow anthropologists – so that we never know precisely *if* it is 'Japan' that is described in print, or if so *why*. Anthropologists thus struggle to uphold at least three discourses – one with the society which they have chosen to study, another with the 'field' that has been prepared before them, yet a third with the academic discipline in which they are employed. In this respect, they are the abalone divers of the scholarly world, although one suspects that they occasionally lack the entrepreneurial adaptability of the people of Kuzaki (Martinez).

Moeran's description of his machinations in the ceramic art world neatly exemplifies this point, which is then elaborated by Ben-Ari in his discussion of how texts translate meanings and enact power relations between cultural systems. The questions posed here concern the way in which the 'art world' of anthropology functions, and how it creates notions of 'value' within and outside – and thereby 'wraps' – its 'discipline'. In accordance with Rabinow's remark (1986: 253) that 'the micropractices of the academy might well do with some scrutiny', Ben-Ari proceeds to look critically at the power of publishers to influence directly the finished product of any ethnographic writing; at the role of the tenured professional in initiating experiment; and at the social context underlying the creation of 'ethnographic knowledge'.

This analysis is by no means intended to be exhaustive, but it raises problems that anthropologists would do well to discuss more openly (Rabinow 1986: 253–4). Given that publishers *do* pay heed to the recommendations of 'eminent' academics, that they 'edit' texts, and demand glossaries, indexes, and certain types of illustration (or none at all), we need to look very carefully at the way in which they operate in the academic world. Let's face it, academics 'rank' publishing companies, in the same way that they 'rank' university departments, and such ranking often follows the classic inverse relation between quantity and quality found in art: what is good does not have to sell and, by corollary, what does not sell must somehow be good! Thus, university presses tend to be ranked higher than commercial publishers, and those university presses that fail to distribute their books, but which win prizes for their design, tend to be ranked higher than those that at least make an effort to serve their authors' financial needs.

Academics' own place within the disciplinary hierarchy, then, depends upon their ability to publish with the 'right' publisher – in the same way that Japanese potters are ranked according to whether they manage to hold their one-man shows at a national museum of art, a Tokyo department store, or a private gallery in a provincial city (Moeran 1987: 32–3). The analogy may be taken further in that both younger academics and inexperienced potters can benefit considerably from the 'patronage' of a former teacher or senior colleague. Ultimately, then, it would appear to be power connections that permit the circus of anthropology to continue with its animal acts (Nuer cows, Balinese cocks, New Guinea cassowaries), theoretical juggling and intellectual acrobatics – relieved only too infrequently by the occasional clown (Barley 1983).

Whether the world of anthropology is peopled with the kind of 'mafiosi' who inhabit the Japanese art world is probably a matter for debate. What no doubt worries those who have aspirations to go up in this world is the question of 'value'. Surely, they will protest, it is here that the worlds of art and anthropology definitively part? In art, perhaps, there may not be any 'specificity', but in anthropology at least there must be a hard core of 'essential' value that cannot be denied? This, too, can – and should – be debated at greater length, but it looks as if 'style' in anthropology is very much a matter of 'visual ideologies' (Hadjinicolaou 1978) whereby we can depict our 'being there' (Geertz 1988) only according to the written materials already available to us.

Here, of course, we face the problem of how to balance the discourses available to us. In some areas of the world – it seems to me that South-East Asia is one – the discourse of authropology tends to overwhelm that of the society being depicted, and 'theory' (functionalism, structuralism, hermeneutics) takes precedence over 'field' (Orientalism, Japanism). In others, such as Japan, the reverse has been true. The papers in this book attempt to balance these two discourses of anthropology and Japanism, while remaining faithful to the discourse of Japan, so that none of them is either super- or subordinate to the others. Alas! One has a nasty suspicion that such pluralism might itself be just another Japanist idea.

The cherry blossoms turn to snow . . .[9]

Notes

1 The allusion is to poem number 41 in the tenth-century collection *Shinsen Haka* (New Selection of Japanese Poetry, c. 934) (see McCullough 1985: 302–3):

> Miyoshino no
> yamabe ni sakeru
> sakurabana
> shirakumo to nomi
> ayamataretsutsu

> Flowering cherries
> Blossoming in the mountains
> Of fair Yoshino –
> Betrayed by unwary eyes,
> We mistake them for white clouds.

2 This volume thus complements the *Introduction* to the first JAWS collection which focused on the contribution of social anthropology to Japanese studies (Hendry 1986).

3 As, for example, the provision of subsidies for translations of *nihonjinron* books, but not for Marxist analyses of Japanese society, together with the whole range of works chosen for publication in English by the Japanese.

4 A good example of the kind of approach criticised by both Dale and Miller is to be found in Suzuki (1978). See also Said (1979: 320) on Arabic and ideology.

5 Although honorific usage is clearly *socially* defined and it is changes in social definitions of what is correct or incorrect usage that are at issue here, I use the term 'proper' as an *essential* category because that is the way those concerned themselves use it.

6 In his criticisms of an earlier draft of this *Introduction*, Eyal Ben-Ari suggested that there are varying dimensions of conscious manipulation of honorifics by inferiors, and that some marginal groups may 'play' with language in order to further their own ends. In this way, of course, they replicate in inverted form the language of the powerful, so that the idea if a single Power, rather than plural powers, would still seem to hold good.

I would like to take this opportunity – belatedly – to thank both Eyal Ben-Ari and James Valentine for their patience, hard work, and constructive criticism, not only of this Introduction, but of every paper published in this book.

7 A short, but useful, introduction to honorific usage may be found in Neustupny (1987: 173–6).

8 By the sheer number of *nihonjinron* volumes, incidentally, they disprove Said's assertion that there are few Oriental books about the West (1979: 204).

9 The allusion is to a poem by Ki no Tomonori (number 60) in the 10th century collection

Brian Moeran

Kokin Wakashū (Collection of Early and Modern Japanese Poetry, ca. 905) (see McCullough 1985: 25):

> Miyoshino no
> yamabe ni sakeru
> sakurabana
> yuki ka to nomi zo
> ayamatarekeru

> Flowering cherries
> Blossoming in the mountains
> Of fair Yoshino -
> Betrayed by unwary eyes,
> We mistake them for snowflakes

References

Barley, N. 1983. *The Innocent Anthropologist: Notes from a Mud Hut.* London: British Museum.

Barthes, R. 1982. *Empire of Signs* (Trans. R. Howard). New York: Hill & Wang.

Barthes, R. 1986. *The Rustle of Language* (Trans. R. Howard. Oxford: Basil Blackwell.

Befu, H. 1980. The group model of Japanese society and an alternative. *Rice University Studies* 66 (1).

Ben-Ari, E. 1986. A sports day in suburban Japan: leisure, artificial communities and the creation of local sentiments. In *Interpreting Japanese Society*, ed. J. Hendry and J. Webber. Oxford: JASO Occasional Papers, no. 5.

Bendix, R. 1969. *Nation-Building and Citizenship: Studies of our Changing Social Order.* Garden City, NY: Anchor.

Bestor, T. 1985. Tradition and Japanese social organization: institutional development in a Tokyo neighborhood. *Ethnology* 24 (2), 121–35.

Boon, J. 1982. *Other Tribes, Other Scribes: Symbolic Anthropology in the Comparative Study of Cultures, Histories, Religions, and Texts.* Cambridge: Cambridge University Press.

Brown R. and Gilman, A. 1960. The pronouns of power and solidarity. In *Style in Language*, ed. T. Sebeok, pp. 253–76. Cambridge, Mass.: MIT Press.

Clifford, J. 1986. Introduction: partial truths. In *Writing Culture: the Poetics and Politics of Ethnography*, ed. J. Clifford and G. Marcus, pp.

1–26. Los Angeles and Berkeley: University of California Press.

Dale, P. 1986. *The Myth of Japanese Uniqueness*. London: Croom Helm.

Dore, R. 1973. *British Factory – Japanese Factory*. Berkeley and Los Angeles: University of California Press.

Douglas, M. 1970. *Purity and Danger*. Harmondsworth: Penguin.

Ewen, S. 1976. *Captains of Consciousness: Advertising and the Social Roots of Consumer Culture*. New York: McGraw-Hill.

Geertz, C. 1988. *Works and Lives: the Anthropologist as Author*. Stanford, Calif.: Stanford University Press.

Goffman, E. 1971. *The Presentation of Self in Everyday Life*. Harmondsworth: Penguin.

Hadjinicolaou, N. 1978. *Art History and Class Struggle* (Trans. Asmal). London: Pluto Press.

Hannerz, U. 1969. *Soulside: Inquiries into Ghetto Culture and Community*. New York: Columbia University Press.

Haug, W. 1986. *Critique of Commodity Aesthetics: Appearance, Sexuality and Advertising in Capitalist Society* (Trans. R. Bock). Cambridge: Polity Press.

Hendry, J. 1985. The use and abuse of politeness formulae. *Proceedings of the British Association of Japanese Studies* 10, 85–91.

Hendry, J. 1986. Introduction: the contribution of social anthropology to Japanese studies. In *Interpreting Japanese Society*, ed. J. Hendry and J. Webber, pp. 3–13. Oxford: JASO.

Hendry, J. 1988. Respect, solidarity or contempt? Politeness and communication in modern Japan. In *Contemporary European Writings on Japan*, ed. I. Nish. Tenterden: Paul Norbury.

Hobart, M. 1986. Introduction. In *Context, Meaning, and Power in Southeast Asia*, ed. M. Hobart and R.H. Taylor, pp. 7–19. Ithaca, NY: Cornell Southeast Asia Program.

Kelly, W.W. 1985. Rationalization and nostalgia: cultural dynamics of new middle-class Japan. *American Ethnologist* 13 (4), 603–18.

Krauss, E., Rohlen, T., and Steinhoff, P. (eds) 1984. *Conflict in Japan*. Honolulu: University of Hawaii Press.

Labov, W. 1972. *Language in the Inner City: Studies in the Black English Vernacular*. Philadelphia: University of Pennsylvania Press.

Levi-Strauss, C. 1985. Cross readings. In *The View from Afar* (Trans. J. Neugroschel and P. Hoss), pp. 73–87. Oxford: Basil Blackwell.

Lock, M. 1980. *East Asian Medicine in Urban Japan: Varieties of Medical Experience*. Berkeley and Los Angeles: University of California Press.

Brian Moeran

McCullough, H. 1985. *Kokin Wakashū: the First Imperial Anthology of Japanese Poetry*. Stanford, Calif.: Stanford University Press.

Martin, S. 1964. Speech levels in Japan and Korea. In *Language in Culture and Society*, ed. D. Hymes. New York: Harper & Row.

Miller, R. 1971. Levels of speech (*keigo*) and the Japanese linguistic response to modernization. In *Tradition and Modernization in Japanese Culture*, ed. D. Shively, pp. 601–65. Princeton, NJ: Princeton University Press.

Miller, R. 1982. *Japan's Modern Myth: the Language and Beyond*. Tokyo: Weatherhill.

Moeran, B. 1983. The language of Japanese tourism. In *The Anthropology of Tourism, The Annals of Tourism Research*, ed. N. Graburn, Vol. 10, pp. 99–108.

Moeran, B. 1984a. *Lost Innocence: Folk Craft Potters of Onta, Japan*. Berkeley and Los Angeles: University of California Press.

Moeran, B. 1984b. Individual, group and *seishin*: Japan's internal cultural debate. *Man* 19 (2), 252–66.

Moeran, B. 1987. The art world of contemporary Japanese ceramics. *Journal of Japanese Studies* 13 (1), 27–50.

Moeran, B. 1989a. Beating about the brush: on ethnographic writing in Japan. In *Localising Strategies: Regional Traditions in Ethnographic Writing*, ed. R. Fardon. Edinburgh: Scottish Academic Press; Washington DC: Smithsonian Institution Press.

Moeran, B. 1989b. *Language and Popular Culture in Japan*. Manchester: Manchester University Press.

Moore, B. Jr. 1966. *The Social Origins of Dictatorship and Democracy: Lord and Peasant in the Making of the Modern World*. Boston: Beacon.

Morris, I. 1970. *The Pillow Book of Sei Shōnagon*. Harmondsworth: Penguin.

Neustupny, J. 1987. *Communicating with the Japanese*. Tokyo: The Japan Times.

Norbeck, E. 1954. *Takashima: a Japanese Fishing Community*. Salt Lake City: University of Utah Press.

Nussbaum, S. 1985. The residential community in modern Japan: an analysis of a Tokyo suburban development. Ph.D. thesis, Cornell University.

Parkin, D. 1978. *The Cultural Definition of Political Response: Lineal Destiny among the Luo*. London: Academic Press.

Rabinow, P. 1986. Representations are social facts: modernity and post-

16

modernity in anthropology. In *Writing Culture* ed. J. Clifford and G.E. Marcus, pp. 234–61. Berkeley and Los Angeles: University of California Press.

Reynolds, D.K. 1980. *The Quiet Therapies: Japanese Pathways to Personal Growth*. Honolulu: University of Hawaii Press.

Rohlen, T. 1974. *For Harmony and Strength: Japanese White-Collar Organization in Anthropological Perspective*. Berkeley and Los Angeles: University of California Press.

Rohlen, T. 1983. *Japan's High Schools*. Berkeley and Los Angeles: University of California Press.

Said, E. 1979. *Orientalism*. New York: Vintage.

Singer, K. 1973. *Mirror, Sword and Jewel: a Study of Japanese Characteristics*. Edited and with an Introduction by R. Storry. London: Croom Helm.

Suzuki, T. 1978. *Japanese and the Japanese: Words in Culture* (Trans. Akira Miura). Tokyo: Kodansha International.

Trudgill, P. 1971. Sex, covert prestige and linguistic change in the urban British English of Norwich. *Language in Society* **1** (2).

Williams, R. 1961. *Culture and Society 1780-1950*. Harmondsworth: Penguin.

2
Joy Hendry

Humidity, hygiene, or ritual care: some thoughts on wrapping as a social phenomenon

Introduction

The careful wrapping of goods, particularly those to be served to guests or presented as gifts, is not peculiar to Japan, but it is an accomplishment which is certainly highly developed in that culture. It is my view that this is no chance phenomenon, but that attention paid to the wrapping of goods is merely one example of an important and pervasive – but possibly not explicit – ordering principle available to participants in Japanese society. It is, as such, an important component of non-verbal communication, but it can be shown to be manifest at various levels of social awareness. The aim of this paper is to describe examples of this 'wrapping principle', to examine some possibilities for its wider significance and implications, and, finally, to make some tentative suggestions about how the Japanese case may provide a model for cross-cultural comparison.

It should be made clear at once that this is a preliminary attempt to describe and analyse a phenomenon which I observed rather casually during a recent field trip,[1] although it is set in the context of considerable previous research. No single theoretical framework is proposed, although various possible modes of further analysis will be suggested at the conclusion. In the rather recently established but nevertheless valuable ethnographic tradition of self-revealment, however, I will first describe briefly some of the circumstances of the inquiry in question. For this particular nine months I was living as far as possible the life of a 'professional' Japanese housewife, mostly in Tateyama City in Chiba Prefecture. In an emic view, I rated rather low on the scale of quality in this respect, as I left my husband behind in England, subjected my

18

children to a school where they could, for the first few months, understand little of what was going on, and even delegated some of the domestic tasks to a student who agreed to accompany me on this venture. Nevertheless, I spent much of my day, each day, in the company of 'real' Japanese housewives, mostly mothers of school-age children, living parts of the lives they normally lead, and trying as far as possible to cultivate an interest in the matters with which they seemed most concerned. Education was, of course, a subject with which I became greatly involved, but I found little to be gained from a sewing and knitting boom which seemed to be the current fashion, so I spent a few hours a week with those of a younger age-group who were preparing to be housewives, engaged in tasks I had previously neglected such as flower arranging and tea ceremony. Cooking classes were an activity which I attended with my own contemporaries, and these turned out, somewhat surprisingly, to make rather an interesting contribution to the subject of wrapping. I also spent a number of hours participating in another boom activity in the southern part of the Boso peninsula, namely tennis.

Some examples of wrapping

What, then, does all this have to do with wrapping? Let us turn to consider some examples. The phenomenon can be witnessed even at the most mundane levels, where functional explanations might well be applied, but further examination will serve to reveal how it may also be understood as part of a more comprehensively coherent principle. First, on a very basic level, the groceries purchased in Japan are characteristically wrapped with considerable care. Tea-bags, for example, already wrapped and processed versions of the original tea leaves, are usually again individually enclosed in paper packets, and sometimes these paper packets are sealed in further packets of, say, five together, packed with other similar packets in a box, which is then itself sealed in cellophane. Cheese is often accorded similar treatment. In recent years it has become possible to buy quite a wide variety of cheese in Japan, but always prepared and processed in ways which make it ready for use in preparing meals. Packets of grated cheese are ubiquitously available, and another common version is to be found in packets of sliced cheese in which each individual slice is wrapped, first, and then the pack of individual slices sealed again into a larger packet. Camembert comes in a packet, enclosed in a tin, enclosed in a box, finally sealed in cellophane. These forms of cheese are of course available for convenience in most countries, but in Europe, at least, it is not only possible, but by many thought preferable to purchase a slice of the product direct from a fresh slab.

On a social visit between housewives, especially those aspiring to upward mobility, coffee is very often served with individually wrapped spoonfuls of sugar and tiny cartons of cream, a custom reserved in most countries for airlines, trains and coffee shops. Furthermore, in many Japanese homes, the biscuits or cakes which accompany the beverage are also often individually wrapped, biscuits usually in paper packets, but cakes may themselves be made in the form of little parcels, one of the arts imparted in my cooking class. Indeed, it is part of the etiquette of social visiting to know how to deal with the papers, or perhaps fresh green leaves, in which such items are enveloped, and which one needs to know whether or not to consume.

At a purely functional level, various arguments may be put forward for this extra wrapping of especially imported produce.[2] It may be explained as necessary for the protection of such goods from Japan's humid climate, and this is indeed a valid argument. There may also be an element of hygiene involved. If one is served cream, sugar and biscuits in individually wrapped containers, one knows that they have not been handled by one's host, or visited by flies or mosquitoes. Meats marked as 'ham' or 'roast pork' undoubtedly come in vacuum-packed plastic containers for the purpose of preservation, but their further arrangement on satin cushions enclosed in a substantial cardboard box, which, when purchased, comes wrapped further in fancy paper, with *noshi* paper[3] around that, all finally to be placed in a carrier bag, must have some significance other than these practical ones.

The last description applies in particular to a range of goods available for purchase at two specific times of the year, namely New Year, when they are termed *oseibo*, and the summer 'Bon' festival for the memory of ancestors, when they are called *ochūgen*. On these occasions the most ordinary household goods, such as oil, coffee, sugar and soap, as well as a variety of meats and biscuits, are dressed up and decorated in fancy packets and boxes in order to become formal gifts made between people, families and organisations indebted in some way to each other. At this level, these mundane goods have been converted into gifts, and are being accorded the lavish degree of ritual attention which is thought appropriate for such times. They may thus be compared with gifts made on other special occasions such as births, weddings and funerals.

For these events, wrapping is used in most countries, and apparently the idea of providing a wrapping service at the point of purchase was imported from America. The bows and ribbons provided for birthday and Christmas presents reflect this influence, although the use of *noshi* paper for happy celebrations, or black-edged paper decorated with lotus flowers for gifts connected with funerals and memorials, is independent of this outside influence. This layer of wrapping makes it possible to mark the gifts with a clear purpose, and also to write the name of the giver on the gift. Where money is being presented, special envelopes serve a 'similar purpose, and these may even include a space for entering the amount given so that the recipient may keep a record after removing the cash.

However, there are further aspects of wrapping which remain to be explained. One example is the way the money presented in the special envelope just described is often wrapped again in paper inside the packet. Another is the way people writing letters sometimes 'wrap' a single-page letter in an extra blank sheet of writing paper. Many gifts are enclosed in several layers of paper or packaging (cf. Barthes 1982: 45). Indeed, a return gift of small dishes I received for a present I made to the house of a friend whose father had died was wrapped no less than seven times! Native explanations of such practices often include the use of the word *teinei*, which means both 'polite' and 'careful', a concept applied to all sorts of formal and careful behavior in a variety of situations and circumstances. By carefully wrapping an object, one is apparently expressing politeness and care, care for the object, and therefore care for the recipient (e.g. Uno 1985: 118–20). In my view, however, the act of 'wrapping' has even more significance and to understand this, we must look elsewhere.

Wrapping materials

One preliminary way of developing the theme is to look at some of the other ways in which the materials are used in Japanese society. The most common element is paper, and it has recently become prestigious to select, or even make your own traditional white *washi* (literally, Japanese paper) for the purpose of wrapping gifts. Paper is accorded a fairly important role in several other ways, however. It is used in Shinto rites to mark off sacred or ritual space, and to create a staff used by Shinto priests for rites of purification. It is used in the construction of *shōji* (sliding windows) and *fusuma* (room partitions), and in other ways to decorate and to beautify. It is also used by children as well as by adults to create all manner of objects in the 'art' form known as *origami*, some of which may be used for ritual purposes, such as the string of 1000 paper cranes which is regarded as a force for healing. It is, of course, used for writing and painting, as elsewhere, but in Japan particularly valued in its own right for its artistic merits.

Straw is another important material employed in wrapping and packing, and although it is less commonly used for protective purposes in these days of synthetic materials, it can still be seen, for example, in the packing of fish presented as gifts at New Year. Straw also has many important ritual uses. It, too, is used to mark off sacred or ritual space, ranging from a roped-off square in the centre of a building site for the Shinto ritual which precedes the construction of private houses and public buildings, to the marking off of a whole district for the celebration of a festival. It is hung at the entrance to shrines, in the form of a heavy rope plait known as a *shimenawa*, and it is used to create and decorate ritual objects for a variety of occasions, from straw octopus, fish and sake cups hung over rivers at an annual river festival held in many parts of Japan, to the adornment of large sea-bream, presented as a part of betrothal gifts. Thus the materials of wrapping are themselves valued in other ritual and symbolic ways.

Precious objects are often encased in sturdy boxes, usually made of wood if the item inside is valuable enough, and sometimes they seem so carefully made that they are almost *objets d'art* in their own right. They are used for storage as well as protection, and a particularly special object may be wrapped in silk before being enclosed in more than one box. A Korean writer seeking Japanese customs which differ from those of his own often very similar culture mentions 'boxes within boxes' as a Japanese device which gives 'concrete expression' to what he calls 'the principle of inclusion' (Lee 1984: 25–31). The boxes come in sets where a number of them fit inside each other, each slightly smaller than the previous one, and he points out that the same idea is used, functionally, for bowls and pans to allow a large number to be stored in a small space. These boxes are sometimes called Chinese boxes in English, and dolls within dolls are a popular souvenir of the Soviet Union, but it is interesting that this Korean commentator should choose these layers of packaging as particularly Japanese.

Other forms of 'wrapping' and their significance

Lee also argues that the same principle may be observed in Japanese poetry where a series of possessives have the effect of reducing the perception of space down to a manipulable level, and this forms part of an overall argument about a Japanese propensity to miniaturise things. He gives as one example a poem by Ishikawa Takuboku which he renders as follows:

Tokai no	On the white sand beach
kojima no iso no	Of a tiny island
shirasuna ni	In the Eastern Sea
ware nakinurete	Bathed in tears
kani to tawamuru	I toy with a crab (ibid. 25)

Lee argues that the use of the possessive *no* reduces 'the vast, boundless "Eastern Sea" to a "small island" ', then, further, through 'beach' and 'white sand' 'down to a tiny crab, and then, since the poet is weeping, we have in essence the great Eastern Sea in a single teardrop' (ibid. 27). Be the reduction here as it may, the order of the original Japanese version of the poem does move from the large through to the small in a way which can plausibly be metaphorically compared with the 'boxes within boxes'. It can also perhaps be seen as a device which 'wraps' the crab (and possibly also the tear) in layers of the environment in which it is found.

This example may not seem so far-fetched when we look further at broader ideas of 'wrapping' in a Japanese view. As Ekiguchi Kunio explains in a book designed to introduce some Japanese ideas for gift wrapping to the West, the Japanese concept of wrapping, *tsutsumi*, 'plays a central role in a wide variety of spiritual and cultural aspects of Japanese life' (1986: 6). The paper *shōji* and *fusuma* already mentioned as room partitions may, for example, be described as the wrapping of architectural space (ibid), as may the use of straw and paper to mark off the sacred or ritual areas described above. The *shintai*, or 'sacred body', to be found at the most holy centre of a Shinto shrine, for example, is 'wrapped' in a series of compartments inside the inner sanctum of the building which is in itself enclosed in space marked off from the outside world by one or more *torii* or stone arches. For the purposes of prayer or a specific rite, the visitor to shrines proceeds from the mundane world through the boundaries of the increasingly sacred areas by a series of acts of purification, such as the washing of the mouth and hands and the

23

removal of footwear, although the ultimate inner sanctum where the *shintai* is kept is usually beyond the access of all but the most holy of priests.

These ideas of 'spiritual wrapping' are developed in detail in a book by Nukada Iwao (1977: 9, 168–76) entitled *Tsutsumi* (Wrapping), a historical approach which attempts to trace the evolution and cultural elaboration of notions of wrapping. Nukada suggests that the use of paper in Shinto ceremony is related to the fact that the Japanese word for paper is homophonous with that for 'god' (*kami*) so that a white sheet of paper symbolises the purity of the gods (ibid. 139), and he describes how wrapping and folding have themselves been regarded as a means to know the will of god (ibid. 138).[4] Nukada identifies three basic types of 'wrapping'. Two of these, the wrapping of objects and the wrapping of space,[5] have already been discussed above; the third is the wrapping of the body (ibid. 15–16). This sees garments as a form of packaging and examples are cited from Japan and elsewhere to illustrate the symbolism associated with different forms of apparel for both the living and the dead (ibid. 41–63).

Probably the most famous Japanese example of this kind of 'wrapping' is the *junihitoe* of the court ladies of the Heian period, whose twelve layers of kimono were chosen to create an aesthetically pleasing combination of colour contrasts. Such sumptuous attire represents the ultimate expression of the way clothes and their colours were indications of social status (ibid. 149), a phenomenon certainly not peculiar to Japan. Nowadays, these garments are only to be seen at Imperial weddings when they also indicate the extreme formality of the occasion, as do fewer layers for more ordinary mortals. A regular bride in modern Japan often wears at least three layers of garments, the outer one being the most luxurious, but with the inner layers visible at its peripheries.[6] These layers of clothing indicate ritual and formality just as gifts for such occasions are carefully wrapped in a way entirely unnecessary for presents exchanged casually between close friends. Similarly, few families use individually wrapped spoonfuls of sugar and cream at ordinary meals. This notion of 'wrapping' is not only widespread, then, it is also a mechanism with considerable social significance.

'Wrapping' in language

A further example with which I was particularly concerned during the Tateyama research project is the use of polite and respectful language (*keigo*). *Keigo* is very often associated with the expression of hierarchical differences, but much of its use, especially amongst women, is concerned with quite different, though not unrelated matters.[7] Prominent amongst these is the way *keigo* is used more to express phrases and sentiments considered appropriate to a particular situation or occasion than to communicate much in the way of fact or feelings. It is said to be the opposite of *hadaka hanashi*, or naked speech, which may be regarded as the most frank language. Indeed, *keigo* is often described as a form of language which is used to hide one's real feelings.

Oishi Hatsutarō has used the word *kakine* (fence) to describe this role of *keigo* (1975: 63), and it has been compared by more than one writer with Geertz's (1972: 173–4) (possibly inaccurate) expression for Javanese honorific language, namely that it builds 'walls of etiquette'. It is Uno, however, who points out that the use of other expressions of respect (*keii hyōgen*), such as careful wrapping, demonstrate care for the recipient in the same way that the use of *keigo* demonstrates care for the person being addressed (1985: 118–19). People use polite formulae, verbal and non-verbal, to express respect for those with whom they interact, but at the same time protect themselves from the harshness of direct exchanges by wrapping their *honne*, their individual opinions and views, in an appropriate layer of politeness.

At an extreme level, there may be very little communication with the 'real person' inside the parcel. For example, the lift attendants in department stores, whose language is usually not only polite and respectful, but uttered in high and stilted tones, are simply presenting an image of the company's choice. They could conceivably be replaced by machines, and in the case of the similar role played by bus guides, they often are. According to some of the girls inside these 'packages' it would be virtually impossible to carry out such a boring task all day long if one did not separate one's inner self from the activity. The outer layer of etiquette also apparently provides protection from the possible abuse or amorous advances of the lift and bus users. At a symbolic level, the ubiquitous white gloves worn by these employees, as well as by drivers, guides and other functionaries, 'wrap' and thereby separate and protect them from the public with whom they deal.

At the other end of the scale, close friends use little *keigo* in everyday conversation, especially when exchanging confidences, just as they evince little need to use much wrapping when they give things to one another. There are, of course, occasions when polite formulae are expected, and these may be quite nicely correlated with the garments the participants understand it is appropriate to wear. Language definitely rises a notch or two,[8] or should I say a layer or two, when its users are dressed in kimono, although both factors are no doubt precipitated by the occasion which demand the formality. On the other hand, ladies whose everyday language is really rather polite, seem to drop most of the forms of adornment when they are dressed in the casual, sometimes rather skimpy attire of the tennis court. This idea could no doubt be pursued in other arenas such as bath-houses or hairdressers' shops.

Of course, there are certain social circles, such as those associated with Yamanote in Tokyo and Akashi in Kobe, where extremely polite forms are used all the time between members. In this case, the endings of the polite verbs vary depending on the occasion and the degree of intimacy of the speakers so that, for example, *meshiagarimasuka,* a polite way of offering food, becomes *meshiagaru,* still a polite verb, but with a less formal ending, in intimate company within such circles. Thus, the words which raise the level of the language for other people, are used almost like a dialect for the inside members of such groups, expressing solidarity between them (cf. Brown and Gilman 1972). However, members of such groups drop these exalted levels when they are speaking to people who are unable to use them in the same way, so that in this case the language may be seen as serving to wrap and protect their elite groups from outside intrusion.

Processes of penetration or unwrapping

The pinnacle of Japanese society, the Imperial Court, is almost completely closed off to the outside world. The language used in this context is particularly formal and polite, even somewhat archaic, so that if an ordinary person had an opportunity to meet a member of the Imperial family they might well find themselves tongue-tied. Indeed, some Japanese living in Oxford at the time of the study visit of the Emperor Hirohito's eldest grandson, Prince Hiro, resorted to English when they were presented to him for that very reason. In fact the chances of such an encounter for an ordinary Japanese are really rather slim. The whole Imperial Household is wrapped, just like the ancient castles were, in layers of gardens and moats on the outside,[9] and, no doubt, with elaborate arrangements of *shōji, fusuma* and screens on the inside. Those who penetrate these layers of wrapping physically must also be equipped with the necessary skills of formality to communicate effectively at the inner levels.

To a lesser degree, similar principles are at work in many hierarchical organisations, so that it is common for higher positions to be cushioned and separated by layers of spatial wrapping. In traditional country houses, for example, the master's seat in the *zashiki*, was reached by passing through not only the *genkan* (or porch), but also through rooms called the *gozen* and the *tsugi no ma* (two rooms which separated the front porch from the chief reception room). There may well have been an alternative, more direct route through the garden, but only people whose ranks were close to the master's could avail themselves of this short-cut. A modern example is the way the *kōchō* (head) in a school sits in an enclosed office beyond the staff room, and anyone who enters this inner sanctum, even – so I am told – the headmaster's previously close friends, notches up their language a little. The head is not to be bothered with the humdrum *honne* of everyday frustrations. His is a world of *tatemae* (public face), and the appropriate language is *keigo*.

In general, in the same way that people in 'high' positions are 'wrapped' spatially and the forms of address appropriate for them involve layers of polite language and other expressions of formality such as bowing, those aspiring to (culturally) high forms of living use the 'wrapping principle' in other ways to represent degrees of cultural elaboration. Thus, a simple cup of tea may become an elaborate ceremony – literally, in the case of the tea ceremony itself, but also in ostensibly quite informal gatherings where the goods served are used to express these aspirations. The cakes at such tables, and the knowledge required for their consumption, have already been mentioned. These illustrate the principle very well, for many, if not most are themselves made in a way which involves some form of wrapping. The basic ingredient is often a kind of bean paste (*an*), enclosed in a variety of substances, usually made from rice, and these are then often enough enclosed again in a leaf or paper of some sort.[10]

To feel comfortable with all this cultural elaboration, one needs to be used to it, because participants judge each other on the basis of their demonstration of knowledge of rules of etiquette. Only if one can relax in such situations can one break through the barriers of formality and find intimacy within. High-status groups tend to insulate themselves in this way, proclaiming a lifetime of experience necessary for in-group member-ship, but in modern Japan there are also many arenas to which one can train to belong. The tea ceremony is one example. Every part of the ritual involves the performance of fixed movements, and it is only through years of practice that one may reach the stage of being able to participate without fear of making mistakes. It is, however, theoretically possible for anyone to achieve the ultimate heights of enlightenment and non-verbal communication promised, and the training process is one of the ways in which people seek to 'improve' themselves. This and other traditional Japanese arts, such as archery and flower arranging express cultural elaboration *par excellence*.

An interesting analysis of the tea ceremony, which also illustrates another aspect of the 'wrapping principle', is to be found in an article by Dorinne Kondo (1985). She describes in some detail quite an elaborate variant of the ritual known as *chaji*. Her analysis depicts the various activities and movements involved as a symbolic journey from mundane space and time through stages of greater and lesser formality to a ritual climax which offers the participants the possibility of a 'distilled form of experience set apart from the mundane world' (ibid. 302). Here, too, rites of purification such as the changing of clothes, removal of sandals, and washing of hands and mouth bring participants gradually closer to this central climax, which is also achieved through the manipulation of different linguistic and material symbols. Interestingly, as one approaches this ultimate expression of *tatemae*, translated by Kondo as 'the graces necessary to maintain harmonious social interaction', one can expect to 'forget the contingencies of everyday life'. The *honne* of one's mudane thoughts and feelings become irrelevant as one 'unwraps' this higher plane of transcendental existence.

The rites of purification involved in penetrating the 'wrapping' of a Shinto shrine are very similar at some points to those of participants in a tea ceremony approaching the tea-house, but lay people can only go so far. The priests who protect the inner layers also use very formal language to put supplications to the gods on behalf of ordinary mortals, and, at first, it seemed that this would serve again to wrap the gods, like an extreme form of *keigo*, perhaps to be compared with the language of the

Imperial Court. A conversation with some high-ranking priests at Awa Shrine, near where I was working, served to alter this view, however. They pointed out that the language of the *norito* is indeed formal and fixed, and it is to some extent polite and respectful, but it is not the same as *keigo*. It is the language of worship, unchanged for 1200 years, and it is appropriate for the rituals in which it is used. However, unlike the case of the Emperor, anyone may speak to the gods, and when they do they speak from the heart. There is no need for them to wrap their feelings up in language, indeed many do not articulate their requests at all. This form of communication they describe as *kotodama no shinkō*, a kind of communication from the inside of the body – quite the reverse of the wrapping of politeness formulae. It is particularly interesting, then, that gifts offered to the gods are properly offered unwrapped, placed perhaps on appropriate dishes and tables, but open for the world to see, and for the gods to accept and consume.

For human interaction, too, there are ways through to the *honne* in any situation, and here again one penetrates a ritual wrapping to reach a more direct form of communication. To take a mundane example drawn from my housewifely experiences, the form of PTA (or indeed any number of other) meetings will illustrate the point. Such a gathering opens with *aisatsu*, brief and very formal speeches made in polite language suitable for speaking to large gatherings of people. There is very little content in the utterances at this stage of the proceedings; the form of the language is the important issue. The next items on the agenda are grouped under the heading of *hōkoku*, announcements. The matters under consideration are brought up and made known to the assembled company, but they are still being broached in fairly formal language, although it is somewhat less fixed than that of the *aisatsu*. It is only in the following section – *giji* – that the nitty-gritty of real discussion is reached. The language is now much more direct, and, in the case of the meetings I attended in Tateyama, the local dialect breaks through.

By moving through the layers of formality, by gradually unwrapping the layers of politeness and deference, one is able acceptably to come to the point where real opinions are expressed. A completely informal gathering without any such structure would, on the other hand, possibly fail to elicit any direct comments in the company of a large number of people. The process is not dissimilar to that described by Moeran (1984) in a paper on sake drinking. Again, an occasion for drinking usually opens with a first stage of formal greetings, and Moeran identifies four further stages as the participants become increasingly intoxicated, and increasingly move from the public language of *tatemae* to the more intimate and direct language of their *honne* or 'words . . . from the heart'.

One could adduce further examples of this process taking place in different arenas. The principle of wrapping as a social phenomenon would appear to operate on many different levels, and in my view an understanding of its importance in Japanese society can aid an understanding of many of the so-called paradoxes pointed out by commentators on Japan. Writers have discussed the institutionalised discrepancy between the public (*tatemae*) and private (*honne*) faces people use (e.g. Koschmann 1974), and these concepts help to explain apparently contradictory behaviour; but the different layers of *tatemae*, and principles of moving from one to another, have not been examined in detail. Moreover, once an idea of these mechanisms has been understood in one context, there emerges an element of predictability about how they are used in others.

The wrapping principle in theoretical and comparative perspective

This paper has so far concentrated on describing a principle which has proved to be pervasive in Japanese society, but I hope that the idea will also have some applicability elsewhere. Ultimately, confirmation of this expectation relies on the opinions of specialists in other areas, but parts of the material presented already lend themselves to analysis within various pre-existing theoretical frameworks. In this final section I would like to mention some of the possibilities which could throw open the Japanese phenomenon to cross-cultural analysis and thereby demonstrate some likely ways to make the 'wrapping principle' more widely applicable. In this way, I hope to suggest a contribution Japan could make to general anthropological theory, and thereby comply with the overall aim of this book.

One excellent, though now classic example is Goffman's (1971) work on the presentation of self in everyday life. This approach, which sees self-presentation as a kind of performance concerned with the creation and management of impressions, could certainly be invoked to describe and explain some of the behaviour we have been discussing here. There is little doubt that many of the Japanese women with whom I worked choose their language, as well as their clothes, cakes and gift wrappings carefully, bearing in mind the impression they will create on the people with whom they interact; the 'wrapping' of the elevator girls, as another example, is on the other hand very much concerned with the image and impression of the establishment in which they work.

I have already elsewhere referred to Goffman's work in a discussion of the polite and respectful language known as *keigo*, particularly to his (1956) distinction between deference and demeanour. This was in an effort to broaden the view of *keigo* as 'respect language' to include cases where it is used reciprocally between women who would appear to be more concerned with how their speech will be interpreted than with expressing deference for each other (Hendry 1985). This would suggest that they are concerned rather with their own demeanour. In this way, too, their language can be described as a form of 'wrapping', along with other elements of their self-presentation, in this case instigated by individuals, but in the case of the stylised speech of the elevator girls, by the 'teams', to use Goffman's (1971: 83–108) terminology, to which they belong.

To develop further the manipulative aspect of wrapping, particularly in the use of language, and the way skills may be developed to 'unwrap' situations and people, the wrapping principle could possibly make a contribution to transactional analysis, which in turn may illuminate the material and other symbolic exchanges involved. For example, Gilsenan's (1976) discussion of 'Lying, Honor and Contradiction' in a Lebanese village is quite reminiscent of the conscious level of the 'wrapping' idea in that his informants are also concerned with their self-image and building this up in a way which will impress those surrounding them. In Japanese too, some examples of the use of polite speech as a distancing mechanism, to deter an uncomfortable degree of intimacy, involve the use of what outsiders might term 'lies', although the choice of such a negative word would be unlikely in Japanese.

I have also found some sociolinguistic theory useful in examining certain aspects of the wrapping principle. For example, the way women 'wrap' their elite society by dropping their extremely polite forms when they encounter people who are unable to use them is quite reminiscent of Gumperz's 'code-switching', described for Norwegians alternating between standard Norwegian and a local dialect. In the Gumperz (1971) case, the local people manage to maintain a community of equals in an unequal wider society which regards them as inferior and unsophisticated, whereas the Japanese ladies discussed above would appear to be trying to maintain their sophistication and (in their own view, at least) superiority. In both cases, the solidarity of the group in question is expressed in the language they choose to reserve for their own use.

There are, in Japan, too, other movements between different speech levels and registers, including the way, directly comparable with the Gumperz data, that local people in particular regions switch to standard Japanese in the presence of outsiders, sometimes necessarily because their dialect is incomprehensible to them, sometimes simply because outsiders are by and large socially too distant to be addressed in the intimate and informal terms of the local language. In my view, an analysis in terms of 'wrapping' allows a frame of reference wide enough for comparison at all these levels. In most of these regional examples, as Gumperz also noted, we are often dealing with less conscious and manipulative interaction than in some of the examples given above, and this is a point also made by the Japanese linguist, Ide Sachiko, in her discussion of the application of Brown and Levinson's (1976) theories of politeness to the Japanese case (Ide *et al.* 1986).

All these examples have the limitation of dealing only with the level of behaviour, however, and my feeling is that the strength of the wrapping principle lies as much in its paradigmatic as in its syntagmatic qualities, to borrow Ardener's (1971: lxxvi) distinction. In other words, analysis of the genre described by Ardener as 'social anthropology A', or 'sociol-inguistics A' offers more scope for an all-encompassing theoretical framework. At the level of language, then, the term for the envelopment of gifts, 'wrapping', could be seen as providing a model for metaphorical usage in the various other ways which have been discussed in this paper, but it might also be possible to see the 'wrapping principle' as a cognitive category or set of cognitive categories underlying the arrangement of material goods and space, and the organisation of time.

The broad range of its application would suggest that this is a very basic category in the Japanese case, a fundamental ordering principle only imperfectly described as a metaphor derived from the material manifestation. The theoretical implication here is that if such a basic ordering principle exists for the Japanese case, providing explanations for phenomena found in so many different arenas, one is likely to find similarly all-pervasive principles in other societies. It may or may not be helpful to look at material wrapping as a starting-point elsewhere. I think it would almost certainly be helpful to look at the way in which the use of language is related to intentionality in communication.[11] 'Wrapping' could also be examined, for example, in terms of barriers and boundaries, or an (emic) opposition between nature and culture (cf. Nukada 1977).

In Japan, those whose language is too blunt and direct tend to be classed by terms whose meanings resemble 'uncouth' or 'uncultured' by the more 'polite' members of society, and residents of the old capital of Kyoto, whose speech is said by natives and outsiders alike to be the furthest removed from their actual thoughts and feelings, tend to think that they are the only really civilised people in the country. In a completely different society, 'frank' language may be classified as an ideal, whether or not it is valued in practice, and those who make their indirectness too obvious could be spurned as devious or downright dishonest. In yet another social situation, dissimulation skills could be seen as evidence of cultural development, too much honesty as plain stupidity.

Evidently 'wrapping' in each of these cases needs to be interpreted in its own social context, where its value, positive or negative, may be found to be related to other social arenas. In the Japanese case, the notion of 'wrapping' works very well across the board, and it already has enough metaphorical usage in English to allow the word to be picked up for the title of this volume. Its wider cross-cultural value is a subject which remains open for further investigation and some preliminary conversations encourage me to suggest that it could prove a fruitful line of enquiry to develop, although the type of analysis I have in mind would be of an order distinct, though probably complementary to the behaviourist ones. Ultimately, I hope that a greater understanding of such a notion, and its converse, 'unwrapping', will lead to a deeper understanding of forms of communication in general.

Notes

1 This paper is based on research funded by the Economic and Social Research Council (UK), reference number: G0023 2254/1.

2 It is probably not insignificant that the products which one purchases well wrapped are imported from abroad. As well as the functional reasons discussed later, there is also a certain prestige attached to serving imported items such as cheese and 'black' tea, and these are therefore sold in a suitably presentable form.

3 *Noshi* paper has developed out of a custom whereby people in Japan used to afix a small slice of abalone to their gifts as an indication to the recipient that they were not in a state of pollution, which could be transmitted with the gift. If they had been in such a state, fish would be prohibited to them so they could not use the abalone. Nowadays

noshi paper depicts the abalone graphically.

4 Protective amulets purchased in shrines are often made of paper or fabric folded and wrapped in a ritually significant way (e.g. Nukada 1977: 159–60).

5 The notion of 'wrapping' space is also discussed in some detail by the architect Maki Fumihiko (1978) in an article about the concept of '*oku*' ('depth' is one possible translation).

6 The white inside layer of the wedding kimono has its own symbolic significance in a Japanese view, variously representing the purity of the bride, a *tabula rasa* as the bride begins a new life (Hendry 1981: 169–70), and, because white is said to be the colour of the gods, indicating that she is first the bride of the gods (Ekiguchi 1986: 6).

7 I have examined some of these different concerns in more detail in Hendry (1985, 1988), and in a forthcoming paper presented at the Tokai University symposium 'Rethinking Japan', held in Venice, October 1987.

8 In practice women's voices often do rise slightly in tone when they are using *keigo*. This is particularly evident on the telephone.

9 This arrangement, in the centre of Tokyo, inspired the depiction of the city by Roland Barthes (1982: 30–2) as having an 'empty centre'.

10 At the cooking class I attended, considerable time was spent practising the art of enveloping one substance in another, and this indeed involves quite intricate techniques. There are various ways of finishing the envelope, sometimes so that no 'seam' should be visible, others so that the outer layer should take on a specific form. Apart from cakes, other food used on ritual occasions involves a type of wrapping or layering, *tenpura* and some varieties of *sushi* being just two examples. Seaweed, for example, is prepared in a form which gives it a quality resembling paper and makes it an excellent wrapping material.

11 As the final revisions of this paper are written, work is already in progress on a book developing much further some of the ideas presented here. Discussions are also under way for a conference/workshop to bring together scholars who have found material which may be compared with the Japanese case.

References

Ardener, E. 1971. Introductory essay. In *Social Anthropology and Language*, ed. E. Ardener. London: Tavistock.

Barthes, R. 1982. *Empire of Signs*. London: Jonathan Cape.

Brown, P. and Levinson, S. C. 1976. Universals in language usage: politeness phenomena. In *Questions and Politeness*, ed. E. Goody. Cambridge: Cambridge University Press.

Brown, R. and Gilman, A. 1972. The pronouns of power and solidarity. In *Language and Social Context*, ed. P. P. Giglioli. Harmondsworth: Penguin.

Ekiguchi, Kunio 1986. *Gift Wrapping: Creative Ideas from Japan*. Tokyo, New York and San Francisco: Kodansha International.

Geertz, C. 1972. Linguistic etiquette. In *Sociolinguistics*, ed. J. B. Pride and J. Holmes. Harmondsworth: Penguin.

Gilsenan, M. 1976. Lying, honor and contradiction. In *Transaction and Meaning* ed. B. Kapferer. Philadelphia: ISHI.

Goffman, E. 1956. The nature of deference and demeanor. *American Anthropologist* 58, 473-502.

Goffman, E. 1971. *The Presentation of Self in Everyday Life*. Harmondsworth: Penguin.

Gumperz, J. J. 1971. Social meaning in linguistic structures: code-switching in Norway. In *Language in Social Groups*, comp. A. S. Dil, pp. 274-310. Stanford, Calif.: Stanford University Press.

Hendry, J. 1981. *Marriage in Changing Japan*. London: Croom Helm.

Hendry, J. 1985. The use and abuse of politeness formulae. *Proceedings of the British Association of Japanese Studies* 10, 85-91.

Hendry, J. 1988. Respect, solidarity or contempt? Politeness and communication in modern Japan. In *Contemporary European Writings on Japan*, ed. I. Nish. Folkestone: Paul Norbury.

Hendry, J. (forthcoming). The armour of honorific speech. in *Rethinking Japan*, ed. A. Boscaro, F. Gatti and M. Raveri. Folkestone: Paul Norbury.

Ide, Sachiko *et al.* 1986 *Nihonjin to Amerikajin no Keigo Kōdō*. Tokyo: Nan'undo.

Kondo, D. 1985. The way of tea: a symbolic analysis. *Man* (N.S.) 20, 287-306.

Koschmann, J. V. 1974. The idioms of contemporary Japan VIII: Tatemae to Honne. *Japan Interpreter* 9, 98-104.

Lee, O-Y. 1984. *Smaller is Better: Japan's Mastery of the Miniature*. Tokyo, New York and San Francisco: Kodansha International.

Maki, Fumihiko 1978. Nihon no toshi kukan to 'oku'. *Sekai*, December, 146-62.

Moeran, B. 1984. One over the seven: sake drinking in a Japanese pottery community. *Journal of the Anthropological Society of Oxford* 15 (2), 83-100.

Nishimura, Kunio 1987. Wrapping your heart. *Look Japan*, April, 36-7.

Nukada, Iwao 1977. *Tsutsumi*. Tokyo: Hosei Daigaku Shuppansha.

Oishi, Hatsutarō 1975. *Keigo*. Tokyo: Chikuma Shobo.

Uno, Yoshikata 1985. *Keigo o dono yō ni kangaeruka*. Tokyo: Nan'undo.

On the borderlines:
the significance of marginality
in Japanese society

Two traditions in the concept of marginality

There are two main traditions in social research on marginality: the sociological and the social anthropological. It is a sad example of academic segregation that each rarely makes reference to the other.

The sociological tradition, in terms of 'marginal man', stems from Park (1928) in the Chicago school of sociology, although Park himself refers back to Simmel on 'the stranger' (1917). 'Marginal man' was seen to be between two cultures: an optimistic picture, both in terms of gradual assimilation (if this is seen as optimistic), and in terms of the potential for creativity amongst those in marginal situations, Park's ideas were followed up by Stonequist, but in a less optimistic vein. He interpreted marginality psychologistically in terms of marginal personality and its problems (1935: 10).

This latter approach was criticised by Dickie-Clark (1966), who emphasised the sociological study of marginal situations rather than the psychological study of marginal personality. A key component of marginal situations would be some sort of exclusion: exclusion from social participation, from wealth and material rewards, privilege and power. The idea of exclusion is already suggested by the notion of borders and barriers inherent in the concept of marginality. Yet, if the exclusion were definite, consistent and permanent, then the case would no longer count as marginal, but rather outside: 'complete exclusion and complete inclusion are incompatible with the notion of marginality' (1966: 32). The question of whether one is an insider, a marginal, or an outsider, is thus a matter of degree rather than of kind.

Perlman (1976), in a study of Brazilian shanty dwellers, criticises a more recent approach to marginality in the sociology of development. She notes that marginality is often thought to imply insignificance, especially economic insignificance (as in 'of marginal importance'); and argues in contrast that marginals are highly significant, and are intimately bound up with the mainstream, which is too often ignored in focusing on marginals out of context, as if they are not in any sense integrated (1976: 245).

The anthropological tradition does not usually make this mistake of taking marginality out of the context of the whole. This tradition tends to start from a holistic view of the culture and its principal categories, and to regard marginality as that which somehow falls between the categories, on the borderlines or threshold of its normal classification system. Van Gennep (1960) on *rites de passage* thresholds, Victor Turner (1974) on the liminal, and Mary Douglas (1970) on the power and dangers of boundaries and margins, all work within this tradition. Douglas shows how features of the natural and human world, activities and actors, may defy a classification system, being either anomalous (a member of a category that belongs properly elsewhere) or ambiguous (where belonging anywhere is uncertain, weak and confused) (1970: 49–53). Such marginality may be interpreted as having positive sacred power, or negative power of pollution, or indeed both, but in either case is found to be disturbing.

What is the contribution of Japanese Studies to these traditions of research on marginality, and indeed what is the significance of marginality for understanding Japan?

Japan on the margins

In the development of concepts and theories of marginality, and indeed of other areas of social life, Japan has generally been ignored, despite the wealth of relevant Japanese material.[1] Sociologists have tended to focus on Western industrial societies or on underdevelopment, while non-industrial societies have been the principal, though by no means exclusive, area for anthropological research. It seems almost as if Japan has been out of bounds for both disciplines, falling between their main areas of concern, a borderline case, of marginal significance for mainstream social science.[2]

Thus in the classic works in both sociological and anthropological traditions of marginality there is a remarkable lack of reference to Japan, even though the oft-claimed social and cultural homogeneity of Japan would appear to render marginality especially threatening and significant. For instance, Japanese examples are notably absent from the wealth of illustrations used by Douglas to develop her argument in *Purity and Danger*; yet at first sight a concern for purity, and the dangers of impurity, would seem especially pertinent to Japan. Indeed Japan is relevant to Douglas's argument, not only because of its highly developed ideas of purity and pollution, but also because of its emphasis of social form and boundaries, and its accompanying exploration and utilisation of ambiguity, notably in religion and the arts. Douglas argues that the Lele are a people preoccupied with form (1970: 200): the same might be said of Japanese society.

It is often noted that it is vital in Japanese social interaction to adopt suitable form, to know how to behave appropriately. In order to accomplish this one must define the situation correctly, and in particular know who the other is, where s/he belongs (Lebra 1976: 23). Especially crucial is the designation of the other as belonging inside (*uchi*) or outside (*soto*).[3]

Since you are defined by where you belong, your frame (Nakane 1973: 2), it is important that you do not change it too often, or your belonging is liable to become uncertain or ambiguous. Ambiguity in current belonging may mean that your loyalty is suspect, although distaste for double loyalties is not peculiar to Japan, as is suggested by Douglas's reference to those in marginal positions in Tikopia and Taleland: 'their double loyalties and their ambiguous status in the structure where they are concerned makes them appear as a danger to those belonging fully in it' (1970: 123). Ambiguity in origins may further imply a suspect identity altogether, and may be regarded with repulsion. Hence Lebra's concise and telling statement that 'ambiguity in belonging arouses suspicion or contempt' (1976: 24).

This emphasis on fully or purely belonging, and distrust of ambiguity in belonging, should make Japanese society especially revealing for the study of marginality. Belonging has to be a major focus in any study of marginality, as those who fully belong are in a sense the opposite of those who are marginal. The notion of ambiguity in belonging brings together the anthropological concern with the disturbing character of thresholds and ambiguities, and the sociological emphasis upon uncertainty and inconsistency of exclusion, to suggest criteria for a high degree of marginality, which may be applied to potential types of marginal situations.

Types of marginality in contemporary Japan

In acknowledging different degrees of marginality, certain potential cases appear to be more adequately designated complete outsiders than marginals, just as other cases suffer insufficient social exclusion to warrant the term marginal. Thus there is a range, extending from outsiders, through borderliners, to marginals in particular contexts.[4] A person on the borderline is subject to doubts about the possibility of truly/fully belonging and yet is not seen as properly outside. To complicate matters, the most borderline can ironically become the most outside, more excluded than the proper outsider. For example, an *ainoko* (of mixed Japanese and foreign parentage) is more marginal, yet at the same time more rejected, than a 'pure' *gaijin* (foreigner).[5] Through such rejection s/he paradoxically becomes in some senses more outside than the complete outsider.[6]

In assessing the degree and significance of not fully belonging, some element of exclusion is crucial. The greatest degree of marginality will be where there is an element of exclusion from social (including material) participation, where the barriers to participation are of great scope (if not, the marginality will lack significance), and where these barriers are inconsistent, ambiguous and/or of uncertain duration (Dickie-Clark 1966: 48). If the barriers are clear, definite and immutable, then the case is likely to be more that of an outsider than of a real marginal. The possibility of avoiding recognition as marginal, that is, 'passing', and in contrast the physical recognisability of marginality, is thus a relevant factor in assessing the degree of marginality: complete passing and physical recognisability may, at each extreme, render the case too much that of an insider or outsider respectively.

Amongst those cases that qualify as highly marginal, various sources of marginality may be differentiated. These sources refer more to the kinds of condition which the mainstream regards as crucial in entailing marginality, than to any real attribute of the marginals themselves. According to these sources, one may construct groupings of marginal types, though these categories are not mutually exclusive.

In constructing these groupings, several methods[7] of investigation were pursued, including content analysis, interviews and participant observation. A content analysis of Japanese newspapers[8] from 1984 to 1986, focusing on articles pertaining to different kinds of marginality, contributed to the construction of an interim list of types that could be used in interviews and participant observation, which subsequently led to amendments and additions to the list in the dialectical process inherent in interpretation. Unstructured interviews were conducted with mainstream and potentially marginal informants, and with Japanese researchers on marginality, some of whom also considered themselves to be marginal. Participant observation of marginality was principally through interaction with co-residents in a traditional mercantile and artisan (*shitamachi*) ward of Tokyo where I lived for seven months. In addition, as a foreign researcher, one can oneself become part of the subject matter of the research, though more plausibly as an outsider than a true marginal.

This research thus led to the construction of a list (by no means intended to be exhaustive) of potential types of marginality in Japanese society, grouped tentatively according to supposed source of marginality:

'Foreign blood' – that is, not of 'pure Yamato race'
This classification is obviously inherited, and is often accompanied by an ideology of physical difference, usually thought to be recognisable even if it is not. Cultural differences are also assumed, even where not in evidence. This grouping includes the Ainu, Okinawans, Koreans, Chinese and *ainoko*.

Of these cases, the most marginal would appear to be the *ainoko* and the Koreans. In the case of the *ainoko* this is because cultural difference is unlikely if they are brought up in Japan. Yet their being physically recognisable may render them more outside than marginal, especially if the race of the non-Japanese parent is regarded as distinctly low in status, as in the case of offspring of Japanese and black Americans.[9] Koreans, however, are especially marginal (along with Okinawans, who are less subject to exclusion), since, in spite of contradictory ideology, they are not physically recognisable. They can therefore pass physically, although in other respects attempts to pass are beset with great difficulties.

Burakumin (members of outcaste communities) may well constitute a category of their own, yet in terms of the inheritance aspect and of mainstream ideology[10] they might come under this grouping, and be seen as a kind of ethnic minority (depending on the definition of ethnic), especially since 'blood' and 'race' are in any case ideologies. In terms of degree of marginality, *burakumin* may be grouped with Koreans, although their exclusion may be greater and their sense of ethnic identity less strongly developed (Price 1967: 12–13).

Foreign contact

The contact may vary from short to long term, and will include returnees of various kinds and lengths of stay abroad: at the extremes of short/long stay, they may be too inside/outside to count as truly marginal. Examples of such returnees are those born abroad (such as children of emigrants, orphans left behind in the Japanese empire, etc.); emigrants; employees returning from service abroad (again there are differences in status depending on the country of service abroad); children of such employees, who become returnee schoolchildren (Goodman, Chap. 9). A further case of foreign contact is marriage to a *gaijin*, although marrying a foreigner from a low-status country may render one more outside than marginal.

Pollution through illness/damage

Those who suffer certain kinds of illness or damage are regarded as marginal and potentially polluting in Japanese society.[11] A recent example would be people with AIDS (and those known to be HIV positive), but these suffer the added stigma of the perception of AIDS as affecting marginal groups and as a foreign disease.[12] People with AIDS may thus be seen as the embodiment of pollution through foreign contact: their marginality is then multiple.

Others within this grouping will include the mentally ill, handicapped, environmental pollution victims, and bomb victims (*hibakusha*) (cf. respectively Ohnuki-Tierney 1984: 60–1; Mihashi n.d.: 11; Tsurumi 1977: 20; Harada 1983: 10). The last three cases are often physically recognisable, and hence cannot pass. This may make them more outsiders than marginals.

Deviance: criminal and/or ideological

This grouping includes criminals, and members of certain political and religious groups. Criminals may in some cases be outsiders rather than marginals: for example, the *yakuza* (organised criminal gangs); and perhaps ex-convicts, given their difficulty in passing back into mainstream society. Political radicals should probably be of the left rather than of the right to qualify as sufficiently excluded; they may also be subject to police investigation. Amongst members of non-mainstream religious groups, one might be tempted to include followers of the so-called new religions, but it is unlikely that they suffer sufficient exclusion to be deemed truly marginal; the same may be said of Christians, although some informants identified themselves as marginal and subject to discrimination.

Other kinds of deviance may form part of a wider grouping of those associated with the liminal:

Association with the liminal

Artists, in spite of their association with the liminal (Turner 1974: 115), and the idea of their being not quite respectable (a legacy, for some types of artist, from the Tokugawa era – Yamaguchi 1984: 7), constitute a dubious case of marginality. This is clearly the case with those who are sanctified and receive public honour (such as a dancer who is deemed a 'Living National Treasure'). Yet even for less esteemed artists, the barriers may not be very great, they may not feel excluded, or they may wish a form of exclusion which is involved in belonging to the artists' world: doubts about belonging may thus not arise.

Those working in less respectable entertainment industries, including gambling or sex, are often already marginal in other respects. For those who work in erotic occupations,[13] compartmentalisation may prove difficult, and their employment may define their wider social identity. The vast majority of 'sexual deviants', however, can and do pass in Japanese society. They manage to compartmentalise this aspect of their lives, do not suffer exclusion, and thus do not qualify as marginal.

Association with life – death thresholds may incur temporary heavy pollution, and hence temporary ritual marginality, through close association with blood or death, as in the case of relatives of the dead, menstruating women, and women after childbirth (Befu 1971: 106–7; Yoshida 1981: 91). One reason for not including such cases in a list of highly marginal types would be that they *are* temporary and compartmentalised, and that any exclusion involved terminates as a matter of course. This is to a lesser extent true for the very young and the old, whose association with life – death thresholds is longer term, yet still temporary.[14] The young, of course, will grow out of their marginal status; yet the old can move out of their age status only through death, and thus appear more properly marginal, depending on their degree of

42

exclusion and loss of role and function (Wöss 1984a: 229).

Unusual family circumstances

The clearest case of marginality here is the unmarried man beyond early middle age. For a woman a career may count as a legitimate 'excuse' for remaining unmarried, yet she may not escape marginality under another category (see below). Other women may not have a recognized career, or may be pressurised to leave to get married (Lunsing 1989: 341): for these the choice is also marriage or marginality.

Other unusual family circumstances are more dubious as types of marginality, as the degree of exclusion is debatable: possible cases include the divorced,[15] and children of divorced or unmarried parents.

Unusual at work

Two cases that initially appeared marginal turned out to be rather doubtful: men who change company frequently (although this is thought to be difficult to achieve, if accomplished it will involve little exclusion); and *madogiwazoku* (those 'beside the window', referring to the less successful salary-men who are given less significant tasks and no further chance of promotion) – again, despite their marginal sounding title (*giwa* = *kiwa*; side, edge, or verge) most informants did not think these, being just the commonly unsuccessful, qualified as marginal.

More plausibly marginal are men who do not drink alcohol: it is difficult for them to participate fully in the socialising that forms a vital part of occupational life. For the same reason, not drinking alcohol is considered a handicap in a political career (cf. Moeran 1986: 240).

The most obvious case of marginality at work is the professional woman, or at least a woman in a 'man's occupation'. It is sometimes suggested that Japanese women are all in a sense marginal: but can a majority rather than a minority be marginal? In general it seems the exclusions are too unambiguous and permanent, and further that there is a definite idea of a woman's proper place. Professional women, however, are neither in that proper place, nor fully accepted into what is conceived as the man's world of professionals (with the exception of 'women's professions' of course), and hence are very much in-between and potentially rejectable by both sides.

Although the above types are supposed to share a high degree of marginality, any characterisation of types in terms of degree of marginality may not tally exactly with particular cases: for example, Koreans may be marginal in different degrees, depending on their circumstances and how they cope with marginality. The degree of marginality will thus be affected by the means of coping with it.

Means of coping with marginality

Of the various ways of coping, not all will be available to any one type of marginal. Some of the ways will moreover not only reconcile a person to marginal status, but will alter that status. This may be the intention of some means, and the unintended consequence of others.

There are three basic means of coping which may alter marginal status: 'passing' as an insider, forming support groups and compartmentalisation.

Passing

It has already been noted above that passing will affect the degree of marginality. If passing is too easy, exclusion is too readily avoided, and the case no longer qualifies as really marginal. If it is too difficult, as in the case of physical recognisability, then one is more likely to be seen as an outsider than on the borderline. Passing should not of course be seen in purely physical terms: passing does not just depend on looking the same, since, even where there is no physical difference, there is great variation in capacity for passing. Amongst all cases of a high degree of marginality, passing will be a possibility, though with different degrees of difficulty involved.

Amongst Koreans in Japan I found a contrast between those who took pride in proclaiming themselves Korean, and those who attempted to pass as Japanese. In attempting to pass, one pays a high psychological price,[16] including the price of doubts about one's own identity, the price of continually hiding and having anxieties of discovery, and the price of having to distance oneself from, and perhaps be shunned by, those who proudly proclaim their Korean identity. These latter follow an alternative path of mutual support.

Support groups

Although not all marginals are able to form support groups, such groups are a common response to marginality, as Cohen notes in his study of belonging in British rural cultures:

> The consciousness and valuing of difference – the awareness of commitment and of belonging to a culture – is . . . a ubiquitous feature of peripheral communities. Peripherality does not have to be understood in geographical terms alone, but could include marginality as well. . . . When peripherality as a self-image is complemented by a positive commitment to 'the culture', one often finds something like a widespread 'politicisation' of social life . . . There is often in such a milieu a fierce desire for self-determination.
>
> Cohen (1982: 6)

In Japan the emphasis on belonging makes the formation of support groups especially likely, and such groups may become as exclusive as the insider groups from which they are excluded. Smith (1983: 90–4) refers to the emphasis on the distinctiveness of each group, 'the clear boundaries that surround the group and set it off from all others', as providing evidence for exclusivity, and implies that this principle operates also among Japan's minority populations. This tendency towards mutual exclusiveness of insider and outsider groupings is, like 'belonging' (as in the title of Cohen's 1982 book), hardly peculiar to Japan: Cohen's more recent book, *The Symbolic Construction of Community* (1985) argues throughout that identity, including community identity, is defined in contradistinction to others. This exclusiveness is, however, particularly overt in Japan. Although exclusiveness means that support groups of marginals are likely to be seen as outside rather than marginal, at least they gain the advantage of support, and the potential for concerted action to improve their status or challenge the barriers and categories that render them marginal.

If marginals do not form or join support groups, this may mean that they remain or become all the more marginal, not only because they continue to defy insider–outsider status, but because they defy the common Japanese perspective which views people as existing in groups or networks.[17] A marginal who is seen as not properly in any network or relationship would accordingly contradict the Japanese conception of people: thus it may be that a grouping is assumed, supposed, or invented for them. For a Japanese marginal, who is likely to share the Japanese conception of others *and* self in group/network terms, it may in turn be difficult to come to terms with a self-conception as individually marginal and thus unrelated. In interviews, I found that several marginal and unattached Japanese individuals saw themselves as not really Japanese, as in some way foreign, and would try to find some explanation for this, even in terms of a previous life as a non-Japanese.

45

If they wish to avoid outsider designation resulting from alternative group solidarity, marginals may have to remain peripheral individuals. Thus the choice for marginals may be either to be deemed outsiders or to lack support for an alternative identity. This would be in line with the rather tragic portrayal of marginals in wider social research since Park's more hopeful account of 'marginal man'. Yet we should avoid assuming that marginals are always doomed to misery.

Compartmentalisation

In some cases compartmentalisation may be possible, which may lead either to special status and perhaps even privileges within that compartmentalised world, as with some kinds of artists and entertainers, or to tolerance of marginal roles as of minor significance. These latter roles may not then define who/what one is.

If one's identity is conceived in terms of belonging, then variation in private behaviour is less relevant to social identity and is tolerated as long as it does not interfere with the social obligations inherent in belonging: 'so long as a limited number of public things are done in a socially approved way, there simply is no reason to take note of variation in the realm of private behavior, much less condemn it' (Smith 1983: 93). What occurs apart from one's primary belonging must thus be either compatible with it or complementary to it (Lebra 1976: 167), and is thus acceptable if it does not challenge the paramount reality of where one belongs. Similarly, if a marginal role gives rise to double loyalties, a method of coping with this would thus be to grant clear priority to a principal loyalty: double loyalties may then not be a problem if one's obligations in primary loyalty are properly performed, and thus only become a problem if one's primary loyalty is unfulfilled or in doubt.

Compartmentalisation of some types of marginality may thus lead to toleration. Yet for other types, including deviance that is criminal or ideological, compartmentalisation is not an option. Criminal deviance attaches a public label defining the person rather than just the act, and hence precludes compartmentalisation even after penalties have been paid. Ideological deviance may be difficult to compartmentalise, even if there is the wish to do so: in some cases ideological deviants may not wish to compartmentalise if their ideology informs their life more generally.

However, if compartmentalisation is readily possible, then what might be marginal in another society, as defining who/what one is, may not be conceived as such in Japan, and may thus not count as really marginal. To put it another way, the tolerance is towards a marginal activity or role, that therefore does not constitute a marginal identity or self with the consequences of exclusion that are essential to a truly marginal situation. Tolerance of marginality here is perhaps in terms of one of the other possible meanings of marginality (i.e. marginal = insignificant), in contrast to the definition of marginality in terms of highly significant exclusions.

Possibilities for compartmentalisation in Japan suggest that, whereas in some ways being marginal looks at first sight more problematic in Japan, due to the more definite insider–outsider distinction, in other ways it may be surprisingly easier to cope with marginality in Japan than in other societies.

Ease of coping: a less tragic view

In particular, the preoccupation with suitable form, with acting in terms of an appropriate *omote* (front), may allow marginality, *ura* (behind, as in 'behind scenes'; back, as in 'backstage'),[18] to go undetected and without interference. There may thus be greater opportunities for passing or compartmentalisation, although this will only be the case with certain types of marginality, and the easier it is to pass or compartmentalise, the less marginal the case will be in our terms.

Even the importance of the *uchi–soto* distinction may make coping easier in some respects: it may increase the likelihood of support groups forming, while at the same time allowing those who remain marginal to any group at all to be relatively undisturbed. The preoccupation with your own circle means that others, recognising your not belonging, may find you no longer relevant, and hence accept you as marginal, which means in a sense accepted but left alone. You have your niche, and for the most part no one will bother you. Yet, while perhaps you escape direct interference, the price will still be material and social exclusion. Furthermore, the acceptance of (or indifference to) marginality again depends very much on the type of marginality in question, is more feasible (along with compartmentalisation) in urban than rural areas, and is more likely to apply if the marginality is chosen rather than ascribed.

The potential for some marginals in Japan to remain marginal to any group, thus lacking collective support for a strong alternative identity and world view, may encourage detachment from fixed perspectives on self or society, and give the individual a sense of cultural relativism that, despite social and material difficulties, constitutes a form of awareness which is prized in itself or at least as compensation.[19] Such detachment has been seen by Schutz and others as essential for the development of creativity and intellectual insight (1964: 104), particularly in sociology itself, and it is noteworthy that in discussions with Japanese sociologists many identified themselves as marginal.

Furthermore, marginals can play a vital role in introducing a sense of cultural relativism into the mainstream. Official circles have recently been emphasising the need for Japan to internationalise, and the prominent Liberal Democratic Party politician Miyazawa Kiichi has advocated a new *kaikoku*, opening up of the country, which he argues should be self-determined. The drive to open should come from within Japan, rather than as a response to external pressure. I would argue that, in this 'opening', marginals within Japanese society may hold the key; but to be effective they must be treated with ambivalence rather than rejection or indifference.[20]

In contrast, then, to the negative and passive picture of marginals that predominates in much of the literature, some marginals may actively choose their marginal situation, may embrace their marginal status, or at least play upon it, individually or in groups, for their own advantage or to attempt wider social change. Marginality may grant you a niche that distances you from the social pressures of full belonging; it may secure you a privileged status (though within a compartmentalised sphere – otherwise lack of exclusion belies true marginal status); it may be valued for its associated relativistic viewpoint; and it may be used to push at the very categories to which it is marginal. This is not to overrate the power of interactive negotiation, or underrate the power of the mainstream to impose its categories and enforce compliance: potential for negotiation versus compliance will vary according to the type of marginality involved.

What marginality reveals about Japanese society and vice versa

The foregoing analysis of the ways of being and coping with being marginal in Japan may be of relevance to the study of marginality in anthropology more widely, as when considering the interaction between means of coping and degree of marginality (noted above under 'ease of coping'). It may also reveal significant aspects of Japanese culture and society, not only at the more specific level of marginality in Japan, but at the more general level of key features of Japanese orientation and social organisation. It is worth remembering here Perlman's point that the study of marginality is often carried out in its own terms, without reference to the mainstream it implies (1976: 97); yet this mainstream, implicitly revealed by marginals, should be confronted explicitly.

One way in which marginality reveals the mainstream is in terms of the threats it poses, from the universal dangers inherent in the margins of society (Douglas 1970: 136),[21] to the challenges it presents to the categories of a particular culture: 'Each culture has its own special risks and problems' (ibid. 145). On the general – but less than universal – level, one may ask why marginality should be seen as threatening in terms of different social structures.[22] In the case of Japan, what is it about Japanese social structure that makes marginality threatening? Two general aspects of Japanese society noted at the outset have been supported by the investigation of marginals: the Japanese ideology of social and cultural homogeneity, and the emphasis on unambiguous belonging.

Marginals in Japan, even where standing in between social categories, are usually conceived by the mainstream as peripheral. In Japanese academic discourse, a range of terms for marginality can be distinguished: the loanword borrowed from American sociology *mājinaru*, and the Japanese terms *shūhen* and *kyōkai*. While *shūhen* implies periphery, *kyōkai* would refer more to the situation of those who are in between rather than on the edge. It is significant that *shūhen* is the more commonly used term in discussions of marginality in Japanese society.[23]

This mainstream interpretation of marginal as peripheral implies a view that looks from the centre outwards, and reflects the predominant sense of social and cultural homogeneity in Japanese society (but not, of course, its reality, which is denied by the very fact of marginality). This contrasts with the immigrant experience and melting-pot ideology of the USA in which the Western sociological conception of marginality, as a borderline situation in between two groups or cultures, was developed. The Japanese sense of homogeneity of insiders is sometimes graphically expressed in terms of Japan being a circle (Yoshida 1975: 133–9), in which case marginals are represented as on the circumference, furthest from the centre.[24]

The interpretation of marginal as peripheral rather than in-between may also reflect the difficulty of managing 'one foot in each camp' in

Japan, and recalls the emphasis on unambiguous belonging. The norm of primary belonging, of clear allegiance, makes it difficult to belong significantly to more than one competing group. Marginals thus belong peripherally, or, if they are seen as properly belonging elsewhere, are treated as outsiders. Support groups may even further this process as we have seen, tending to become exclusive themselves, and thus to be conceived as outsiders rather than as true marginals.

On a more particular level, specific types of marginality reveal the mainstream through the threats they pose to cultural categories in between which they fall. They reveal the key categories that they transgress, such as Japanese/foreign (the ultimate *uchi*/*soto* boundary of the culture), or physically like us versus physically different from us. Where more readily understood as peripheral rather than in-between, marginals may still reveal fundamental concerns. The *burakumin* clearly reveal the cultural emphasis on purity, as indeed do those cases seen as polluted through illness or damage. Ohnuki-Tierney (1984: 38) argues that the principles (such as outside=impurity) governing categories of thought have been stable in Japanese culture, although the specific forms of their expression (for instance, who is marginal and thus impure) have undergone transformation. This view is supported by the findings described above.

It has already been suggested that one is likely to be less marginal, and deemed rather outside, if one cannot pass at all due to physical recognisability. This indicates the great significance given to physical signs of difference. Even where not physically recognisable, marginals are often thought to be so in the prevailing ideology; and, where outward appearance is not thought to manifest difference, this may still be explained in physical terms. There seems to be a preference for physical explanations of difference if at all plausible. Thus, if one's marginal status is considered to be involuntary, the factors responsible tend to be conceived as physical, rather than social or psychological. For example, physical explanations are often invoked to account for unmarried men.

Reactions to marginals as threatening or disturbing may reveal what are the most significant margins, but these must not always be assumed to be the boundaries of the society as a whole. One must thus ask whether particular types are marginal and threatening with respect to the whole society, or to a particular group or institution within it. Although this question may not be answered altogether unambiguously, it may prove revealing or at least suggestive.

Most Japanese studies of marginality reflect the common assumption in Japan that marginality refers to ethnic or pseudo-ethnic groups that are not fully assimilated into mainstream Japanese society, and hence experience social discrimination. This assumption excludes consideration of other types of marginal situations, especially those that are marginal with respect to particular social institutions rather than to society as a whole. Some groupings of types of marginality clearly threaten the whole society in one or two ways: a threat to national purity (the 'foreign blood' grouping plus *burakumin*) or to social order (some cases of criminal and ideological deviance). But other groupings suggest more particular threats: 'unusual family circumstances' and 'unusual at work' imply that one may be marginal to kinship and occupational institutions rather than to the wider society and its sense of purity and security.[25]

Even so, a threat to a particular institution may be taken as a wider social threat. For example, a threat to the family is seen as a more widescale challenge, flouting key social norms, than is a threat to a particular work-group. This is perhaps because the latter threatens only that particular group: elsewhere in society those concerned do not constitute a threat. In contrast, divorced women perhaps, and more probably unmarried men, can be seen as undermining one of society's basic institutions, the family, and hence as threatening the whole. Professional women, though classified above as marginal at work, clearly also challenge family and wider sex-role norms, and thus seem to count as marginal at all levels.

Some cases of potential marginality in Japan may prove to be not truly marginal because of possibilities for passing or compartmentalisation (a point already noted in the discussion of methods of coping and the preoccupation with *omote*). Yet the possibility of passing also helps to explain the attempts made to ensure that those categories of marginality that define who the person is, that are in this sense 'absolute' and cannot be compartmentalised, do not pass into the inside. It is worth noting here the way in which one's household register (*koseki*) may be used to maintain exclusion and keep one marginal. Restrictions on access to the *koseki* have merely increased the employment of private detectives to check on social background before marriage, or before acceptance as a permanent employee of a large company. In a sense this reveals a preoccupation not only with *omote,* but with *ura* too – as further evidenced by the popularity of magazines and television programmes that try to get behind *omote*. This of course is hardly unique to Japan, and suggests that *omote* and *ura* should perhaps gain wider currency in anthropology.

The idea of 'absolute' marginality suggests a reference to what you are rather than what you do, a quality of the person rather than of the behaviour,[26] and indeed (in contrast to Nakane's general view, 1973: 2) what you are in terms of attribute rather than the social frame of particular relationships or immediate social situation. Thus, while it is often argued that the Japanese are not absolutists, the case of some marginals would contradict this view, or at least show the social limits to situationism.[27]

Those who are marginal through 'foreign blood' or pollution are the most obvious cases here; but ideological deviants, in particular political radicals, unable and perhaps unwilling to compartmentalise, are specially interesting in this context. Ideological deviants may be seen as double deviants, since they deviate not just in terms of ideology but by the very fact of being ideological and hence in a sense absolutist: their application of absolute standards in turn receives an absolute rejection from the mainstream.

The assumption that absolutism is not a feature of Japanese culture is often applied to stratification in Japan. Just as it is argued that people are not absolutely designated in terms of social class in Japan, but rather situated in a variety of context-bound particular hierarchical relationships (some more significant than others), so it might be concluded that individuals are not absolutely marginal in Japan, but rather marginal only in particular contexts. Yet while hierarchy in Japan may as a rule operate specifically rather than in general, this is with the significant exception of certain marginals and outsiders, who are absolutely defined as below the mainstream, and excluded from its particular hierarchies.

Absolute marginals thus challenge two common assumptions or stereotypes about Japan: that Japan is a homogeneous society, and that Japanese culture is characterised by particularistic situational relativism. In response to these claims, we may wish to say with Ruth Benedict '*but also*' the opposite is true (1967: 1), and indeed, in the case of supposed homogeneity, marginals, especially as peripherals or pushed to being outsiders, do not just exist 'but also' but 'precisely because' (of the supposed homogeneity).

In considering what marginality reveals about Japanese society, we have arrived again at the usual hermeneutic circularity 'problem': the document tells us about the culture, which is necessary to interpret the document, and so on (Valentine 1986: 126). In particular, marginality will tell us something about the concerns of Japanese culture, which are perhaps necessary in order to spot marginality in Japan. There is a similar circle or dialectic, in that if marginality is especially revealing about Japan, because of its significance for Japanese social structure and cultural orientations, then Japan will be a significant arena for the exploration of marginality more widely, for its refinement as a concept, and for our more general understanding of methods of becoming, being and coping with being marginal.[28] If marginality helps to define the lines of social structure, and is inherent therein, as Douglas argues (1970: 136), then the study of marginality in a society in which it has special significance will be of relevance to anthropology more generally: research on marginality, as indeed research on Japan, is not after all so marginal.

Notes

1 This was a major impetus for the research underlying this paper. It is based on seven months' fieldwork in Japan in 1986, supported by the Japan Foundation, the Japan Foundation Endowment Committee and the Carnegie Trust for the Universities of Scotland.

2 This 'marginality' of Japan is also partly self-induced by Japanologists who refuse to look at Japan cross-culturally, thus reflecting and reinforcing the Japanese myth of uniqueness (*nihonjinron*).

3 This distinction is, however, not a fixed element of the social structure, but a variable frame (Lebra 1976: 112), a continuum of possibilities ranged in terms of social distance from self (Bachnik 1986: 69).

4 A situation not to be confused with marginality is that of duality (Rose 1983: 58–9), in which the person belongs fully to two worlds without being excluded from either.

5 Hamabata makes a similar point about Japanese Americans in Japan who, although physically Japanese, are culturally American, and thus pose a special threat (1986: 369): instead of being considered a talented foreigner speaking some Japanese, one may be thought of as an 'incomplete Japanese' (1986: 356).

6 Compare Ohnuki-Tierney: 'there are two kinds of "outside" – the clear-cut outside, which is the opposite of the inside, and the outer margin. In terms of meaning, the former is assigned dual power, beneficial and destructive, whereas the latter is designated as impure' (1984: 47). Similarly Bowes argues that Kibbutzniks prefer those 'strangers' (volunteer workers) who can be comfortably categorised as a group of 'total outsiders' (1980: 666).

7 These are included in the 'methods of marginality' (used by the researcher and the researched) discussed more fully in Valentine (1987).

8 The analysis of Japanese newspapers was suggestive, as the marginal tends to attract media attention, whether of condemnation or awe; cf. Buruma on 'real life' television programmes (1985: 41).

9 One may note here the Japanese fascination with *ainoko*, and indeed with other cases in this grouping, including Chinese, and the use of such marginals in the entertainment industry. Fascination and disturbance/distaste are two sides of the same coin however, and this does not mean they do not suffer exclusion in other fields.

10 Hane notes the persistence of the popular belief that *burakumin* are of different racial origin from the Japanese (1982: 139).

11 Compare Ohnuki-Tierney: 'My emphasis is on the close association between the notion of purity as it applies to the body and the general health of the Japanese, and that of moral purity' (1984: 35).

12 For example, in 1986 foreigners became excluded from certain bath-houses: the predominant belief was that you were safe from AIDS if you avoided contact with foreigners.

13 Brameld notes an estimate that the number of females employed in Japan in 'erotically stimulating occupations' is about 1 million (1968: 196).

14 Wöss (1984b) argues for the marginality of the young and the old in Japanese society.

15 Several male informants suggested divorced women were marginal, an opinion generally not shared by female informants. Divorced men were rarely considered to be marginal.

16 Compare De Vos and Wagatsuma on the 'anomic marginality' of *burakumin* who pass (1967: 247).

17 Bachnik (1986: 50) quotes Nakamura as saying that Japanese consistently describe people as 'always . . . existing in a network of human relationships' (1968: 192); and quotes Smith (1983: 49) on the Japanese seeing people as 'invariably identified as acting in some kind of human relationship, never autonomously'.

18 This front/back distinction is not of course peculiar to Japan. Goffman distinguishes front and back regions in his analysis of presentation of self (1971: 114).

19 This was noted in particular by some Korean informants.

20 Compare Goodman (Chap. 9) on the ambivalent position of returnee schoolchildren; and Weimann (1982) on the bridging function of marginals in the flow of information between groups.

21 Anthropologists have pointed in particular to the association between the margins and formlessness (Douglas 1970: 118) or chaos (*konton*) (Yamaguchi 1974: 15).

22 Perlman addresses this question for Latin American societies (1976: 92).

23 As for *majinaru*, rather than this loanword having a precise academic meaning, it is often used to describe general social problems. For example, the 'Majinaruman' (Marginal Man) issue of *Gendai no Esupuri*, February 1985, is revealing in terms of what is considered to count as marginal: the table of contents reads like a list of currently topical social problems, such as educational suicides, badly behaved young women, childish adults, absent fathers, lonely old people, and orphans returning from China. This last case, more obviously marginal in our terms, was given substantial coverage by Japanese television in 1986. Similarly the 'marginality' of individuals or groups, as described in Western publications, is often translated into Japanese as the *mondai* ('problems') of these people.

24 Yamaguchi argues that, for most of Japanese history, the emperor was a marginal/peripheral figure. In this sense both the top and the bottom (the peripheral minorities) of the social scale would be marginal. Moreover they shared a moral and spiritual ambivalence as both sacred and polluting (1977: 173). During the Tokugawa period certain groups lost this ambivalent character, and with the Meiji Restoration the

emperor became defined as central, though the emperor and despised minorities remain two sides of the same coin implying each other: sacred centre and polluted periphery. The inference made by the political left is that the exclusion of the despised peripheral minorities cannot be eradicated without the abolition of the sacred centre. An alternative view is implied by Amino, who traces connections between the central *Tennō* (imperial) family and the freedom of peripheral peoples in pre-Tokugawa Japan, thus proposing 'the relation of the Tennō to the world of peace and freedom' (Ishii 1987: 14).

25 This is reminiscent of the three fundamental spheres of human self-formation – language/interaction (with an interest in homogeneity of cultural understandings), work and family – that Habermas (1968: 9–10) adopts from Hegel's Jena writings.

26 Compare Foucault on the new persecution of 'peripheral sexualities' in Europe, when practice is transformed into personage, acts into species (1981: 42–4).

27 This is indeed implied by Lebra, in discussing the difference between social relativism and situationism (1976: 14).

28 This side-steps the current fruitless debate on whether or not Japan is unique: of course Japan is different in some respects from other societies, and hence relevant for purposes of contrast; and of course Japan is the same as some other societies in many respects, and hence of relevance for comparative purposes. Japanese Studies wins either way in its potential contribution to general anthropology.

References

Bachnik, J. M. 1986. Time, space and person in Japanese relationships. In *Interpreting Japanese Society*, ed. J. Hendry and J. Webber. Oxford: JASO.

Befu, H. 1971. *Japan: an Anthropological Introduction*. San Francisco: Chandler.

Benedict, R. 1967. *The Chrysanthemum and the Sword*. London: Routledge & Kegan Paul.

Bowes, A. M. 1980. Strangers in the kibbutz: volunteer workers in an Israeli community. *Man* (N.S.) **15**, 665–81.

Brameld, T. 1968. *Japan: Culture, Eduction, and Change in Two Communities*. New York: Holt, Rinehart & Winston.

Buruma, I. 1985. *A Japanese Mirror: Heroes and Villains of Japanese Culture*. Harmondsworth: Penguin.

Cohen, A. P. (ed.) 1982. *Belonging: Identity and Social Organisation in British Rural Cultures*. Manchester: Manchester University Press.

Cohen, A. P. 1985. *The Symbolic Construction of Community*. Chichester: Ellis Horwood; London: Tavistock.

De Vos, G. and Wagatsuma, H. 1967. Group solidarity and individual mobility. In *Japan's Invisible Race*, ed. G. De Vos and H. Wagatsuma. Berkeley and Los Angeles: University of California Press.

Dickie-Clark, H. F. 1966. *The Marginal Situation*. London: Routledge & Kegan Paul.

Douglas, M. 1970. *Purity and Danger*. Harmondsworth: Penguin.

Foucault, M. 1981. *The History of Sexuality*, Vol. 1. Harmondsworth: Penguin.

Goffman, E. 1971. *The Presentation of Self in Everyday Life*. Harmondsworth: Penguin.

Habermas, J. 1968. *Technik und Wissenschaft als 'Ideologie'*. Frankfurt: Suhrkamp.

Hamabata, M. M. 1986. Ethnographic boundaries: culture, class, and sexuality in Tokyo. *Qualitative Sociology* 9 (4), 354–71.

Hane, M. 1982. *Peasants, Rebels, and Outcastes: the Underside of Modern Japan*. New York: Pantheon.

Harada, K. 1983. The atomic bomb survivors of Hiroshima and the social aftereffects on their lives. Paper presented at Essex University.

Ishii, S. 1987. Review of Y. Amino, Nihon chūsei no hinōgyōmin to tennō. *Japan Foundation Newsletter* 14 (6), 12–14.

Lebra, T. S. 1976. *Japanese Patterns of Behavior*. Honolulu: University of Hawaii Press.

Lunsing, W. 1989. Fujin Kōron 'hagaki tsūshin' ni miru nihon josei. *Fujin Kōron* 1, 338–45.

Mihashi, O. (n.d.) Body situation: a sociological essay on contemporary Japanese society. Unpublished paper, Wako University, Tokyo.

Moeran, B. 1986. One over the seven: sake drinking in a Japanese pottery community. In *Interpreting Japanese Society*, ed. J. Hendry and J. Webber. Oxford: JASO.

Nakane, C. 1973. *Japanese Society*. Harmondsworth: Penguin.

Ohnuki-Tierney, E. 1984. *Illness and Culture in Contemporary Japan:* Cambridge: Cambridge University Press.

Park, R. E. 1928. Human migration and the marginal man. *American Journal of Sociology* 33, 881–93.

Perlman, J. E. 1976. *The Myth of Marginality: Urban Poverty and Politics in Rio de Janeiro*. Berkeley and Los Angeles: University of California Press.

Price, J. 1967. A history of the outcaste: untouchability in Japan. In *Japan's Invisible Race*, ed. G. De Vos and H. Wagatsuma. Berkeley and Los Angeles: University of California Press.

Rose, P. I. 1983. *Mainstream and Margins: Jews, Blacks and other Americans*. New Brunswick, NJ: Transaction Books.

Sakada, G. (ed.) 1985. *Majinaruman. Gendai no Esupuri* no. 211.

Schutz, A. 1964. The stranger: an essay in social psychology. In *Collected Papers II: Studies in Social Theory*. The Hague: Martinus Nijhoff.

Simmel, G. 1950 (originally 1917). The stranger. In *The Sociology of Georg Simmel*, ed. K. H. Wolff. New York: Free Press.

Smith, R. J. 1983. *Japanese Society: Tradition, Self, and the Social Order*. Cambridge: Cambridge University Press.

Stonequist, E. V. 1935. The problem of the marginal man. *American Journal of Sociology* 41, 1-12.

Tsurumi, K. 1977. Social price of pollution in Japan and the role of folk beliefs. Research Papers Series A-30, Sophia University, Tokyo.

Turner, V. W. 1974. *The Ritual Process*. Harmondsworth: Penguin.

Valentine, J. 1986. Dance space, time and organization: aspects of Japanese cultural performance. In *Interpreting Japanese Society*, ed. J. Hendry and J. Webber, pp. 111-28. Oxford: JASO.

Valentine, J. 1987. Methods of marginality in Japanese society. Paper presented at social research methods seminar, Department of Sociology and Social Policy, University of Stirling.

Van Gennep, A. 1960. *The Rites of Passage*. London: Routledge.

Weimann, G. 1982. On the importance of marginality: one more step into the two-step flow of communication. *American Sociological Review* 47, 764-73.

Wöss, F. 1984a. Escape into death, old people and their wish to die. In *Europe Interprets Japan*, ed. G. Daniels. Tenterden: Paul Norbury.

Wöss, F. 1984b. Existence on the brink of life: traditional Japanese concepts on childhood and old age. Paper presented at Social Anthropology of Japan Conference, Nissan Institute, Oxford University.

Yamaguchi, M. 1974. *Bunka to ryogisei*. Tokyo: Iwanami Shoten.

Yamaguchi, M. 1977. Kingship, theatricality, and marginal reality in Japan. In *Text and Context: the Social Anthropology of Tradition*, ed. R. K. Jain. Philadelphia: ISHI.

Yamaguchi, M. 1984. Theatrical space in Japan, a semiotic approach. *Japan and America: a Journal of Cultural Studies* 1, 1-8.

Yoshida, K. 1975. *Japan is a Circle*. London: Paul Norbury.

Yoshida, T. 1981. The stranger as god: the place of the outsider in Japanese folk religion. *Ethnology* 20, 87-99.

The feminine in Japanese folk religion: polluted or divine?

Introduction

It has been widely reported that traditionally women were ritually prohibited from entering certain mountains and other sacred places in mainland Japan (e.g. Miyata 1979: 59–66; Miyake 1987). In the fishing villages in which I conducted fieldwork women are not allowed to get on a fishing boat because they are said to be ritually polluted or because the *funa-dama* (guardian spirit of the boat) is female and will become angry since she is jealous of female crews.[1] This prohibition and its associated ideas seem to exist in many other Japanese fishing villages. Women, and menstruating women in particular, must not participate in village festivals in a number of rural communities. In most places it is Shinto priests who conduct the festivals, and men predominate in ritual activities.

However, in the south-western archipelago it was, and still is in many villages, mostly women rather than men, who conduct festivals and rituals as *kaminchu* or priestesses. There are a few men who participate in rituals as priests (*kaminchu*), but even so they perform somewhat secondary roles as assistants to the priestesses. Other men are not allowed to participate in rituals at all. Nor, traditionally, can men enter sacred places. For example, on the island of Kudaka there are certain sacred places in the villages which men are not allowed to enter.[2]

Thus, on the one hand, Japanese women were, and still are, considered to be ritually polluted in certain parts of Honshu (mainland Japan), Kyushu and Shikoku. On the other hand, in the south-western archipelago they are regarded as sacred priestesses, and men are mostly excluded from ritual activities.

Although there exist a great number of studies of villages in Okinawa as well as mainland Japan, there are few studies concentrating on pollution beliefs about women aside from Namihira's work (1984). It would seem, therefore, that this subject deserves more careful examination.

After reviewing some Japanese folklorists' views on apparently conflicting ideas about the feminine, I will first briefly describe prohibitions and taboos concerning menstruation, pregnancy and childbirth in two fishing villages – one in Kyushu, and the other in Wakayama – and then examine whether such prohibitions and pollution beliefs exist or not in Okinawan villages. The material used derives both from fieldwork and library research. I will then try to discover certain underlying notions concerning the feminine in Japanese folk religion. Finally I will briefly examine Douglas's theory of pollution.

Pollution beliefs associated with women

Yanagita Kunio and Segawa Kiyoko have tried to explain these contrary ideas on the feminine in historical terms. First, Yanagita states that 'originally, most of the important activities in rituals and prayers were performed and controlled by women. Mediators with gods were in principle women. Formerly, every housewife served gods, and the most talented woman among them became the leading priestess' (1948: 14). Segawa, for her part, writes that,

> while menstruation is tabooed in mainland festivals, in the southern islands such taboos are lacking and in Okinawa menstruation is even considered to be an expression of divinity. Even today rituals are performed there by women as priestesses. It is said that in ancient Japan priestesses officiated in rituals. Is this contrast due to the influences of Buddhism, Confucianism, Taoism and others from abroad?

> (Segawa 1984: 103)

It seems to me that these scholars argue that, in ancient Japanese society, ritual activities must have been performed by women, as in contemporary Okinawa, but that indigenous pollution beliefs became more pronounced under the influence of Buddhism in Honshu, Shikoku and Kyushu. However, such beliefs did not develop in the Amami and Okinawa islands because Buddhistic influences have never been strong in those islands.[3]

Although this interpretation suggests what probably happened, it should be noted that it is *not* the introduction of Buddhism which produced such pollution beliefs. After all, beliefs in the pollution of childbirth are obvious in the (pre-Buddhist) *Kojiki* and *Nihonshoki*. According to the Japanese historian Shigeo Okada, it was in the ninth century that beliefs in the pollution of childbirth became stronger. While the 'pollution' period of childbirth was seven days in earlier times, this period was extended to a month in the late Heian period (794–1185). In other words, from this time women who bore babies were not allowed to enter the compounds of a shrine for a month after giving birth (Okada 1982: 331–4; Namihira 1985: 131–2). This prohibition is still observed in many Japanese villages.

With regard to the notions of women, pregnancy and childbirth in contemporary Japan, there exist local variations within the mainland itself. In the fishing village of Katsumoto-ura, located on the island of Iki, Nagasaki Prefecture, the husband of a women who has just borne a baby must not go out fishing for three days after the birth and must purify himself with sea water before going to fish on the fourth day. In this same village pregnancy is also considered to be polluting and villagers say that, if there is a crew member on the boat whose wife becomes pregnant during a fishing trip, there will be poor catches. Thus, when the wife of one of the crew members becomes pregnant, not only the husband but all crew members and the boat must be purified by a Shinto priest from the village shrine. Moreover, women were tabooed from fishing itself because traditionally it was believed that if a woman boarded a fishing boat, the fishermen's guardian spirit of the boat (*funa-dama*) would become angry (Yoshida *et al.* 1974: 6).

While pregnancy and childbirth are believed to bring about poor catches of fish in Katsumoto-ura, in the fishing village of Koza, located on the southern tip of Wakayama Peninsula, pregnancy was thought to bring good luck until the end of World War II, even though menstruation and childbirth themselves were considered to be ritually polluting.[4] A fisherman then would face his pregnant wife's belly, putting his hands together just as if praying to a deity, and prayed for a large catch. It is said that then a good catch would result because menstruation stops when gestation begins. Yet people also say that they must try not to talk with pregnant women before they go out to fish. Just as in Katsumoto-ura, women in Koza are prohibited from getting into a fishing boat. Although wives during menstruation used to cook, wash clothes and perform other daily household tasks, they also spent every night during menstruation in the girls' hut (*anya-yado*, or *musume-yado* in standard Japanese). According to Segawa Kiyoko such menstruation or childbirth huts (variously called *kariya*, *taya*, *koya* and *yogore*) were to be found more frequently in south-western, than in north-eastern, Japan and these huts were more frequently found in fishing villages than in inland farming areas (Segawa 1984: 45).

In Koza it was a convention that men should not enter a room where there was a pregnant women. Menstruating women should not enter a room where a household altar (*kami-dama*) was placed; they were not allowed to worship at a shrine; nor could they enter the compound of a shrine or other sacred places. Moreover, they were forbidden from participating in shrine or other festivals and rituals, as well as in wedding or other rites of passage. Finally, they were not supposed to prepare the lunch boxes that were to be eaten on board fishing boats. These taboos, however, are not observed that frequently nowadays, particularly by young people (cf. Takei 1987).

Further practices associated with folk beliefs included the purification of the whole house by sprinkling it with salt. In the case of poor catches of fish there was a custom called *ryotsuke* (to make a good catch) in which girls before puberty, or women after menopause, exposed their pudendae to the guardian spirit of the boat (Takei 1987).

Keiko Takada notes that in mountain villages engaged in lumbering and farming in Kozagawa-cho, Wakayama Peninsula, women used to give birth in their husband's house (instead of in their natal house) where the 'back room' was used for childbirth until a hospital was built in the post-war period. Most of the traditional practices associated with childbirth disappeared when they began to give birth in hospitals built nearby. Before then, the afterbirth, which was considered to be ritually polluted, was buried either under the house or near the graveyard, after being purified with salt. A naming ceremony was performed on the 11th day after birth for a boy, and on the 9th day after the birth of a girl. During the period from childbirth to the naming ceremony, the woman who bore the baby was not allowed to go outside the room where she had given birth, except for obvious reasons. In particular, she was not to approach the house oven, otherwise she would 'contaminate' it. Also, she was not to go out into the sun, and both her own clothes and her baby's diapers had to be dried in the shade, not in the sun. Prohibitions were to some extent slackened after the naming ceremony, although the mother was considered to be 'dirty' up to the 33rd day after birth. During that period she could not do such things as enter the village tutelary shrine, or attend village festivals. On the 33rd day, the mother, carrying her baby, visited the tutelary shrine – often in the company of her husband and mother-in-law – to pray for her baby's luck and health. Clearly pollution is here associated with childbirth (Takada 1987).

Priestesses in Okinawa

It is widely reported that there exist few prohibitions of the kind just described in the south-western islands (Segawa 1984; Namihira 1985: 132–3). Shamans called *yuta* whom we interviewed in the Amami and Okinawa Islands may hold seances or performances (*kami-goto*) even when they are menstruating. According to my fieldwork, this is in contrast to, for instance, Balinese shamans (*sadeg*) who stated explicitly to me that they never performed seances during the time of menstruation.[5] Not only *yuta* but priestesses (*kaminchu*), including the high priest (*noro* or *nuru*) and other priestesses in the south-western archipelago, perform communal rituals during their periods.

Just as it would be simplistic to state that in the mainland, Kyushu and Shikoku women take no part in ritual activities,[6] it would also be misleading to assert that there exist no pollution beliefs associated with menstruation in Okinawa. In the village of Bise (with population 816; 265 households in 1985), situated in Motobu Peninsula, Okinawa Prefecture, some women, who are not only priestesses in village festivals but also act as *yuta* in daily life, state that while a priestess can perform rituals during menstruation, ordinary women who are not priestesses do not come to rituals during their periods.[7] Also, another older priestess states that during her menstruation she refrains from entering the village shrine (*asagi*) although she participates in the performance of rituals outside the shrine. While most of the households of Bise consist of farmers engaged in sugar-cane and vegetable cultivation, some twenty household heads are engaged in fishing as a subsidiary occupation. According to one informant, fishermen do not let their wives touch their fishing equipment just before going to fish. While there is no prohibition against women getting into a fishing boat, it is taboo for a man and a woman (not necessarily a husband and his wife) to get on the same boat because the deity of the sea, being a female deity, gets jealous.

Incidentally, there is no belief in the *funa-dama* in Bise village; it is all right for two men and a woman to get on a boat; theoretically, it is even all right for a man and two women to get on a boat, but it is preferred that fewer women than men get on a boat at the same time. Fishermen here traditionally do not believe that menstruation is polluting, but they try not to meet women, menstruating or not, when going to fish, and they believe that menstruating women should not touch pickles; if they do, they spoil them.

However, compared to the mainland, pollution beliefs associated with women in Okinawa seem to be weak. This is evidently related to the ritual superiority of women in Okinawa. Here attention should be paid to the processes by which priestesses are selected.

Altogether, there are 32 *munchū* (lineages) in Bise, but priestesses (*kaminchū* or *kamingua*) are selected from only 3 of these (Nakada 1983). The priestess system in Bise is basically similar to that of the small village of Noho (34 households, population of 85) on the island of Iheya, north Okinawa. In Noho there are 12 *kaminchū* (9 women and 3 men). While the priestess systems in both villages are similar, in that the *kaminchū* are selected only from certain *munchū*, they differ in the ways they select *kaminchū*. In Noho they are selected from 10 *munchū* after discussion among the members of each *munchū*. When there are several candidates, the successor priestess is decided by a lottery. The present priestess, called *nuru*, was decided in the latter way, and she succeeded the preceding *nuru* who died several years earlier (Shirakawa, personal communication). In Bise, however, while the priestesses are selected on the basis of certain *munchū* as in Noho, they are considered qualified to be priestesses only when they have experience of the *kamidāri*, which refers to certain psychological and physical disorders which are regarded as a mark of the divine. It is still believed that this abnormal psycho-physical state can only be cured if a woman becomes a priestess, succeeding her predecessor, because the gods want her to become a priestess. If she refuses to do so, her illness will not be cured.

It seems that the *kamidāri* which usually afflicts women from 14 to 35, includes various sorts of abnormal behaviour, unconsciousness and hallucinations, such as, for example, seeing the image of an old man with a white beard during the day, and at night dreaming of being taught how to perform rituals and other mystical things. One priestess named Muta Umosa had a dream, when she was 14, in which she prayed at various sacred places of the village, making offerings to the small shrine, dedicated to the sea goddess and located in the middle of the village. Another priestess, who acts also as *yuta* (medium or shaman), was seriously ill when she was in her early thirties, and was confined to bed for several months. They both recovered from these disorders when they became priestesses.

It is the *yuta* who judge through supernatural means whether certain illnesses are *kamidāri* or not. For example, when a girl becomes mentally ill, her parents or other relatives consult the *yuta*. In Bise there were four *yuta* in 1987; two of them are just *yuta*, but another two are priestesses as well; the latter have married out of the village and have been practising as diviners, folk curers of illness, shamans possessed by ancestral spirits; while one lives in Tancha and another in Nago City, both of them return to Bise at the times of annual rituals to act as priestesses.

Religious context

Female superiority in religious contexts, as opposed to male dominance in secular, political contexts, is obvious in the ground plan of Okinawan houses described in detail by Mabuchi (1968) and Ouwehand (1985: 31–8). In Iheya, too, the symbolic oppositions, east/west, south/north, male/female, correspond to superior and inferior in everyday life. Thus the 'first room' (*ichibanza*) on the east side, is used for receiving formal visits. Male guests sit in the most eastern side of the room, women to the west, the inferior side. Normally, the 'second room' (*nibanza*), located west of the 'first room', is used. It is in this room that the head of the house, his wife and children sleep. However, when rituals are held – as, for instance, the annual festival of the *unjami* (ritual worship of the sea goddess), which I observed in Dana, Iheya island, in 1982 – the priestess is situated on the most eastern side of the 'first room' while her *munchū* members gather in the 'first' and 'second' rooms of her own natal house to have a feast after the ceremony. In this connection it is to be noted that, as elsewhere in Okinawa, the *munchū* membership of women here does not change after their marriage. Therefore, those *kaminchu* who married out due to virilocal rules return to their own natal house to act as priestesses at the times of village rituals. Watanabe and others regard *munchū* as a patrilineage (Watanabe 1986: 175–6).

The 'back rooms' (*uraza*), situated at the back, northern, or inferior side of the house are used as bedrooms for a young married couple or marriageable daughters, and for childbirth. In Hateruma, during the period after delivery 'the east side of the house is screened with *shimenawa* and salt is strewn because of its purifying effect' (Ouwehand 1985: 34). Also, 'since mother and child are considered to be polluted for a certain period after the delivery, the other members of the household and particularly the baby's father, must observe certain taboos' (Ouwehand 1985: 34). Thus, in spite of the striking overall superiority of women, certain prohibitions are associated with childbirth in Okinawa.

The east–west axis of the house described above is occasionally reversed in Noho and in Bise, depending on the location of the sacred places. In the village of Noho in certain houses located on the eastern side of the sacred mountin (*gushiku*) the 'first room' is situated on the west side of the house, and the 'second room' on the east side; the toilet is situated in the north-eastern corner of the yard, whereas it is located in the north-western corner of the yard in ordinary houses. These houses are called 'divine houses' (*kami-yashiki*). While in ordinary houses the kitchen is located west of the 'second room', in the 'divine houses' the kitchen is on the east side. This reversal of the house plan shows that the location of the *gushiku* is encountered first along the east–west axis. In Bise some 17 'reversed' houses are all located on the eastern side of the 'sacred' road which gods are believed to pass along.

In order to understand the notion of 'woman' in Okinawa, it is also useful to pay attention to the ritual tug-of-war performed as part of the all souls *bon* festival. In Noho and other villages on Iheya island the tug-of-war was performed by the inhabitants of the two sides of the village, the eastern half representing the male side and the western half the female side, as in many other areas in Okinawa (Mabuchi 1980). It is stressed here and elsewhere that if the female side wins, fertility will increase. In Bise, the ritual tug-of-war was performed on the 25th of June according to the lunar calendar, between the inhabitants of the northern side and of the southern side of the village consonant with the division of the village into a north side and a south side. Bise village, which faces the sea to the west, is a long community extending from north to south along the coast of Motobu Peninsula, Okinawa Mainland. In this village the northern side represents the female, the southern side the male. Villagers say that these terms 'male' and 'female' derive from the way in which the two ropes used in the tug-of-war are knotted. Namely, one rope is called 'female' with a large loop in the end, and the other called 'male' with a small loop. The loops of the two ropes are tied around a stick. In Noho the 'female' rope is placed to the west, while the 'male' rope is placed to the east, while in Bise, the 'female' rope is placed on the northern side and the 'male' rope on the southern side. In the latter village, it is said that when the northern or 'female' side wins, abundant crops and large catches of fish will be had, but that they will suffer hunger if the southern or 'male' side wins. According to the high priestess (nuru), once the contest starts, both sides try to win, and, although men do not make the female side win, strangely enough, it is usually the 'female' side that does win. The ritual tug-of-war is now much simplified due to the decrease of rice straw. The nuru's statements imply that the feminine is associated with fertility, while maleness is associated with hunger and scarcity.

Thus the notions associated with women in Okinawa cannot be understood without taking into account its cosmology. The notion of female superiority in rituals seems directly related to a widespread Okinawan belief in the spiritual predominance of the sister over the brother; Mabuchi writes, this is the belief 'that the spirit of the sister, either living or dead, has the power to protect her brother from evil influences . . . the brothers, especially the eldest brother, are regarded as obliged to help their sisters in economic affairs when they are in need' (1961: 79). This belief seems to be found in most Okinawa islands and survives to this day (cf. Ouwehand 1985: 96–9). Thus sisters serve as spiritual patrons for their brothers while the brothers try to protect their sisters in secular life (Mabuchi 1961: 79; 1980). During World War II sisters gave brothers leaving for the war a towel, a quilted belly-band (senninbari), or a lock of hair to protect them. Thus the brother–sister relationship is not only social but deeply religious, and reflects Okinawan cosmology;[8] also, this relationship is basically the same as that between men and women in general in Okinawa.

Aspects of Okinawan cosmology are expressed in various sorts of rituals, which are far greater, both in frequency and intensity, than those on the Japanese mainland. For example, in the village of Bise they still perform a great number of annual communal rituals every month except October and November, according to the lunar calendar; for example, in July seven such rituals are performed. On the occasion of the ancestral bon festival from the 13th to the 15th of July ancestors who died during the last thirty-three years are worshipped. In the ritual called upuyumi performed on the 20th of July, for the purpose of securing good harvest and large catches of fish village priestesses pray to the nirai-kanai, which is believed to be the world of ancestors who died more than thirty-three years ago. The *nirai-kanai* is also regarded as the sea deity. Also, there are several sacred places to be worshipped: the *gushiku* (sacred mountain) is situated on the top of the hill, east of the village; the deity of the 'mountain', believed to be a male deity, is said to descend from the sky; men were traditionally forbidden to enter this place: only priestesses could enter there to worship. There is a small concrete shrine, *ryūgū*, situated in the middle of the village spread along the west coast, where the sea deity, considered to be a female deity residing at the bottom of the sea, is enshrined. On the eastern and inland side of the shrine, that is, the central part of Bise, the village shrine, *asagi*, is located; here the *hinukan* (the deity of the fire) is enshrined. On the northern edge of Bise there is a small island to the west, and one can walk there at low tide; while this island is considered to be entirely sacred, on the island there are two places of worship for the sea deity; one is new, the other, old; in Bise there are four sacred wells, one of which is used for getting the *wakamizu* (water used at the New Year Ceremony). All of these and the other sacred places in Bise are worshipped in succession by priestesses on prescribed days and at the times of annual rituals.

Although the use of tablets for the dead and the practice of holding the ancestral *bon* festival seem to have been introduced to Okinawan society from the mainland of Asia (Mabuchi 1980), the ideas of pollution associated with women appear to have had no place to flourish there because of the overwhelming importance of women in religious activities. In other words, women cannot be polluted beings in Okinawa where rituals and festivals are almost exclusively conducted by them; where inhabitants' personal problems are solved by women *yuta*; where men are spiritually protected by their sisters; where the *bon* and other ancestral and communal village rituals are performed by the priestesses; and where the fire deity, which is represented by three stones in the sand of a container placed on an altar in the north-west corner of the kitchen, located in the north-west corner of the house, is expected to be worshipped only by the wife of the head of the household. In brief, as both men and women admit, it is only through women's religious activities that all villagers can be assured health, fertility and welfare.

Childbirth and fire

In the tripartite division of categories, *hare* (the state of celebration), *kegare* (pollution) and *ke* (the daily or ordinary state) in Japanese folk religion,[9] I think, as Namihira argues (1984: 21–34), that the categories *hare* and *kegare* should not be treated as a rigid opposition but as interchangeable categories. According to a result of our field research on Katsumoto-ura and other villages (Yoshida 1981), a 'polluted' corpse adrift in the sea is believed in many fishing villages in the mainland to bring about good catches if it is buried in one's graveyard. In view of the fact that pregnancy is considered a form of pollution (*kegare*) in Katsumoto-ura, but as a sign of fortune in Koza, the ideas of pollution and *hare* are clearly interchangeable, and the symbolic meanings of pregnancy are associated with powers producing negative and positive results. As is often found in Japanese folk beliefs, a polluted thing can be used as a magical power to drive away demons or evil. Human excrement, for instance, was used for that purpose.

I indicated earlier that in many instances women had to give birth in a special hut because of the pollution associated with childbirth. However, such huts were at times considered sacred as well as polluted. Iijima writes that in many Japanese villages when a woman had just given birth in a childbirth hut (*ubuya*), it was customary for villagers to hang sacred straw hung with cut paper (*shimenawa*) around the hut (1986: 167). This implies that the hut is considered to be a sacred space even though a woman has borne a baby in it. Iijima also reports that in Yaeyama they piled up the firewood near the kitchen to be used for warming a woman who was going to give birth in a hut, and screened it with *shimenawa* while drying it. Also, since they started collecting the firewood on an auspicious day (1986: 107), the custom suggests that it is associated with the divine. Segawa also writes, 'the custom in which a women gives birth in an *imiya* or tabooed hut screened with *shimenawa* exists in Amami and Okinawa' (1984: 102).

The practice of warming with fire a woman who has just given birth has been widespread in the south-western islands and in certain places on the mainland (Iijima 1986: 105). In Amami, according to Osada, the fire of the hearth was thought to squeeze out the 'poison' in the sweat of the woman who had just given birth (1978: 91), and Ebara writes that in Amami, the fire to warm the woman just after delivery should not be extinguished from between four to seven days after childbirth (Ebara and Sakihara 1977: 119). The custom of warming with fire just after delivery was practised in the village of Bise, Okinawa, until the 1940s; a woman in labour used to enter a room with a hearth (*jiru*), and was warmed near the hearth before and after the delivery. The room was screened with a 'left-rope' – that is, a rope made by twisting strands by pushing one's left hand forward clockwise, namely, in the opposite way to usual – into which branches of a shrub, *tobera (Pittosporum tobira)*, were placed in order to ward off the demons (*ma*). The afterbirth was buried at the entrance to the kitchen, situated in the north-west corner of the house (Nakada 1983: 151). As I have reported elsewhere (Yoshida 1986: 138), in Amami formerly a 'left-rope' was used for warding off demons, and the shrub *tobera* was used for magical purposes probably because of its special smell. On the island of Iheya a woman who had just given birth was warmed intensively with strong fire from the hearth, whether it was summer or winter, for about ten days. The firewood used for this purpose was especially prepared. This custom, however, was abandoned during the middle Taisho period (around 1915) following a doctor's suggestion (Moromi 1981: 61).

Why then did they warm in childbirth? First, most of the local explanations for the practice are that it is good for both mother and child. Second, a polluted state must be purified at once with the fire. However, few inhabitants explicitly stated this as a reason. Certain women said that the practice had just been customary. Third, the fire was used to ward off demons. This is actually an *emic* interpretation given by villagers. In the south-western islands both the woman who has just given birth and her newborn child were believed to be most likely to be attacked by demons, so that the latter must be exorcised by fire. In the examples mentioned above, in addition to the use of fire, certain devices were made to ward off demons. For the same purpose an edged tool or the *susuki (Miscanthus sinensis)* were also used to drive away demons at the time of childbirth (Iijima 1986: 109). In Amami, when a woman gave birth, it was customary for villagers to stick a pair of scissors into the ash of the hearth to ward off demons (Setouchi-cho Editorial Committee 1977: 167). In Sokari, Amami, a woman bore a baby in a 'back' room on the north side of the house, and her own relatives stuck nails or a pair of scissors into the earth under the eaves of the house to ward off the *kenmun* (demon) (Setouchi-cho Editorial Committee 1977: 91–2; Yoshida 1986: 136–9). Fourth, fire was employed to squeeze out the 'poison' in the sweat of the woman just after delivery. This is another *emic* interpretation.

A fourth interpretation, which is of an *etic* nature, concerns the fact that fire might have been used for 'cooking' women who had just given birth. Interestingly, the practice of warming a woman who has just given birth is not unique to Japan, but is widespread in South-east Asia, Micronesia and among North and Middle American Indians. After reviewing some examples from those areas, Lévi-Strauss writes, 'they "cook" the individuals deeply involved in a physiological process: the newborn child, the woman who has just given birth, or the pubescent girl' (1964: 432). In the summer of 1986 on the island of Yap in Micronesia, I was told by an old Yappese man that there used to exist until the 1940s the practice of warming with fire a woman who had just given birth. Itabashi (1988) reports that on Yap the custom of warming the pubescent girl with fire was practised until the 1940s. The practice of warming with fire a woman just after delivery exists also among the Chamula Indians, a Tzotzil-speaking group, in south Mexico (Yoshida, 1989). Also, in view of the fact that in many places in Japan a new bride had ritually to step across a fire put at the gate of her bridegroom's house (marriages being generally virilocal) (Iijima 1986: 91), it may be that, as Iijima argues, the fire served as a transformational agency or a mediator by which a woman in childbirth was brought back to this everyday, ordinary world from the other, extraordinary world, which is polluted and divine, and which she enters when labour begins (Iijima 1986: 105–11).

Concluding remarks

By way of conclusion I would like to stress the following points with regard to the feminine in Japanese folk religion. First, the notions of pollution and sacredness or divinity associated with women cannot be rigidly opposed, but are often blurred, depending on the contexts. Second, there exist significant regional variations in prohibitions and taboos associated with menstruation and women. This cautions against hasty generalisations in the study of Japanese society and culture. Third, in order to account for the weak prohibitions and taboos associated with women in the Amami and Okinawa islands, social, historical and cosmological dimensions are to be considered.

As for the social dimension, we might try to apply the hypothesis of Mary Douglas: 'when male dominance is accepted as a central principle of social organization and with full rights of physical coercion, beliefs in sex pollution are not likely to be highly developed', while 'when moral rules are obscure or contradictory there is a tendency for pollution beliefs to simplify or clarify the point at issue' (1970: 168–9). One might then argue that pollution beliefs did not develop so much in the Amami and Okinawa islands because the roles, statuses and relations of men and women are more clearly defined than in south-western Honshu, Shikoku and Kyushu where ideas of pollution associated with women are more pronounced than in the north-eastern type of community in Japan (Namihira 1984: 241–2). However, this does not account either for the pronouncement of pollution beliefs on the south-western mainland or for the weakness of such beliefs in Amami and Okinawa, because Okinawan social organisation is not so different from, but basically similar to, the south-western type of community in Honshu, Shikoku and Kyushu. According to my field researchers on five rural communities in Kyushu and Shikoku and in the San'in region, when compared to villages dominated by hierarchically organised *dozoku* (patrilineally related families) often found in north-eastern Japan,

> these villages in the southwest have more different social relationships and groups which are not only functionally important but are cross-cutting each other and pulling against each other . . . In those villages personal kindred (*shinrui*) which includes affines as well as both maternal and paternal kin is functionally more important than the *dozoku* principle in daily mutual activities.
>
> (Yoshida and Ueda 1968: 377–8)

While in Okinawan lineages the patrilineal principle seems stronger than in the mainland counterpart, as in the south-west, lineages (*munchu*) are not hierarchically organised, and coexist with personal kindred, bilateral and cognatic systems (Watanabe 1986: 173–80); age grade systems, often found on the south-west mainland, Kyushu and Shikoku, are functionally important in southern Okinawan communities (Omoto 1978; 1980). Thus it seems clear that there exist various kinds of relationships and principles in Okinawan society. Therefore, it seems to me difficult to prove that there exists less obscurity in Okinawan social relationships than on the south-west mainland, Kyushu and Shikoku.

Douglas also states that: 'When the principle of male dominance is applied to the ordering of social life but is contradicted by other principles such as that of female independence . . . then sex pollution is likely to flourish' (1970: 169). In Okinawa in the sense that men themselves admit the importance of, and their indebtedness to, women who are their sisters, wives, mothers, grandmothers, aunts and daughters, for their religious roles, it can be said that male dominance is not checked by female dominance in the religious aspects of life, and that female dominance in ritual contexts and male superiority in secular, political contexts are very well defined. It may be argued that this could be one reason why pollution beliefs associated with women did not flourish in the Amami and Okinawa region, especially since in the south-west including western Honshu, Kyushu and Shikoku, principles of social organisation tend not to be so clearly defined as in the north-eastern mainland where pollution beliefs are not pronounced.

On the other hand, we could also say that male dominance is checked by other contradictory principles in Amami and Okinawa, where the male is dominant in political and economic life while the female predominates in religious activities. In this sense it can be said that contradictory or opposing principles coexist side by side. Thus it is more important to examine the contexts in which a power, whether it is political or mystical, is used, than to see whether contradictory principles exist or not.

However, Douglas's hypothesis of pollution is congruent with this fact. Pollution beliefs associated with menstruation and women are pronounced in the south-western type of community where the relationships of the stem and the branch families are more frequently formed independent of the landlord–tenant and patron–client relationships, and where other social relationships such as fictive kinship relations, kindreds, neighbourhoods, religious associations (*kō*), mutual aid associations, and age groups perform various activities and are formed mostly cross-cutting each other. But they are much less pronounced in the north-eastern type of community often found on the north-east mainland (e.g. Ishigami, Iwate Prefecture reported by Ariga 1939), where the landlord–tenant and patron–client relationship is established along the stem–branch family relationship which is, in turn, strengthened by the landlord–tenant and patron–client relationships, and where the village is dominated by hierarchically organised *dozoku* and not by other social relationships as in the south-western type of community (Yoshida and Ueda 1968; Namihira 1984: 239–41). Therefore, when compared to the north-eastern type, the south-western type of community has more structural conflicts between social relationships, and social rules tend to be obscure and ill defined.

Yet the Okinawan material seems to indicate the inadequacy of Douglas's theory of pollution, in that when contradictory or opposing principles exist in the same society, if they operate in completely different contexts, pollution beliefs are not likely to develop. But these contexts are best understood in relation to Okinawan cosmology.

My last comment on Douglas's theory of pollution is a theoretical one. In my view Douglas's sociological approach fails to recognise that collective notions, ideas and beliefs as part of cosmology cannot be *produced* by social organisations alone. While cosmology can be influenced by social organisations, the latter can also be much affected by the former. Various ethnographies seem to indicate that there is not a one-way determining relation. As Needham clearly illustrated in the early 1960s, social determinism of this kind, originally derived from Emile Durkheim is ethnographically untenable, and is unjustifiable when considered under a more theoretical aspect (Needham 1963: vii–xiviii; 1979: 25–7). Needham also states that: 'In no single case is there any compulsion to believe that the society is the cause or even the model of the classification' (1963: xxv). I think that this can be applied not only to classification but to social ideas and beliefs. Thus it is clear enough that notions and beliefs associated with woman cannot be understood in relation to social dimensions alone.

As for the historical dimension, whereas the introduction of Buddhism seems to have strengthened the pollution beliefs concerning women in the mainland, Buddhistic influences have never been strong in the south-western archipelago, so that pollution beliefs have not flourished. Since there exists no evidence with respect to differential regional influences of Buddhism on the mainland, the pronouncement of pollution beliefs associated with women in south-western Japan, excluding the Amami and Okinawa islands, cannot be explained by the introduction of Buddhism.

Male dominance in political and economic contexts and female dominance in religious contexts are closely related to the cosmological dimension. The earlier discussions dealing with Okinawan cosmology indicate that, while man is symbolically related to superior, secular, east, front, south, mountain and hunger, woman is related to inferior, religious, west, back, north, sea and fertility. Female dominance in religious contexts is too overwhelming to allow pollution beliefs associated with women to develop. In Okinawan cosmology women assume the role of spiritual patron for men and both individual and communal terms. Whether Japanese women are regarded as polluted or as holy beings, traditionally they are seen to have certain spiritual or mystical powers that can bring about ill fortune or prosperity and fertility in Japanese folk religion. Which is occasioned depends, like so much else in Japanese culture, largely upon the context.

Teigo Yoshida

Notes

1 A typical example is found in Katsumoto-ura, a fishing village on the island of Iki (Yoshida *et al.* 1974).

2 This observation is based on my fieldwork jointly undertaken with Sakumi Itabashi, Emiko Namihira and Takuma Shirakawa at different times (from 1978 to 1987). Most of those studies were financially supported by the Scientific Research Fund of the Japanese Ministry of Education. My visit to the island of Kudaka was made, assisted by Takuma Shirakawa, in May 1983, for the purpose of helping Prof. and Mrs Claude Lévi-Strauss on their visit to the Okinawa islands with the financial aid for which I am grateful from the Japanese Federation of Economic Organisations. Fieldwork in Bise, Noho and other communities on north Okinawa has been conducted under my leadership since 1986, provided with a research grant for 'A Social Anthropological Study of Religion of North Okinawa' by the Scientific Research Fund of the Japanese Ministry of Education. This is a three-year research project begun in 1986. Therefore this joint study in which Michio Suyenari, Takuma Shirakawa and Yoshio Kimura are collaborators is still in progress. I wish to thank them for their co-operation. I wish also to thank Shoichi Nakanishi and Kuniya Ishibashi for helping in data collection. I am also grateful to Joy Hendry, Andrew Duff-Cooper and Brian Moeran for revising the English style of the present paper and for supplying helpful comments on it.

3 I do not deny certain Buddhistic influences in Okinawan culture (cf. Mabuchi 1980: 14–15).

4 This fieldwork was jointly conducted with Takuma Shirakawa in the summers of 1983, 1984 and 1985 as a training programme for anthropology students of Keio University. Among them Shoichi Nakanishi, Yuji Nakanishi, Keiko Takada and Hiroko Takei were particularly helpful in data collection concerning the indigenous notions of 'woman'. I wish also to thank Mr Ichio Katamori, Village Chief of Koza, who has been an excellent informant. I make quotations from, and references to, the graduation theses of both Keiko Takada (1987) and Hiroko Takei (1987).

5 This is based upon my fieldwork conducted from 1974 to 1975.

6 According to Noboru Miyata, in festivals in certain villages on the mainland significant roles are played by women (1983: 50–58).

7 For a detailed study of the social organisation centring around kinship of Bise village, Ogo's report (1965: 123–56) was useful. I have benefited from the graduation thesis of my ex-student, Yorimichi Hamada, a field study of the '*kamidāri*' of Bise women (Hamada 1985).

8 This is based upon Mabuchi's papers (1964; 1980).

9 Balinese in Indonesia also use a tripartite division as seen from their views that man consists of body, soul and evils, that man consists of 'head', 'trunk' and 'legs', that 'head' is related to gods, 'legs' to the underworld, and the 'trunk' is placed between them, and that the house yard consists of shrine, house and bath place (Swellengrebel 1960: 44; Yoshida 1983: 159–60). They also divide the universe into three worlds: *akasa* (the upper world), *madyapada* (the human world), and *neraka* (underworld) (Hobart 1978: 16). The Kaguru of Tanzania also employ a triadic classification (Beidelman 1966; Needham 1979: 9). Dumézil stressed the tripartite division in ancient Indo-European societies (e.g. 1958).

74

According to Sakurai (1982: 242–5), Yanagita, the founder of Japanese folklore, discussed a dual division of *hare* and *ke* independent of the Western division 'sacred' and 'profane'. The first attempt at employing the tripartite division as an analytical framework to investigate Japanese folk religion was apparently by Namihira, whose paper dealing with it was first published in 1974 and reprinted in her book (1984) (Miyata, personal communication).

References

Ariga, K. 1939. Nambu Ninoe-gun Ishigami-mura ni okeru daikazoku seido to nago seido (Large family system and *nago* system in Ishigami Village, Ninoe County, Nambu Province). Tokyo: *Attic Museum Report*, no. 43.

Beidelman, T. O. 1966. *Utani*: some Kaguru notions of death, sexuality, and affinity. *Southwestern Journal of Anthropology* 22, 354–80.

Douglas, M. 1970 *Purity and Danger*. Harmondsworth: Penguin.

Dumézil, G. 1958. *L'idéologie tripartie des Indo-Européens*. Brussels: Latomus.

Ebara, Y. and Sakihara, T. 1977. *Okinawa Amami no shukuji* (Celebrated events of Okinawa and Amami). Tokyo: Meigen Shobo.

Hamada, Y. 1985. Okinawa no kamidari ni kansuru chosa hokoku (Report of the *kamidari* in Okinawa). Graduation thesis, Keio University.

Hobart, M. 1978. The path of the soul: the legitimacy of nature in Balinese conceptions of space. In *Natural Symbols in South East Asia*, ed. G. B. Milner, pp. 1–28, University of London: SOAS.

Iijima, Yoshiharu. 1986. *Kamado gami to kawaya gami* (God of oven and god of toilet). Tokyo: Jinbun Shoin.

Itabashi, S. 1988. Yap tō no kegare no kannen ni tsuite (On the concept of pollution on Yap). In *Kosumosu to shakai* (Cosmos and Society), ed. T. Yoshida and H. Miyake, pp. 237–57. Tokyo: Keio Tsushin.

Lévi-Strauss, C. 1964. *Mythologique: le cru et le cuit*. Paris: Plon.

Mabuchi, T. 1961. Spiritual predominance of the Sister. In *Ryukyuan Culture and Society*, ed. A. H. Smith. Honolulu: University of Hawaii Press.

Mabuchi, T. 1968. Toward the reconstruction of Ryukyuan cosmology. In *Folk Religion and the World View in the Southwestern Pacific*, pp. 119–40. Tokyo: Keio University.

Mabuchi, T. 1980. Space and time in Ryukyuan cosmology. *Asian*

Folklore Studies. **39**, 1–19.

Miyake, H. 1987. *Omine San Kamigadake no Nyonin Kinsei* (Taboos for women of Kamigadake, Omine Mountain). *Ashinaka.* **202** (8).

Miyata, N. 1979. *Kami no Minzokushi* (Folklore of Gods). Tokyo: Iwanami Shoten.

Miyata, N. 1983. *Onna no reiryoku to iye no kami* (Spiritual power of woman and god of house). Tokyo: Jinbun Shoin.

Moromi, S. (ed.) 1981. *Iheya-sonshi* (History of Iheya Village). Naha: Editorial Committee of History of Iheya Village.

Nakada, E. (ed.) 1983. *Bise shi* (History of Bise). Motobu-Cho: Editorial Committee of Bise.

Namihira, E. 1984. *Kegare no kōzō* (Structure of Pollution). Tokyo: Seidosha.

Namihira, E. 1985. *Kegare* (Pollution). Tokyo: Tokyodo Shuppan.

Needham, R. 1963. Introduction. In *Primitive Classification,* E. Durkheim and M. Mauss. Chicago: The University of Chicago Press.

Needham, R. 1979. *Symbolic Classification.* Santa Monica, Calif.: Goodyear.

Ogo, K. 1965. *Kami-motobu Son Bise no shakai soshiki* (Social organization of Bise, Kami-Motobu village), *Okinawa no shakai to shyukyo* (Society and religion of Okinawa). Tokyo: Heibonsha.

Okada, S. 1982. *Kodai no imi* (Taboo in ancient period). Tokyo: Kokusho Kankokai.

Omoto, N. 1978. Miyako jima ni okeru mogo shudan (Associations on Miyako Islands). *Shakai Jinruigaku Nenpo* (Annual Report of Social Anthropology). Tokyo Metropolitan University **4**, 207–22.

Omoto, N. 1980. *Okinawa ni okeru nenrei kaiteisei* (Age grade system in Okinawa). *Minzokugaku Kenkyu* (The Japanese Journal of Ethnology) **45** (1), 32–50.

Osada, S. 1978. *Amami Joseishi* (Description on Amami women). Tokyo: Tokyo Shoseki.

Ouwehand, C. 1985. *Hateruma: Socioreligious Aspects of a South-Ryukyuan Island Culture.* Leiden: Brill.

Sakurai, T. 1982. *Nihon minzoku shyukyo ron* (Japanese folk religion). Tokyo: Shyunjyusha.

Segawa, K. 1984. *Onna no minzoku-shi* (Ethnograpy of women). Tokyo: Tokyo Shoseki.

Setouchi-cho Editorial Committee (ed.) 1977. *Setouchi-cho Shi* (Description of Setouchi Town). Setouchi-cho: Setouchi choshi Henshu Iinkai.

Swellengrebel, J. L. 1960. Introduction. In *Bali: Studies in Life, Thought, and Ritual*, ed. W. F. Wertheim *et al*. The Hague and Bandung: W. van Hoeve.

Takada, K. 1987. *Girei to fujokan* (Ritual and pollution). Graduation thesis, Keio University.

Takei, H. 1987. *Koza ni okeru josei* (Women in Koza). Keio University.

Watanabe, K. 1986. *Nansei shotō* (Southwestern Islands). *Nihon no minzoku-gaku* (Ethnology in Japan 1973–1983), ed. The Japanese Society of Ethnology *(Nihon Minzoku Gakkai)*, pp. 173–9. Tokyo: Kobundo.

Yanagita, K. 1948. *Imo no chikara* (The power of the sister). Tokyo: Sogensha.

Yoshida, T. 1981. The stranger as god: the place of the outsider in Japanese folk religion. *Ethnology*. **20** (2), 87–99.

Yoshida, T. 1983. *Shyukyo to sekaikan* (Religion and cosmology). Fukuoka: Kyushu University Press.

Yoshida, T. 1986. Gods, ancestors and mediators: a cosmology from the southwestern archipelago of Japan. In *Interpreting Japanese Society*, ed. J. Hendry and J. Webber, pp. 131–46. Oxford: JASO.

Yoshida, T. 1989. *Kyokaisei, jikan, metamorphosis* (Liminality, time and metamorphosis). In *Shocho to shakai* (Symbol and Society), ed. T. Yoshida, pp. 301–47. Tokyo: Hirakawa Shuppan.

Yoshida, T. and Ueda, H. 1968. Spirit possession and social structure in southwestern Japan. *Proceedings of the VIIIth International Congress of Anthropological and Ethnological Sciences*, vol. 2, pp. 377–8. Tokyo and Kyoto: Science Council of Japan.

Yoshida, T., Maruyama K. and Namihira E. 1974. Technological and social changes in a Japanese fishing village. *Journal of Asian and African Studies*. **9** (1–2), 1–16.

5

Keiko Tanaka

'Intelligent elegance':
women in Japanese advertising

'When I use a word', Humpty Dumpty said in rather a scornful tone, 'it means just what I choose it to mean – neither more nor less'.

(Lewis Carroll, *Through the Looking-Glass*)

Introduction

This paper discusses the language used in contemporary Japanese advertisements which target young women. The projection of the image of women in advertising has been the subject of a vast literature in various disciplines, such as linguistics, anthropology and sociology. The focus here is on words which are frequently used in relation to women in advertisements. 'Feminism', 'intelligence' and 'individualism' have been chosen to illustrate this process.

Moeran (1983, 1984) has studied some words which continually recur in various social and cultural spheres, including advertising literature; he calls them 'keywords'. In particular, his 1984 article approaches the way in which Japanese society is trying to cope with the problem of individualism.

His analysis is based on the notion of a 'key verbal concept' developed by Parkin (1978), which 'shapes people's perceptions of changes in the group's environment of opportunity, which may in turn redefine the lexicons and taxonomies' (ibid. 26). Parkin has studied the Luo community in Kenya and shown how keywords were used differently depending on social context: while they were used by people in power to reinforce their authority, they were reinterpreted in private speech.

Moeran has adapted this approach to the study of some Japanese keywords, such as *kokoro* (heart) which, he argues (1984: 260), make up the concept of *seishin* (spirit). He points out (1984: 258) how it has been argued that *seishin* has been a keyword with which the Japanese like to describe their own culture and society, and indeed 'Japaneseness'. Moeran goes on to argue (1984: 259) that *seishin* is used in parallel with the group model and in contrast with Western capitalism and individualism.

Now, Moeran observes (1984: 262) that the word *kokoro* is also found in association with the word *kosei* (individuality). Does this mean that the word *kokoro* is used to represent Western individualism as well as Japanese group ideology? He says (1984: 262) that he is not convinced that *kosei* actually is equivalent to what is known as 'individualism' in the West. He argues (1984: 262) that Japanese has two words to cover 'individualism'; the positive side is *kosei* and the negative side *kojin-shugi*. Moreover, he argues (1984: 262-3), while the latter corresponds to Western individualism, in which they see no good, the former is regarded as entirely original and hence 'uniquely Japanese', and is adapted into *seishin*, that is, 'Japanese spirit'. Moeran has taken up a certain semantic field which is roughly covered by the word *seishin*, studied words which are contained in the field, and analysed how those words are related to each other.

I shall take my study in a different direction. Instead of taking a semantic field as the object of my study, I shall focus on how the few words listed above are used in one particular form of communication, namely advertising. I am concerned to reveal what these words actually mean within this one narrow medium, and what values they represent, by analysing how they are used in a number of concrete cases.

Recent linguistic theories tend to stress that meaning is derived as much from the way in which a word is used as from its dictionary definition.

> Is it not possible that the word 'intelligent' is used by speakers of English in a variety of circumstances among which we can perhaps discern certain family resemblances, but which have no common defining property?
>
> (Lyons 1977:212)

'Intelligence' is one of the words which is frequently manipulated in persuasive discourse, and it is one of the examples used below. In essence, advertising uses the appeal of certain words to particular groups in society, while simultaneously distorting, even contradicting, their meaning. The sophisticated linguistic theories developed since Lyons, which help one to understand better how this process works, are analysed and applied in my thesis (Tanaka, 1989).

What follows is not a systematic sociological study of the manipulation of Japanese women by advertisers, but rather an attempt to see how studying the language used by advertisers may indicate some of the avenues of manipulation. Moreover, as Smith (1987: 1) points out, it is a mistake to focus too narrowly on the position of women in Japanese society. He says that the focus should be broadened out to encompass gender as a whole, but it could be arugued that one needs to broaden it out further to a consideration of how any subordinate group is manipulated, for 'the decisive factor is less purely gender than power in the real world' (Lakoff 1975: 57).

The examples have been culled from a systematic search through monthly magazines for young women, *J.J.*, *Can Can*, *More*, *With* and *Cosmopolitan*, between September 1984 and December 1987. It is worth noting that these magazines all have English titles. As will be seen later on, a certain 'cultural dependence' on the West informs much of the interpretation of these words.

Women in contemporary Japan

Smith (1987: 2) notes that many discussions of the place of Japanese women in society begin with an assessment of how far they have come since feudal times. There was a dominant view as to women's status among the warrior class during the preceding period, which followed the Confucian teaching that a woman should obey three men in turn throughout the course of her life: her father in her youth, her husband in her maturity, and her son as head of the household in her old age. This Confucian view strongly influenced the Civil Code of 1898, which established the household as a legal entity headed by a male, who was given extensive authority over the lives of its members, in such matters as marriage and divorce. Women's legal status changed drastically after 1945, for Article 14 of the 1947 Constitution stated: 'All the people are equal under the law and there shall be no discrimination in political, economic, or social relations because of race, creed, sex, social status, or family origin'.

However, Smith goes on to say (1987: 3) that social reality has changed much less than the law. He argues that the family has remained the fundamental unit of society, and that it is seen ultimately as the product of the wife's investment of her adult life in her husband and their children. Equality between the sexes is seen as a threat to the survival of the family. He argues that the traditional roles of the man and the woman are still valid today; that is, while the man is the bread-winner, the woman rules the home. Moreover, he suspects that the majority of women still adhere to a conservative view of their proper conjugal role. One of the aims of this paper is to consider whether there has been any major breakthrough in the portrayal of female role models in advertising and whether any changes in values can be observed. It would, of course, be worth following up the present study with an investigation of the actual response of women to advertising in Japan.

Feminism

First let us look at the following example of a caption used in a series of advertisements for Tokyo Gas, one of the city gas companies. This series was so successful that it won the 1984 Asahi Advertising Prize.

(1)	Toshi	gasu-tie	feminisuto	ne.
	city	gas	feminist	tag-q

City Gas is a feminist, isn't it?[1]

(Tokyo Gas)

Why is the gas company called a feminist? The answer may lie in the pictures shown in the advertisements. One of them shows a large pot boiling over on a gas cooker. Another depicts a woman wearing an apron and holding a plate, doing the washing up. Yet another shows the same woman's reflection in a mirror, putting on lipstick. She is not looking at herself, for her attention seems to be diverted by something else. These advertisements are for a gas cooker with a special sensor, which automatically stops the gas supply when the fire is extinguished, a gas boiler with similar sensor equipment, and an alarm for the gas leaks. These are all new pieces of apparatus produced by the company. The company is described as 'feminist' on the grounds that it has come up with these instruments to help women with their housework.

The use of the particle *ne* marks the utterance as distinctively feminine. The audience is encouraged to imagine a woman's voice praising the gas

81

company for improving kitchen equipment and thus helping women in their household chores.

It is obvious that the loan-word *feminisuto* in these advertisements does not mean what the original English word means. A Japanese audience would know what the word *feminisuto* means in Japanese, whether or not they know what the word 'feminist' means in English. However, it is not necessary for the audience to know the meaning of the word in advance. If someone who knew English saw the advertisement and read the description, she would realise that *feminisuto* does not mean the same thing as the original English 'feminist'. Apparently, it does not take very long for students doing Japanese at a British university to learn, once they are in Japan, that *feminisuto* is someone who readily opens the door for women whereas a feminist might get offended by such a chauvinistic gesture. They learn it not because of their previous knowledge of the English word, but despite their knowledge of the word, through the contexts in which the word is used.

The word *feminisuto* is used in the advertisements to describe a 'desirable' quality. It is meant as a compliment to Tokyo Gas that they should be called *feminisuto*. The company is being praised for improving kitchen instruments, because they help women to perform their household chores. It is chauvinism, rather than feminism, to assume that a way of gaining women's praises is to improve kitchen instruments. Despite the use of the word *feminisuto,* which originated from the English 'feminist', the attitude behind the advertisements is sexist. These kitchen instruments are made for the use of women. And women do not even question why this is so; they simply compliment the gas company by calling it *feminisuto*. For these women, housework is part of being a woman, just as putting on lipstick is. The very concept of feminist might be foreign to them.

What seems to have happened to the word is that when the English word 'feminist' was absorbed into Japanese, it only retained part of its meaning, namely, the part indicating being nice to women and being worth receiving women's praises. The part indicating being nice to women by treating them equally was ignored. Looking at it from the point of view of the original meaning of the word, the Japanese usage was 'loose' (Sperber and Wilson 1986: 234). And it would have been an unacceptable 'loose use' of the word within an English-speaking community, for it contradicts many of the logical and contextual implications of the word 'feminist', such as accepting women as equal to men. When the word was introduced into Japanese to express male chauvinistic behaviour, there was no clash between the way the word was used and people's knowledge of the word, given that the word did not exist. Thus it was a completely acceptable use of the word. It could be argued that the Western notion of feminism was introduced into Japanese-speaking society in a distorted form. Moreover, the Japanese meaning has ended up by being more contrary than similar to the original meaning. It could further be argued that the distortion in the meaning of the word is an indication of the fact that Japanese society was not prepared for feminist concepts.

Intelligence

The next examples are to show how the words *chisei* (intelligence) and *chiteki* (intelligent) are used in Japanese advertising. In advertisements found in the magazines studied, they are ubiquitous. Their popularity has been growing since the end of the 1970s, when Kadokawa Paperbacks used the following as a caption in their advertisements:

(2) Chisei   no sa   ga   hyoojoo[2]   ni deru rashii-yo.
intelligence of degree subj. expression in show they say

Komatta-ne.
troubled-tag Q

They say that the degree of intelligence shows in one's expression. I am in trouble, aren't I?

Shimamori in her book on women in Japanese advertising argues (1984: 170) that this trend followed some signs that women were looking for new meanings in life. She points to phenomena such as the publication of allegedly new types of magazines for career women, for example, *Croissant*, and *More*, or flourishing cultural centres frequented mainly, if not exclusively, by women. However, one might point out that these facilities were still reinforcing women's social and cultural 'ghetto'.

Let us now examine how 'intelligent' women have become popular in advertising.

(3) Chiteki-de   joohin-na shiruku burause.
intelligent   noble   silk   blouse

(Tokyo Blouse)

An Intelligent and noble silk blouse.

(4) Chotto   ereganto-de   chotto   interijensu-na   inshoo. . .
     a bit   elegant   a bit   intelligent   impression

                                                              (Paco Rabanne)

     The impression of being a bit elegant and a bit intelligent . . . .

(5) Intelligence. (written in English)

     Sore ga   kimi   no   utsukushisa.
     that subj. you   of   beauty

     Kite-iru fuku   ni chisei   o   kanjiru.
     wear-ing clothes in intelligence obj.   feel

     Tatta   ippon   no   kuchibeni   kara   mo
     only   one   of   lipstick   from   even

                                                                   (Kanebo)

     Intelligence. (in English)
     That is (the secret of) your beauty.
     Your intelligence is seen in your clothes. Even
     in the lipstick you wear.

(6) Chisei   to   yasei,   San   Rooran   no   ganchiku
     intelligence   and   wildness Saint Laurent   of   suggestion

                                                          (Yves Saint Laurent)

     Intelligence and wildness, Saint Laurent's suggestion.

These are only a few among many examples of advertisements using *chisei* (intelligence). They are all for women's fashion and they all suggest that women should express their intelligence through their clothes, lipsticks, handbags and so on. This suggestion is in direct contrast with the fact that in Japanese society intelligence is regarded as a desirable quality in a man, but not in a woman, and that it is regarded as desirable that women should not be as intelligent or well educated as men. Can we thus take this phenomenon as a sign that Japanese society is changing, and that now intelligent women are accepted and encouraged? This may be a premature conclusion. It is obvious in the examples above that *chisei* (intelligence) in these advertisements is a superficial quality, a sort of quality which clothes, cosmetics and accessories can given women. It seems to be synonymous with 'elegance', or 'femininity', or 'sophistication', rather than 'brightness', 'cleverness' and so on as a thesaurus would tell us. It is used for appearances, rather than for one's mental state.

Words such as *chiteki* and *chisei* are usually, though not exclusively, used for women in advertising, that is, they describe women in advertisements which are targeted at women. It may be that women are being seen as a *chiteki* gender, *chiteki* in a limited, superficial sense. And this is all 'desirable', even though women are still not encouraged to exercise their mental ability to the full. Perhaps women are accepted as *chiteki* in their own small ways, so long as they do not cross the border and invade men's fields and threaten them. Example (7) provides support for this suggestion:

(7) Egao   mo   onna   no   chisei   kashira.
    smiling face also   women   of   intelligence   it appears

(Narisu Cosmetics)

It appears that a smiling face is also women's intelligence.

In (7), the caption refers to a smiling face as 'women's intelligence', implying that there is a distinction between intelligence for women and that for men, and that a smile belongs to the former, not the latter. It might be that 'intelligence' as we have observed in the examples above is not 'intelligence' in an ordinary, general sense, but in a 'market' sense, that is, intelligence for and only for women.

It has been argued above that 'intelligence' in these examples is synonymous with 'elegance', 'femininity' and 'sophistication'. To be sure, 'sophistication' entails some mental quality (after all, it is derived from the Greek for wisdom), but again the word is used here in a limited sense. It manifests itself in one's outfits and make-up. It might be that it is desirable for a woman to be intelligent in her choice of clothes and cosmetics. It is not that a woman is encouraged to be intelligent in a general sense, nor is it that she is encouraged to be silly. It is virtuous for a woman to be intelligent, but only in a restricted way. Japanese women are expected to rule the home, as mentioned above, and it is they who are responsible for its day-to-day operation, the care of the children, and the management of the household budget. They are encouraged to exercise their brain in their jobs, as managers of households, as mothers and as consumers.

It is possible to argue that Japanese society has long valued women's mental qualities, for an ideal woman has been described since the Meiji era as *ryoo-sai ken-bo*, that is, 'good wife, wise mother' (Smith 1987: 7). One could argue that a *chiteki* woman as depicted in contemporary advertising is a kind of modernisation of this Meiji slogan.

It is worth noting at this point that in Japanese society women are the prime consumers not only of commodities but also of art and culture (see Moeran 1983). It is possible that these two facts are connected. Advertisements seem to suggest that a *chiteki* woman is someone who wears smart clothes and decent make-up, smiles sweetly and goes to art exhibitions. Thus, here is an example to illustrate this point:

(8) | Bijutsukan | e | iku | josei | ga | fuete-imasu. |
| art gallery | to | go | women | subj. | increasing |

| Purachina | o | isukeru | josei | ga | fuete-imasu. |
| platinum | obj. | wear | women | subj. | increasing |

(Platinum Promotion Forum)

The number of women going to art galleries is increasing.
The number of women wearing platinum is increasing.

These images of women seem to parallel the kind of education received by women in contemporary Japan. Before the war, there was an enormous difference in the education received by men and women, even though there was no legal basis for such a difference. A one-time Minister of Education explicitly stated that education for women was based on the assumption that 'women marry', and that 'its object is to fit girls to become "good wives and wise mothers" ' (1909). Lest it be imagined that this statement only represents a sentiment from eighty years ago, Smith (1987: 8) offers evidence that this attitude is still current today, in the form of a speech given by a president of an apparel company to his assembled employees in 1985, which reproduces this traditional view.

After 1945, one of the major concerns of the Americans was to improve educational opportunities for women. Article 3 of the Fundamental Law of Education reads: 'All people shall be given the opportunity to receive an equal education corresponding to their ability. There shall be no discrimination in education because of race, creed, sex, social status, economic position, or family origin.' In 1984, a slightly higher proportion of girls than boys advanced from junior high school to senior high school, the figure for girls being 95.0% and that for boys 92.8%; in that same year, 32.7% of female and 38.3% of male senior high school leavers went on to attend college or university. It appears as though Japanese women are enjoying equal educational opportunities.

However, if one looks into the kind and quality of education received by men and women, one realises that this conclusion is premature. Figures from 1980 show that 82% of four-year college students are men, and 90% of two-year junior college students are women. Moreover, more than 50% of the courses offered in the junior colleges are in home economics and education. Smith is right to remind us that junior colleges are called 'a modern version of the old schools for brides' (1987: 11). Of the small proportion of women who attend the coeducational four-year colleges and universities, the great majority are in the humanities. In my own experience, home economics, education, language and literature, and arts were 'girls' subjects', and the rest of the subjects were for boys. There was little overlap. Thus, as Smith (1987: 11) puts it, 'apparent parity masks a significant difference' in reality.

It has been argued that the meaning of the word *chisei* (intelligence) is restricted to 'intelligence' which is to be manifested in limited domains. These are traditionally categorised as women's domains, such as fashion, the household, and the consumption of commodities and culture. Sometimes the mental quality of the word even seems to be repressed altogether, leaving the word to mean simply some kind of desirability and appeal to men.

It is revealing to look at a feature carried out by *J.J.* (October 1986). It is entitled *'Chiteki eregansu no teian'* (Suggestions for *chiteki* elegance), and includes the following suggestions:

(9) a. In choosing a dress . . . 50% of the creation of an impression of intelligence depends on your neck-line. An appropriate round-neck and golden buttons are the key to success.
b. The main trend of this year's suits is towards those which have a tightly shaped waist . . . a tight waist-line leads to an expression of intelligence.
c. You cannot omit black, for it is a front runner for a *'chiteki'* colour.

This gives us a good idea of what an 'intelligent' woman should look like: she wears a black dress with a round neck and a tight waistline, with golden buttons.

There is no reason why a round neck should be more 'intelligent' than a v-neck, for example. Nor is it self-evident why a small waist, the colour black, and golden buttons should be associated with 'intelligence'. The point is that all these features are in fashion at present. Moreover, this ensemble conforms to what Japanese men find 'desirable' in women, as pointed out below.

Let us look at another example:

(10) Chiteki   eregansu, Jetta.
     intelligent elegance Jetta

     Chiteki-na machi o   chiteki-na josei to
     intelligent town obj.   woman with

     Chiteki-ni hashirmasu.
     intelligent drive

                                                    (Volkswagen)
     Intelligent elegance. Jetta.
     It drives through an intelligent town with an intelligent woman in an intelligent manner.

87

Whatever 'intelligent elegance' may mean, clearly the word *chiteki* here means something different from the English word 'intelligent', or even from what the Japanese word *chiteki* is supposed to mean. In Japanese, let alone in English, 'intelligent town' and 'the car drives in an intelligent manner' are pragmatically unacceptable, and 'intelligent elegance' pragmatically questionable. Only 'intelligent woman' is well formed. However, what does it mean to say that a woman is *chiteki* (intelligent) here? Because the same word is used for a car and a town, which cannot have the quality of being 'intelligent', it is dubious whether the advertiser has meant to describe the woman along these lines. The word is used to express some desirable quality, but not one exactly to do with intellect. It is some sort of pleasant quality for a woman to have, such as being 'fashionable' or 'sophisticated'.

It is worth noting that although the car advertised is German, the background to the advertisement is a European-style red-brick building with a sign indicating that it is a French restaurant. Apparently, a French restaurant is seen as 'intelligent'. Possibly, the word *'chiteki'* is synonymous with 'fasionable', since that is how France is regarded by Japanese women. Or, it might be that German technology and French cooking are seen as *chiteki* assets of the respective countries.

It has been argued here that the words *chiteki/chisei* (intelligent/ intelligence) are used in Japanese advertising for women to mean not so much a mental quality as desirability. The following example says it all:

(11) Kono aki   no   shuryuu   wa yahari   chiteki-de
      this   autumn of main stream subj. as expected intelligent

      sekushii.
      sexy
                                                            (Robe)
      The main trend this autumn, as you may have guessed, is to be
      intelligent and sexy.

Can Can carried a feature entitled 'The declaration to become a "desirable woman" ' ('Ii onna' e no henshin sengen) (December 1987). The suggestions made there almost completely overlap with those in *J.J.'s* suggestions for 'intelligent elegance', including the colour black, a small waist and golden buttons. The feature also recommends visits to art galleries. Furthermore, one of the three cars listed as 'Cars for the "desirable woman" ' was the Jetta mentioned above, for the very reason of being chiteki – looking. Thus, 'intelligence' and desirability, that is appeal to men, seem to be virtually interchangeable. Moreover, the criteria which apply to both attributes, on the face of it, appear much more related to desirability than to intelligence.

Perhaps things have changed a little for women after all, but for the worse. It might be argued that more is demanded of women today. Men want not only the types referred to by Smith (1987: 22) as traditionally valued, the *sewa nyooboo* (caring wise – a close approximation for the good wife and wise mother) type or the *joobu de nagamochi* (healthy and durable) type. On top of these qualities, which are still valid, a woman is also expected to be *ii onna* (desirable woman), that is, well dressed and made-up, feminine and sexy.

Individualism

It has been known that in Japan there has been a strong ideological emphasis on the importance of the group over the individual and the necessity for the individual to subordinate her interests to those of the primary group to which she belongs. However, there have been an increasing number of advertisements which place an emphasis on the importance of *kosei* (individuality). Does this mean that Japanese group ideology is seriously threatened, a point raised by Moeran (1983: 105 and 1984: 262)? Let us examine some examples.

(12) Watashi wa   interia-dezainaa. . . .Ronjin   no Konkuesuto
     I   subj.   interior designer   Longines   of Conquest

     wa. . . chisei-bi   ookusoosei ni ature,
     subj.   intelligence-beauty   originality of full

     kiwadatte   kosei-teki
     strikingly   individualistic

                                        (Longines)
     I am an interior designer. . . . Longine's Conquest is full of intelligent-beauty
     and originality, and is strikingly individualistic.

Here, it is worth noting that the watch is described in terms of *chisei-be* (intelligent-beauty). What is 'individualistic' about the Longines watch remains to be explained. The illustration shows on the left a young European-looking woman, apparently an interior designer, in black and white, and on the right a pair of Longines watches in full colour. It is worth noting that the woman is engaged in a so-called *katakana* profession, that is, a profession which is described in *katakana* script, which is the distinctive form of writing used for Western loan words. *Katakana* professions, due to their Western flavour, are regarded as 'fashionable' and therefore 'desirable'. The design of the watches is not dissimilar to that of the classic Rolex 'Oyster', which is regarded as prestigious and is in fashion in Japan at this time.

The clues to what is meant by the word *kosei-teki* may be found in the way in which the word is used in the same magazine, *With* (July 1987):

(13) a. This year's popular colour, green, plays an important role in emphasising individuality . . .
 b. You should wear a vivid-coloured polo-neck shirt to emphasise your individuality.
 c. Your fringe should be cut short and 'individualistic' . . .
 d. The key to making you look fresh and individualistic is to have your hair in an off-the-face style.

Example (13a) suggests that green provides you with individuality, for it is the colour in fashion. In the same issue, it is mentioned that green is the most fashionable colour in Paris at the present moment. Example (13b) widens the selection, as it suggests any vivid colour. Examples (13c) and (13d) are suggestions about hair-style; the former recommends a short fringe and the latter an off-the-face style, which is recommended every summer, since it is only sensible to keep one's hair short and off one's face to survive the hot and humid summer in Japan.

What examples (13a) – (13d) are suggesting is that wearing a certain colour or having a certain hairstyle makes one *kosei-teki* (individualistic). It is not to have your own style, but it is to do things which are supposed to be 'individualistic', which include using a colour which is in fashion at the present time. An 'individualistic' woman of 1987 is wearing a vivid-coloured polo-neck shirt, carries a green handbag, has her hair up, and has a short fringe. Using a colour because it is in fashion, or because it is popular in Paris, is hardly an individualistic thing to do. Vivid colours have always been popular in summer, rather than winter, because of their association with the tropics. It has been recommended every summer that a woman should wear her hair short, or, if long, put it up, for commonsensical reasons. The word *kosei* in examples (13a) – (13d) is suggesting 'fashionable', rather than 'individualistic'. It is used to mean doing things which are in fashion and which, therefore, other people are doing, rather than doing things one's own way.

This interpretation of the word *kosei-teki* as doing things which are fashionable is not limited to advertising. A survey in 1972 (see Suzuki

1975) asked the question 'Do you think that you can achieve greater individualism by following fashion?' A positive answer to this question was given by 61.5% of women and 48.2% of men. Whereas only slightly more women than men replied positively, it is interesting to note that nearly twice as many men as women answered with a clear 'no' (41.9% v. 22.9%), whereas a larger number of women were undecided.

Let us look at another example:

(14) . . .Itaria no   ii   iro,   ii   katachi Guccini, Jinsei o
       Italy   of good colour   good   shape   Guccini life   obj.

      kosei-teki   ni tanoshimu josei-tachi no tame ni.
      individualistic in enjoy   woman-pl.   of sake for

                                                              (Guccini)

      Good Italian colour and shape, Guccini. For women who enjoy
      their life in an individual style.

Individualism should be about accepting that every person is different and that each person should be allowed to believe or do whatever she thinks is right. But here in example (14), it means doing a particular thing, namely, buying certain tableware. It comes from Italy, which is regarded as a country which produces high fashion and kitchen-ware. Here are some more examples:

(15) Jibun-rashisa   ni kodawarimasu.
      self-like   to stick

                                                              (Hermes)

      I stick to my own self.

(16) Shinayaka ni watashi no tempo de ikite-yuku.
      gracefully in I   of tempo at live-go

                                                          (Les Sportique)

      I am going to live gracefully at my own pace.

Examples (14)-(16) all promote European goods, all high-class and expensive. Being oneself is using Italian tableware and wearing French suits. They are apparently endorsing the idea of 'doing your own thing', but in practice this means buying European products which are expensive and have high status, and which are, therefore, approved of by society. There is a sense that 'individualism' is equivalent to elitism: doing things European or American is 'desirable', for they are superior. Individualism is accessible only to an elite group, who can afford to buy European or American goods.

Also, there is a hint that being individualistic is doing things Western, as in example (17):

(17) Kono natsu, jibun no kami o
this summer self of hair obj.

Amerika no onna no ko no yoo ni
America of female of child like

Yooroppa no onna no ko no yoo ni
European of female of child like

Jibun de heaa-dezain shichao.
self by hair-design let's   (Benezel)

Let's design our own hair, just like American and European girls this summer.

Thus, designing your own hair is doing what American and European girls do. Here, 'doing your own thing' is acceptable, firstly, because American and European girls are already doing it, and secondly because America and Europe are regarded as 'culturally senior' by Japanese.

Let us look at one more example.

(18) Watashi no iro o motie-inai to, hazukasnii.
I of colour obj. have-not then embarrassing

It is embarrassing not to have my own colour.
                                                        (Casio)

This advertisement is promoting identical wrist-watches in different colours. It is recommended to have one's own colour, for, otherwise it will be embarrassing. Thus, having one's own colour is a way of seeking social approval.

We have examined advertisements which make use of the notion of individuality. References are always superficial, about clothes, accessories, hair-style and so on. Moreover, what is regarded as individualistic in these advertisements is what is in fashion at the time. Thus being 'individualistic' means being fashionable. Whereas individualism should be about each person acting in her particular way, in Japanese advertising it is used to mean a specific thing, such as wearing a suit of a certain brand, having a handbag of a certain colour, and having one's hair done in a certain style. Considering that advertising is a tool of mass communication and is thus targeted at a mass audience, it will mean everybody doing the same thing. What is described as individualistic is something which has already gained social approval, by being in fashion, having high status, originating in the West, and so on. Japanese groupism is far from being threatened by individualism.

What is happening here is some sort of change of word meaning via a loose use of the word. The alteration of the word 'individualistic' is achieved by adding an extra premise to the context: the philosophy of individualism is being able to do what one wants; to the same context, add the premise that what a woman wants is what the rest of society wants; then, in this context, the philosophy of individualism becomes doing what the rest of society wants.

Thus, Japanese group ideology is rescued from supposed threats, absorbing them into the conventional. The use of the word *kosei-teki* (individualistic) in Japanese advertisements is suggesting a way of resolving a clash of cultures by apparently absorbing a notion of the new culture, but interpreting it in the old context against conventional premisses.

This conclusion is consistent with the findings of Moeran (1984: 262) that *kosei* is not equivalent to what we know as 'individualism' in the West and that *kosei* is neatly absorbed in 'Japaneseness' and thus the Japanese have been saved from a clash with group ideology.

However, there is a question yet to be asked: how does the notion of 'individualism' occur in Western advertising? Is its usage consistent with what we know as 'individualism', that is, that each one of us acts in our own particular way? An immediate reaction would be to suspect that individualism in this sense is not promoted. For, if advertising is about selling things to a mass audience, how can it coincide with the ideology that people should be doing different things? The association between 'individualism' and elitism can be traced in advertising in the Western press, as is shown by a Citizen watch advertisement which appeared in the *Sunday Times* colour supplement (13 December 1987). The picture, in grey or neutral tones, shows a naked girl who is said to be 'average' in height, hair colour, age and weight. The only thing that does not make her average is her Citizen watch, picked out in luminous gold on her wrist. The caption reads 'There is no such thing as the average Citizen'. At first sight, the advertisement is simply saying that a Citizen watch confers individuality. But there are two subtexts. The first is the pun on the word 'citizen', which holds the attention. The second, perhaps more important, subtext is that there is in fact nothing average about the girl at all. She is pretty and has an enigmatic expression on her face. The advertisement seems to be suggesting that, in spite of 'average facts' about her, the wearing of a Citizen watch confirms that she is a very special person. Because she is naked and pictured against a featureless grey background, there are no overt signs of membership of any social group or class. However, in some sense the beauty of the model suggests membership of an elite group. Clearly, the distortion of notions such as individualism occurs in the West as in Japan.

Concluding remarks

These observations parallel the findings of a Japanese government survey. It was carried out to commemorate the anniversary of the promulgation of a law in 1985, which was an attempt to guarantee equality of opportunity in employment for women. According to the survey, the proportion of women who believed that women should play a traditional role had increased compared to three years earlier, when there was no such law. The survey also predicted that, unlike in some other industrialised countries, in Japan women would continue to put marriage and children ahead of their careers, even beyond the year 2000.

Nearly 95% of the men and women surveyed responded that men had greater opportunity in Japan to develop their potential than women, and 60% said that discrimination against women continued in the workplace in spite of legislation. According to the most commonly cited figures, Japanese women on average earn only half the wages of men. In contrast, in the UK the corresponding figure is 65% (The Independent, 24 March 1988). About 30% of Japanese women would prefer to be reborn as men. According to Women 2000, an investigation into the changes in modern life reveals that only 16% of their British counterparts wished to be reborn as men.

Most golf and country clubs in Japan bar women from becoming members, while a few will allow women to play but only if a written request is made. As recently as 1987, a male judge granted a man a divorce from a religiously zealous wife, on the ground that she had been neglecting her housework.

This judgement might have been shared by the former Prime Minister, Takeshita Noboru, who is reported in the same Independent article to have made a remark that he believed that women ought not to be running for Parliament in early March 1988. When cornered by Doi Takako, the female head of the opposition party, Mr Takeshita made a rather unconvincing explanation that what he really meant to say was that women must find compaigning physically exhausting, to which Ms Doi apparently replied in a decisive manner, 'Not a bit!' The incident was somewhat embarrassing for Mr Takeshita, who only hours earlier had called for an improvement in the status of women in front of the head of the United Nations committee on the elimination of discrimination against women. Just to avoid the impression that the Japanese Parliament is full of Mrs Thatcher figures, it may be added that at present Ms Doi is among a mere seven female MPs in Japan's 512-member lower house, and the number of women holding office in Japan's ruling party has actually declined by nearly 50% over the past 20 years.

The way language is used to describe women in advertising adds a deeper dimension to this continuing story of the status of women. It has been argued that certain words are used in ways which are contradictory to dictionary definitions of their meaning. Far from these words representing real changes in the way in which women are depicted in Japan, the advertisements in question tend rather to reproduce stereotypical images of women, and in so doing debase the thoughts used. Thus, intelligence and individualism are reduced to mere attributes of fashion, and feminism is employed to endorse attitudes which feminists would consider chauvinistic. Although there is considerable appeal to Western models and values, the net effect of this advertising does not appear to be the undermining of Japanese social attitudes. Rather, the prestige attached to certain concepts is subtly recuperated to reinforce many existing values.

Notes

1 All translations by the author.
2 Note that the putative long vowel is transcribed as the two successive vowels /oo/, rather than a single long vowel /ō/. This follows the observation that the sequence, such as /oo/, can bear two distinctive tones.

    e.g. L HL
        biyooin (hairdresser)
        (L and H indicates low tone and high tone, respectively)

References

Goffman, E. 1979. *Gender Advertisements.* London: Macmillan.

Lakoff, R. 1975. *Language and Woman's Place.* New York and London: Harper & Row.

Lyons, J. 1977. *Semantics.* Cambridge: Cambridge University Press.

Moeran, B. 1983. The language of Japanese tourism. *Annals of Tourism Research* **10**, 93–108.

Moeran, B. 1984. Individual, group and *seishin:* Japan's internal cultural debate. *Man.* **19**, 252–66.

Parkin, D. 1978. *The Cultural Definition of Political Response: Lineal Destiny among the Luo.* London: Academic Press.

Shimamori, M. 1984. *Kookoko no Naka no Onna-tachi* (Women in Advertising). Tokyo: Yamato-shoboo.

Smith, R. J. 1987. Gender inequality in contemporary Japan. *Journal of Japanese Studies* **13** (1), 1–25.

Sperber, D. and Wilson, D. 1986. *Relevance: Communication and Cognition.* Oxford: Basil Blackwell.

Suzuki, Y. 1975. *Onna to ryuukoo* (Women and fashion). In *Nihon-jin Kenkyuu 3: Onna ga Kangaete-iru-koto* (A study of the Japanese 3: what women are thinking about), ed. N. Kenkyuukai. Tokyo: Shiseido.

Tanaka, K. 1989. The language of advertising: a pragmatic approach. Unpublished PhD thesis submitted to the University of London.

Williamson, J. 1978. *Decoding Advertisements: Ideology and Meaning in Advertising.* London and New York: Marion Boyars.

Tourism and the *ama:*
the search for a real Japan

The underlying structure of touristic imagery is absolutely plastic, so its eventual form is a perfect representation of the collective conscience, including those aspects of the collective conscience which strive for clarity, precision and accuracy . . . I do not want to suggest that this freedom is always used. Modernization, even before it begins, runs up against traditional concerns and constraints.

(MacCannell 1976: 143)

We have no relations with the tourists.

(A Kuzaki informant, 1984)

Introduction

Much of the available material on tourism addresses itself to touristic imagery, the first point in the quotation taken from MacCannell. However, his observation that touristic images come up against traditional concerns and constraints is one that is not frequently explored by the growing anthropological literature on tourism. Some of the current material concerns itself with the world of the tourist (cf. Passariello 1983) and much of it is concerned with the construction of the touristic image as well as with the economic and ideological factors which form the infrastructure of tourism in a modern industrialised society (Greenwood 1977; Nash 1977; Said 1978; Graburn 1983a, 1983b; Moeran 1983). In contrast to these approaches, this paper[1] will try to contribute to the anthropology of tourism by exploring the reactions and attitudes of the 'natives' when they find themselves to be the object of domestic tourism.

The central argument of the paper is one which I believe has not yet been addressed by anthropologists of tourism: the flexibility and adaptability of peoples who find themselves to be the object of touristic images. Much of the literature in the anthropology of tourism is about the 'impact' of tourism on a population (cf. Duffield and Long 1981; Cohen 1982; Mendonsa 1983; Farver 1984); and it portrays the native population as somehow bemused, hostile, or helpless in the face of this 'impact'. Some anthropologists have analysed the 'impact' in light of the reaction of the natives, and of the strategies used to fit tourism into an indigenous economy (cf. Peck and Lepie 1977; Meleghy *et al.* 1985); while others have looked at the interface which is created when hosts and guests interact (cf. Pi-Sunyer 1977; Brewer 1984; Cohen and Cooper 1986). In general, however, the host population is portrayed as static, with little or no control over the touristic image; varying control over the economics of tourism; and with no touristic images of their own.[2] In this paper I want to present a rather different perspective: the hosts in tourism often have a vested interest in the touristic image, they may try to maintain it or refine it, and they certainly are quite capable of manipulating it to their own ends – *which may be similar to or very different from that of the guests.* Ultimately, it is not just the touristic image which is plastic, but also the 'traditional' concerns and constraints of the host culture.

In the case of the Japanese fishermen and diving women *(ama)* of the village of Kuzaki in Mie Prefecture, the business of tourism is rapidly becoming a way of life. The people of the village do not feel exploited by tourism nor by its images, but do feel that they have been given the opportunity to earn a living in modern Japan without having to leave their native village and without having to abandon their traditional way of life altogether.[3] Most importantly, tourism has revitalised the village to such an extent that traditional religious activity can be maintained and kept separate from the tourists themselves. As the villager quoted above demonstrates, there are mixed feelings about the tourists (but not about tourism, as will be made clear below): villagers want the business, but do not want any connections or relations with the tourists, who may be Japanese but are none the less outsiders. The only relationship villagers will admit to is the formal economic relationship created by tourism.

Following the ideas expressed in the quotations used at its beginning, the paper will be in three parts. The first section will briefly explore touristic images of the *ama* and how historical sources came together to produce these images. The second will outline Kuzaki's history, for one of the important factors in the villagers' reaction to tourism is the sense of identity which is fostered by the village's unique history; and the third section will expand on the attitudes of the villagers to tourism.

The *ama* and their image

Freshness is one more journey . . . the flavour of the ocean.
Soon, the sun will rise, daybreak, the time of nature's own ritual beginning.
Toba: the panorama of the sea, blue winds, enjoy to the full a splendid trip.
(various tourist pamphlets, my own translations from the Japanese)

Moeran (1983) noted the use of 'English' phrases in Japanese tourist brochures which aimed to attract the young and trendy Japanese to urban sites. In contrast, the tourist brochures designed for the National Park of Shima Peninsula which includes Mie Prefecture, Toba City and Kuzaki use few English words. Rather, they stress tradition, often using words related to the Shinto world of ritual and sacred nature. Just as frequently the single word 'festival' *(matsuri)* will be printed across the brochure photographs. This, of course, relates to the fact that Shima Peninsula is where the most sacred Shinto shrine in Japan is located: *Ise Jingū*. The presence of the shrine has ensured that, over the centuries, pilgrims have visited the area to 'pray, pay and play' (Graburn 1983b). If pilgrimage is the historical antecedent to tourism, then Shima Peninsula was long overdue for the tourist boom which hit it in the 1960s.

Ise was also one of the areas to which overambitious courtiers might be exiled, and a long tradition of poetry written during these lonely exiles has helped create part of the peninsula's image. Some examples of these poems are to be found in the eighth-century poetry collection called *Manyōshū* where they paint an evocative picture of a simple, romantic world.[4] Frequently, the diving women of the area are mentioned:

The sound of oars is dimly audible.
The fishergirls, to cut the seaweed /of the offing seem to have let out/their boats.
(Book VII/85, Pierson 1966: 9)

There is often a sense of longing in these poems, a sense of nostalgia for the beauty and simplicity of life by the sea. Although this sort of nostalgia is often associated with modern industrialised society's attitude towards the past, it is not unique to the modern world. Virgil sought to evoke similar feelings with his praise of nature in the *Georgics* and *Bucolics;* while the Parisian court of Louis XVI in the eighteenth century

99

created the pastoral fashions of its day when Marie Antoinette decided to live a simpler 'pastoral' life. So too with the various poems written by exiled courtiers: the sea and diving women became fixed images.

Why women divers and not farmers' wives? I believe it is because there exists a strong association in Japanese society between water, origins and the female sex: the ocean is female, so is the sea god and so are boats. Blacker (1975: 79) follows Hori and other Japanese folklorists in positing that the Japanese originally worshipped deities who came from the sea; with the unification of Japan under the Emperors, this worship eventually shifted inland, both georgraphically and metaphorically, to the worship of mountains. Structurally, one could represent the following as oppositions:[5]

ocean	land
nature	culture
female	male
countryside	court
sexual freedom	sexual constraint

The last pair concerns sexuality: as Dalby noted (1983: 170) 'women, water and sexual emotions are concepts that have tended to cluster throughout Japanese history'. The world of geisha is part of the 'floating world' or the 'water trade' and she cites various sex-and water-related terms used by geisha.[6] Divers, even more than fishermen, are *of* the ocean: they work immersed in water. If the coast, where exiles were sent, was seen as being literally on the periphery of the civilised Japanese world of courts where rigid etiquette ruled, and the coast-dwellers were seen as simple and free, then the *ama*'s image at that time is a logical extension of this: they seemed more like sea creatures than peasant women. In other words, to borrow Hendry's terms: the world of the court was 'wrapped' and the world of divers 'unwrapped'.[7]

Aside from the poetry and some Nō plays by Zeami and Kan'ami,[8] there were also several prints by Utamaro Kitagawa (1753–1806) which are still sold as postcards all over Japan. In these prints the *ama* are always at their most erotic: half-clothed, resting after a dive, or flirting with small boys. Modern versions of these prints, the tourism posters which one sees on the Tokyo underground or plastered all over Ise and Toba, take the Bo Derek approach by showing young, slim divers staring off into the distance while their white, wet, see-through clothing clings intimately to their breasts. These posters occasionally show the girls carrying some fresh fish or lobster as a reminder that divers are the source of the excellent seafood which can be eaten in any of the multitude of inns which now dot the Japanese coast.

However, it would be an over-simplification to say that the Japanese tourists who take trips to Shima, Noto and Chiba peninsulas do so only because the women are sexy and the seafood is tastier. As mentioned above, the brochures also emphasise another side of these villages: their associations with ancient Japanese traditions, religion and ritual. Graburn's (1983b) analysis of Japanese domestic tourism points out how central the idea of pilgrimage still is to modern tourism. The photographs in the tourist brochures emphasise the lost Japan – lost, at least, they imply, to those who dwell in the cities. Out there, somewhere, they imply, there is still a Japan very much like the one seen on television in various programmes set in the pre-Meiji era. This is a Japan of religious festivals, where most of the men were strong and brave and had samurai haircuts, where the women were often slim and soft-spoken and wore *kimono*, and the peasants were happy and simple and liked to drink. In short, Japanese domestic tourism involves journeys to find a *real* Japan: a mythical, idealised Japan replete with the samurai values that have only recently filtered down to a middle class which emerged after the Meiji Restoration (1868).

This modern identification of the *ama* with ancient values supposedly lost through the post-Meiji Westernisation of Japan is not entirely new. Mishima Yukio's novel, *The Sound of Waves* (1956), is a romance set on a small island where the men fish on large boats and the sturdy, honest women dive for seafood. These women are contrasted with the city-educated daughter of the lighthouse keeper. This young girl's selfishness is compared with the divers' selflessness; and she is tainted by Western ways rather than being pure Japanese – an important theme in all of Mishima's works.

In the past, the image of the *ama* was created by aristocrats. Today, the mass-media image of the modern *ama* continues to be in the hands of outsiders: it is created for and by the Japanese who long for a traditional Japan; and by the Japanese National Tourist Bureau which plays up the sexy image. Even foreigners contribute to the touristic image, for they believe that the *ama* are pearl-divers and read books like Fleming's *You Only Live Twice* (1964) which reinforce the idea of the sexy oriental pearl-diver. The story of how *ama* became associated with pearls and how this became a tourist attraction is one of historical coincidence and, after the 1950s, economic need. This will be explained below in the discussion of Kuzaki village.

The setting

THE MELANCHOLY WHISTLE OF THE WOMEN [sic] DIVER . . . SENTI-
MENTS OF THE SEA
Wearing specially designed clothing, the women divers plunge into the sea in search of
pearl oysters, abalone and other sea harvests. The melancholy whistling sound that these
women produce upon surfacing add [sic] to the sentimental comfort of the tourist.
'Women Divers at Work' is demonstrated every forty minutes.
     (from the English-language version of 'Mikimoto Pearl Island' tourist brochure)

In Shima Peninsula, the association between pearls and divers is inescapable. The exhibits and brochures on the museum island called Mikimoto Pearl Island located in Toba City make clear that the *ama* always dived for various things and not just for the pearl oysters which Mikimoto Kokichi would then buy up for his experiments in the creation of the cultured pearl. No tourist, foreign or Japanese, ever seems to take in this fact. Thus, since the perfection of the cultured pearl in 1893, the image of *ama* as pearl-divers has developed so forcefully that it is almost impossible to convince people that this is in fact false.[9]

It was Mikimoto who also designed the 'traditional' diving costume which has been associated with the divers. Noting the surprise of foreign visitors at the diving demonstration in which the *ama* dived in their loincloths. Mikimoto created the white *amagi* which the demonstrators still wear. Again, this information is to be found under one of the photographs in the museum exhibit and, again, no visitor ever seems to notice it. This is a sort of symbolic invention of tradition, for the image of white-clad women diving into deep blue waters in search of luminescent pearls – pearls which glow like the truth (a Japanese pun frequently used in Pearl Island Museum) – is striking and, obviously, what people remember best from their visits to Mikimoto Pearl Island.

The cultured pearl industry *is* important for the inhabitants of Shima Peninsula, and not only for the tourism it brings. When Shima was made a National Park in 1946, it was to protect Ise Shrine and the cultured pearl industry from encroaching urbanisation and industrialisation. As a result, until 1963, the business of pearls was the major business of Shima Peninsula along with fishing and diving. Many villages with protected bays grew cultured pearls and the Mikimoto company employed the men and women of Shima in all areas of its industry. It was not until the scenic motorway, Pearl Road, was completed in the mid 1960s that tourism came to the small villages on the coast. Thus, following Graburn's analysis of Japanese tourism, Shima National Park can offer both types of attraction which the Japanese tourist prefers: cultural, educational and traditional (Ise Shrine, Pearl Island and the divers) and the more modern sun, sea and sex (the coastal villages) (1983b: 11–36).

The inhabitants of Shima Peninsula were ready to take advantage of this tourist boom. Although the peninsula is protected from industrialisation, pollution from Japanese industry affects the sea there, adding to the problem of overfishing created by the high market prices of the 1950s. With no major industry other than that of cultured pearls, the villages of Shima were losing people to the big cities in the North. That trend is now being reversed: tourism ensures employment in various areas. Villagers dive and fish for the catches which are served in hotels and restaurants; many men do construction work, widening roads for tourist traffic and building hotels for the increased tourism; and most of the young women of the area work as tour guides, in the shops which cater to tourists, or in the hotels of Toba City.

Kuzaki, just twenty minutes from Toba City, is typical of many coastal villages. Squeezed between the mountains and the sea, Kuzaki has a long scenic coast with seven wide beaches and two harbours. Nineteen of its 116 households run inns and most of the other households are involved in tourist-related work. Much of the fish and shellfish caught in Kuzaki waters are sold to the village innkeepers, and most of the people who work outside the village in Toba are engaged in the sorts of tourist-related jobs described above.

However, there are various ways in which Kuzaki is atypical of the villages surrounding Toba. The villagers claim that Kuzaki is 2000 years old and has always existed as it does now, a small village, physically cut off from the villages nearby because of the mountainous terrain. In fact, the characters that make up the village's name are *kuni* and *saki*, which older villagers use to mean 'land's end', giving an idea of how isolated the village once felt itself to be.[10] The village's strongest connection to the outside world was its annual tribute of *noshi awabi*[11] to the sacred Shinto shrines at Ise, a tribute they still make.

According to legend, Kuzaki's relationship with Ise began in 5 BC,[12] when Princess Yamato made a tour of Ise Shrine's domain and came to Kuzaki. There she saw women diving for abalone. Stopping at a point called Yoriozaki, the princess watched the divers and then ordered the fresh abalone brought to her; when she tasted the shellfish, she found it the most delicious she had ever tried and ordered that it be sent to her at Ise three times a year as the village tribute.[13] This tribute consisted, and still consists, of a thrice-yearly offering of fresh abalone for the Ise priests and dried *sazaya* (sea snail) and *noshi awabi* to be given to the gods.[14]

The village history, *Kuzaki Kambeshi* (Records of the Sacred Guild of Kuzaki)[15] notes that the Meiji Restoration in 1868, with its restructuring of the Shinto religion, brought a brief hiatus in the giving of tribute to Ise. However, the village resumed giving *noshi awabi* in 1879/80 (Kuzaki 1939: 66) and, despite the decline in the importance of Shinto religion in modern Japan, continues to do so. Various rituals which the villagers performed throughout their yearly cycle were changed and consolidated at this time and it was also then, according to some of the oldest grandmothers in Kuzaki, that a major shift occurred. The women had made the *noshi awabi* for Ise; with the resumption of Kuzaki's tribute, the women had to teach the men, the grandfathers, this skill.[16] I mention this last because it shows that the villagers were always flexible: changes in religious practice, sacred tasks and other 'traditional' activities have always occurred.

The political history of the village during and after the Meiji Restoration is complicated and cannot be described in so short an article. However, it is important to note that in 1955 Kuzaki was made a ward of Toba City.[17] Thus it would be improper to refer to Kuzaki as a village, were it not that it still maintains its own traditions and a sense of distance from Toba. These traditions are various, but the villagers see them as essential in describing how they differ from their neighbours. First and foremost, Kuzaki still makes the food for the Shinto deities at Ise. As a result of this, Ise Shrine performs various ceremonies for them and for no other village. This includes a festival on the first of July carried out in the village by Ise priests and a rite performed in Ise for the village on November 15th. Kuzaki also has a festival for the god of war, Hachiman, on January 5th and a boat festival (Nifune) for a deity known as 'the young deity' during November. Villagers feel that these festivals, as well as various other minor ritual occasions mark them as different from their neighbours. Even *O-bon*, the Buddhist festival of the dead, is celebrated for far longer in Kuzaki than in surrounding villages (from the 7th to the 23rd of August). Thus, associated with its diving tradition (as the divers for Ise Shrine) is a complex religious tradition which continues to be important for the people of Kuzaki.[18] This tradition gives the villagers a strong sense of village identity and is important in understanding their reactions to tourists. The main difference between Ōsatsu, the village next door, and Kuzaki – the villagers feel – is that Ōsatsu has become so involved with tourism that its village identity is gone. Despite its being as far from Toba City as Kuzaki is, it looks like an extension of the city rather than a village. I was told that with its big hotels and constant construction, Ōsatsu could be a resort anywhere in Japan, or in the world for that matter.

Tourism in Kuzaki

When I first arrived as a research student in Tokyo, I knew nothing about Kuzaki. In fact I had decided to do my fieldwork on *ama* in a village called Shirahama on the Chiba Peninsula. My supervisor at the University of Tokyo told me that I would be silly to go anywhere but Kuzaki which the Japanese Folklore Society had decided was the 'most traditional village left in Japan'. It might be easy to see, from my description above, that far from being totally unique, Kuzaki is typical of all sorts of remote villages in Japan which are slowly being incorporated into larger urban areas. However, this designation of being 'most traditional' has had its consequences for the village. For one, the villagers are well used to having Japanese researchers coming around to write articles about their customs. Aichi University spent eleven years visiting the village, producing a 100-page article on Kuzaki. The folklorist Segawa Kiyoko wrote various articles on diving practices and taboos while Prof. Kurata Masakuni of Tsu University, who kindly introduced me to the village, has published extensively on Kuzaki's rituals. In the heyday of physiologists studying diving women, the 1950s, summers were full of visiting scientists. Currently, numerous groups of Japanese students of anthropology or geography descend on Kuzaki for two-week studies and, finally, the village got its own foreign anthropologist in me.

Obviously, all this prior research is very important. Yet, at the beginning of my work, there were a few disadvantages. One was that all my questions were answered with 'Read this article please, it will tell you all you need to know' or 'You know, a very learned professor from X university asked me exactly the same thing last year and I had to tell him that I didn't know, I just do it'. Also, I was often asked: 'Why do you need a year to study us? No one else has stayed that long'. Another disadvantage was that it was difficult to be sure where 'real' practices ended or began. I wondered if the villagers did what they did, just as described in the articles, because they felt an obligation to continue? Where was the change? Had new 'traditions' been created and labelled as 'ancient' in order to affirm village identity? I began to wonder.

As time went on, I saw that maintaining religious ritual was important to the villagers, and people would tell me where changes had occurred. Grandmothers would say: 'The women used to take part in this ritual but not any longer' or 'We used to do this ourselves but now have no time, so Ise Shrine does it for us'. Despite all the publicity, or perhaps because of it, Kuzaki never scheduled its festivals or the making of *noshi awabi* to allow tourists to take part.[19] Religious rituals are not used by the villagers to attract tourists and I needed permission for all the rituals I attended; once I was asked not to see part of one rite.

This attitude of keeping Kuzaki's religious life separate from tourism is important and has persisted despite the two documentaries which were filmed while I was there. This may change in the future but, for the moment, religious tradition and tourism are kept separate. It is in this way that the villagers feel that they have preserved their village identity and integrity. Keeping religion separate from tourism is a 'major constraint', in the sense which MacCannell (1976) used the phrase. However, I mentioned another side to the tourist trade in Shima Peninsula, the search for the attractive diving woman, and this side of tourism is certainly catered for in Kuzaki. Thus, there is also an area in Kuzaki tourism which allows for flexibility and, perhaps, it is possible to be flexible precisely because religious identity is being kept intact.

Diving as a way of life is becoming less and less lucrative in Kuzaki. The co-operative, which acts as a form of village government and oversees all farming and fishing in the area, also enforces the national laws designed to prevent overfishing in the Pacific Ocean. This means that divers now only dive for an hour daily – at the very most, two hours – rather than spending a whole day in the sea. In Kuzaki, with all its restrictions on diving, but with diving continuing all year around for various seaweeds and shellfish, I have estimated that a diver now brings in around £4129 per year.[20] In a community where the wife's contribution to the household income was quite large in the past, £4129 a year is very little and so the divers have turned to various part-time jobs to supplement their incomes.

Since the most frequent tourists to visit Kuzaki are groups of businessmen who come down for a weekend and expect to be entertained, the most desirable part-time job, because it pays £21 an evening, is as a 'geisha' in one of the village's nineteen inns.[21] Almost all of the divers in the village do this work at one time or another. The role of geisha varies from inn to inn; in some the women wear uncomfortable *kimono* and tight *obi,* and struggle to remember to speak softly and politely to the businessmen who come to spend the weekend in Kuzaki. In others, the divers will wear their best dresses and, in the most popular inns, they will come dressed in the white *amagi* which divers are all shown wearing on the tourist posters. The atmosphere in this last type of inn is the most relaxed, with the men – who spend the weekend drinking heavily – being even more openly flirtatious than usual and the divers happily sliding into their everyday 'rough' and frank language, daring to joke that they are not wearing a brassière and hinting that they might not even be wearing underpants. It is not unusual to get a present or a tip at the end of an evening's work.

How do the villagers regard all of this? That, I found, was a difficult skein to untangle.

The first mistake I made during fieldword was to ask about village – tourist relations. I asked what type of connections there were between the two. 'None' was the loud reply. 'None at all.' The tourists, mostly groups of salary-men who came to spend a night or two drinking and eating in an inn, were absolutely separate from the life of the village; so I was told.[22] Tourists were not encouraged to attend any of Kuzaki's religious festivals nor, as happens in other parts of Japan as well as in other countries, were any festivals changed or moved to facilitate tourist attendance. Thus, tourists are confined to the inns or beaches of Kuzaki. Rarely would one see them venture out beyond these confines. What then, do these non-relations between the villagers and outsiders consist of?

Yoshida's (1981) article on the stranger as deity is relevant here: both stranger and deity are outsiders, special, sacred yet dangerous and potentially polluting. So too with tourists, they are treated with great respect; they are fed the best of seafood, receive wonderful service from the *ama* and are taken to fish in the best spots. If the tourists wander through the village and stop to ask questions of someone cleaning or making nets, the replies are always cheerful and polite.

Yet, the tourists are also seen to be dangerous. In the summer, when the tourist season is at its height, the village hires a night-watchman to make sure that these outsiders do no harm to people's homes. Women who work constantly as geisha in the inn did not hesitate to tell me that the tourists can be bad and dangerous for the village and that their children need this night-watchman to keep them safe. No one was ever clear about what the dangers might be: it was the very presence of outsiders which was threatening.

People would say that one must always be 'gentle' (yasashii) when talking to outsiders, but would bellow out directions to these people much in the manner adopted by those people, who, when speaking to foreigners, shout in the hope that shouting will solve the language problem. Fishermen would take the tourists to the best spots for fishing and then sit back and wait for the amateur to get seasick. Some husbands were jealous of the attention these outsiders paid their wives and would go out drinking with their friends on the nights the wife was at work and complain bitterly about the situation. Some families would be openly disapproving of some of the women who did this work and would lecture me on the unspecified dangers incurred in going to the inns with the divers. The blunt query: 'Why is it bad or dangerous?' would bring the reply: 'It just is, bad things can happen'. No one was ever clear on these 'bad things' but from hints I learned that there was a general feeling that the tourists were only interested in sex and that was not good. Others, especially the women themselves, saw nothing wrong with the sexual atmosphere of the inns. It was mostly jokes and innuendo and little else. In short, attitudes towards the tourists were varied.

There was considerable variation also in the explanations given by villagers as to why tourists came. Kuzaki was scenic, that they knew; the seafood was the best in Japan – so they would say – and the beaches not bad to swim from, if that was what people wanted to do. Save for the religious tradition, which they tried to keep separate from tourism, most villagers felt that there was nothing special about Kuzaki. When I would ask about this, I was told: 'But we are Japanese, just like all other Japanese'. If people wanted to come and spend their money there, very well, no one in Kuzaki was going to stop them. That the tourists might be looking for a lost, older Japan and its traditions did not make sense to them. Weren't they fully modernised with big modern houses, cars, air-conditioners, motor boats and video-recorders? Wasn't Kuzaki essentially just like the rest of Japan?

Of course, there was an awareness that the weekend visiting businessmen, the anthropologists, the reporters and photographers came for the *ama*, and various requests were dealt with as the people and the co-operative felt best. Serious scholars got to see real diving; so did newsmen and, to varying degrees, the television people. Groups of photographers who sometimes came by bus to photograph the *ama* were presented with the youngest, prettiest girls in the village, who were dressed in *amagi* and had never dived a day in their lives. The businessmen, down for a weekend of fun, and perhaps some romance, would get the divers as geisha: the real divers, who were in their forties, and were all sturdy, tall and nothing at all like any tourist poster. I can't say that, after a few drinks, these men minded at all because they knew that these women were authentic divers.

These inconsistencies and contradictions might seem odd but the villagers were aware of the incongruities. One informant, a young woman, told me (with a great deal of amusement I might add): 'There is a lot of PR to get the tourists here, and 50 per cent of the PR is lies'. Most men were given to hysterical laughter when confronted by images of the sexy diving women. For example, during a *karaoke* video in which a bare-breasted diver passionately kissed a young fisherman, I once heard the comment: 'Our women are nothing like that!' 'No', came the laughing reply, 'if only they were!' Somewhere, the men of Kuzaki believe, you might find a sexy, willing young woman like those in the videos; when they go off on holiday, they look for these women in towns like Tokyo. That tourists come looking for such women in Kuzaki might worry some villagers, but in general, villagers see this misconception in a pragmatic way: it brings money into the village.

As for the divers themselves, they enjoy the part-time work, especially when the atmosphere is relaxed and they can tell their favourite diving stories, flirt and, best of all, earn a little money. The general attitude is: what harm can it do? Most of these 'geisha' are mothers and grand-mothers; they need the money to help pay for their children's education so that they will not end up as fishermen and divers. Not that they are ashamed of being divers. They are quite proud of their profession, but they realise that it is a dying way of life and want their children prepared to live in modern Japan. So let the outsiders come in search of their lost Japan and their sexy *ama* – it's good business.

Conclusion

I would like briefly to draw together the different strands of this paper. The internal tourist boom in Japan depends on many things: two aspects of this are the cost of foreign travel (Tokuhisa 1980: 137) and a nostalgia for the lost community, which Moeran (1984: 4–5) relates to modern industrialisation. It is important that Japan has succeeded economically, with the result that the Japanese have the time and money to make trips. Another important aspect of the success of industrialisation, I believe, is the growing trend to look inward in Japanese culture, the search to discover the good in Japan and to reject outside influences. So holidays are spent in places that represent the *real* but lost Japan.

Kuzaki seems to fit the description of this lost past. It is still remote and yet accessible along a road which passes some of the most famous scenery in Japan. One can identify the landscape of dozens of old prints from the Shima Peninsula as one drives towards the village. It is a diving village, a village where some of the households still fish and almost all have a working diver. Thus, it is authentically of a past culture: there have been divers in Japan for well over two thousand years. Kuzaki has an important relationship with Ise Shrine, and although outsiders do not get to see this side of the village, they know that it exists, since there are books and television documentaries which attest to it. Last but not least, there are the divers themselves, part of a long tradition which associates sex and water, *ama* and freedom, nature, eroticism and romance. It does not matter, in the end, that the women are older, heavier, or less attractive than the poster *ama;* nor that they dive fully-clad in thick wetsuits. To many tourists, it still seems the real thing, a village like the one they or their parents came from. They do not see, or perhaps they refuse to see, that the villagers find all this romanticism amusing and naive. To dive, to earn a living fishing, that is hard work; to run an inn or to act as geisha in one is also hard work. The people of Kuzaki also see themselves as part of the modern Japan. What is real and unique about Kuzaki for its inhabitants is its religion, by which they mean its unique ritual traditions and festivals. This religion is not put on display for the tourists because it is simply too important. The important point here is that the villagers accept parts of the touristic image about sexy women and use it in order to keep up the very religious traditions which they keep separate from tourism.[23]

It is also interesting to consider the paradoxes involved in the village being seen as part of the true Japan. Ardener (1987) has written about this in detail in an article on 'remote places' in Scotland. The people in remote places do not see themselves as special, they do not understand nostalgia for the lost community and they are entrepreneurs, interested in making money. This description fits the people of Kuzaki well. For them, the big Japanese cities are just as strange, confusing and dangerous as Toba City of which they are part. City people are just as unkind, rough-spoken and difficult to trust as the people of Ōsatsu, the village next door. Kuzaki has unique seafood, they will admit, but that has to do with the sea – ever changeable. There are nice beaches which the tourists manage to fill with rubbish (adding to the view that outsiders are dirty). The women dive, yes, but they also farm and act as fishing partners for the men – isn't that what a wife is supposed to be, a working partner? If the interest is in Kuzaki because of Ise, 'Yes', the villagers will say, 'for that we are special and blessed; but doesn't every part of Japan have its own customs?'

When the people of Kuzaki go on holiday, they love to go drinking and dancing in the big cities like Kyoto or Tokyo. They are also interested in the search for unusual and exotic places in Japan; especially the men, who believe that women in other places might be more interesting than their own. The women of Kuzaki, as well, like to see what the shrines, temples and 'geisha' in other places are like. Thus, and this might seem paradoxical to the anthropologists who see tourism only as a negative 'impact', the *ama* on holiday have many of the same expectations as do the tourists who come to their villages. They are as capable of practising 'touristic imperialism' as are the visitors to their village, which says a great deal about the universality of the touristic experience. However, as part of a host culture, the *ama*'s comments on the way tourism is handled in other places can be critical ('the service was bad, I would never neglect guests so') or envious ('we could make more money if we did that in Kuzaki'). Yet, like the dwellers in Ardener's 'remote areas', they too are caught up in this search for the real and authentic Japan; a Japan which they both represent and continue to look for in other places.

D. P. Martinez

Notes

1 The fieldwork upon which this article is based was made possible through two grants: the Japanese Ministry of Education Monbushō Grant, initially given to me in conjunction with the Oxford – Tokyo University Exchange Programme, and the Philip Bagby Studentship in Social Anthropology. I am most grateful for the support of these bodies, as well as for all the assistance provided by the Cultural Anthropology Faculty of Tokyo University. I would also like to thank D. N. Gellner, Dr Roger Goodman, Dr Joy Hendry and Dr James McMullen as well as other JAWS members for their comments and advice.

2 I must point out that at the First British Conference on the Anthropology of Tourism, several people did deal with the issue of how host cultures react to and manipulate the touristic image to meet their own needs. Most notably, there was Kohn's paper (1988) on tourism in the Isle of Coll and Bowman's paper (1988) on Palestinian shopkeepers.

3 Kim (1986) argues that the indigenous Japanese household, the *ie,* is not disappearing in rural Japan (as some ethnologists have been predicting) precisely because of tourism. The economic success of tourism allows households – which in Japan includes people and property – to remain together and has slowed down the flight of younger people to the cities. The very same thing is occurring in Kuzaki.

4 I am using 'romantic' here in its original sense, that is: 'characterized by or suggestive of or given to romance, imaginative, remote from experience, visionary' (Concise Oxford Dictionary 1964).

5 I would have liked to include danger and safety here. For example: the dangerous sea and dangerous nature as well as the arduous and dangerous work of the divers, for this element of danger also adds to the image which eventually became associated with divers. However, although I do mention the idea 'danger' (which is, paradoxically, associated with the tourists) later in this article, this paper is too short to go into the complex problems raised by the concept in Japan. I have written a second article on this entitled: 'The tourist as deity' (Martinez 1988a).

6 I also noticed that among Tokyo students sexual slang includes words like *wakame* (the seaweed *Undaria pinnatifida*) for pubic hair. The divers of Kuzaki made a very frank association between the vagina and abalone *(awabi* or ear-shell).

7 This opposition might be strengthened by a comparison of the images of geisha and divers during the Edo period (1615–1867), a connection pointed out to me by the American anthropologist David Plath (personal communication). The multi-kimonoed geisha with their masks of make-up and their various skills in the world of art and culture were considered the most beautiful of women. *Ama,* in contrast, worked almost naked in the sea which coarsened their skins and they were famed for their rough and easy manners. The main difference between these groups of women is that the *ama* were seen as being sexually free while the geisha were sexually attractive: a dichotomy well worth investigating.

8 Zeami wrote *Ama* on which Kan'ami based his *Matsukaze* (14/15th century). Both portray the *ama* as forlorn women, abandoned by their aristocratic lovers and left to die and return as ghosts. Both trace their origin, as does the 'Exile at Suma' chapter of *The*

Tale of Genji, to 'the exile of Ariwara no Yukihara (818–893), a famous poet courtier, and scholar' (Keene 1970 : 18).

9 I have had the experience of telling people (mostly non-Japanese) that the *ama* dived for abalone and not for pearls, only to be told that I must be wrong because at Mikimoto Pearl Island that is what they saw: pearl-divers. This image is so pervasive that recently one of the British television stations broadcast a short film made by Japanese students about an *ama* and her daughter. The programme was described as being about 'pearl-divers' and every mention of abalone-diving was translated only as 'diving'.

10 This folk etymology for the characters that make up Kuzaki is a bit unusual. In general, *kuni* refers to a political area such as nation, country, prefecture, but there is an archaic meaning of *kuni* as that which is 'opposed to heaven and sea' *(Nihon Kokugo Daijiten* 1972–6: vol. 6, p. 553) and it is in this sense which the people of Kuzaki use the term. However, I have not been able to find an alternative meaning for *saki* (generally meaning cape) which would indicate the notion of end or point.

11 Dried and cut strips of abalone or ear-shell.

12 Various sources give different dates for this: the village history, *Kuzaki Kambeshi,* gives the date as *Suinin nijūrokunen* or 3 BC in the era of the Emperor Suinin.

13 This story is told by all the villagers, although they tend to begin it with the words *'sen nen maeni'* (one thousand years ago) the rest of the tale follows the version given here. The researchers of Aichi University in their report on Kuzaki politely cast doubt on this legend, but have documentation on Ise Shrine–Kuzaki relations going back to the 6th/7th centuries AD. Kuzaki's relationship in the form of abalone tribute is well documented for Ise *Naikū* (interior) Shrine since AD 1111 (Aichi 1965: 7).

14 Interesting to note is that another, nearby, village called Ōtsu also paid this tribute to Ise, but since Ōtsu became part of Kuzaki in 1499, the villagers are right in saying that Kuzaki is the only village left in Japan to make the gods' food (Kuzaki 1939: 64).

15 *Kambe* is a term which refers to a group with a special relationship to a shrine and can be translated as 'sacred guild'. Generally the group, as Kuzaki village does, performs a certain service for a shrine and this service, called *mitsugi* or tribute, is taken in lieu of tax. In Kuzaki's case, the tribute was *noshi awabi*.

16 When asked why, my informant said that it was 'because the grandfathers had nothing better to do'. I have found no documentation for this change in the sexual division of labour, although there is an Utamaro print in the Ise Shrine Museum which shows the diving women cutting up abalone as if making *noshi awabi*.

17 A detailed discussion of Kuzaki's history is given in my thesis (Martinez 1988b) submitted to Oxford University.

18 There is no room here to discuss this complex religious cycle. What is important to note is that the villagers see this tradition as the symbolic marker which makes them different from other villages along the coast. For more details see Martinez 1988b.

19 In Shirahama, a Chiba Prefecture diving village, I recorded a divers' festival which, according to the villagers themselves, had originally lasted one day. The villagers have decided that they really need a three-day festival to attract the tourists and so repeat the ritual on three consecutive days. They have also added fireworks and a Chinese dragon. I also found, while travelling in Ladakh, India, that the monastery in Hemis has moved a winter ritual to the summer in order that tourists can see it. Brandes, in his look at Mexican fiestas, notes that the original Night of the Dead in the village of Tzintzuntzan was transformed for tourism (1988: 101–9). In the case of these villagers, government

attempts to change the fiesta back to its 'traditional' form failed: the villagers insisted that the expanded, touristic version was *their* fiesta.

20 These figures were converted from yen at the exchange rate of 240 yen to the pound.

21 If Plath is correct about the symbolic opposition of geisha and *ama* during the Edo period (see above, note 3) then the divers working as geisha represents a conflation of this opposition and the creation of a new 'tradition'. See Dalby (1983: 229–50) for a new opposition of Kyoto versus 'country' geisha.

22 I later learned that the wife of the man who told me this worked as often as she could in inns, that the man himself took tourists out fishing in his motor boat, and that their eldest daughter did summer work as a maid in one of the inns. After I left the village, this family finally put the funds together to build their own inn and, when I returned in 1986, had a thriving business.

23 Boissevain (1988) makes a similar argument about tourism and ritual in Malta in a working paper which he presented at the First British Conference on the Anthropology of Tourism. The money earned by tourism is used to support and even increase the religious rituals practised by the Maltese.

References

Aichi University Community Research Institute. 1965. *Amanomura – Tobashi Kuzakichō* (The *ama*'s village, Toba City, Kuzaki Ward). Special Issue of the Memories (sic, Memoirs) of the Community Research Institute of Aichi University. Toyohashi City: Aichi University.

Ardener, E. 1987. 'Remote areas': some theoretical considerations. In *Anthropology at Home,* ed. A. Jackson. London: Tavistock.

Blacker, C. 1975. *The Catalpa Bow: a Study of Shamanistic Practices in Japan.* London: Allen & Unwin.

Boissevain, J. 1983. Tourism and ritual in Malta. An unpublished paper presented to the Group for Anthropology in Policy and Practice (GAPP) First British Conference on the Anthropology of Tourism.

Bowman, G. W. 1988. F**king the tourists. An unpublished paper presented to the GAPP First British Conference on the Anthropology of Tourism.

Brandes, S. 1988. *Power and Persuasion: Fiestas and Social Control in Rural Mexico.* Philadelphia: University of Pennsylvania Press.

Brewer, J. D. 1984. Tourism and ethnic stereotypes: Variations in a Mexican town. *Annals of Tourism Research* 11 487–501.

Cohen, E. 1982. Marginal paradises: bungalow tourism on the islands of southern Thailand. *Annals of Tourism Research* 9 189-228.

Cohen, E. and Cooper, L. 1986. Language and tourism. *Annals of Tourism Research* 13 533-63.

Dalby, L. C. 1983. *Geisha.* Berkeley: University of California Press.

Duffield, B. S. and Long, J. 1981. Tourism in the Highlands and Islands of Scotland: rewards and conflicts. *Annals of Tourism Research* 8, 403-31.

Farver, J. A. M. 1984. Tourism and employment in the Gambia. *Annals of Tourism Research* 11 249-65.

Graburn, N. H. H. (ed.) 1983a. The anthropology of tourism. *Annals of Tourism Research* 10 (1), 9-34.

Graburn, N. H. H. 1983b. *To Pray, Pay and Play: the Cultural Structure of Japanese Domestic Tourism,* (Series B no 26, Centre des Hautes Etudes Touristiques, Université de Droit, d'Economie et des Sciences). Aix-en-Provence: Centre Des Hautes Etudes Touristiques.

Greenwood, D. J. 1977. Culture by the pound: an anthropological perspective on tourism as cultural commoditization. In *Hosts and Guests*, ed. V. Smith, pp. 129-38. Oxford: Basil Blackwell.

Hobsbawm, E. and Ranger, T. (eds). 1983. *The Invention of Tradition.* Past and Present Publications. Cambridge: Cambridge University Press.

Keene, D. (ed.) 1970. *Twenty Plays of the Nō Theatre.* Illustrated with drawings by Fukami Tanrō and from the Hōshō texts. New York: Columbia University Press.

Kim, O. P. M. 1986. Is the *ie* disappearing in rural Japan? The impact of tourism on a traditional Japanese village. In *Interpreting Japanese Society,* ed. J. Hendry and J. Webber, pp. 185-90. Oxford: JASO.

Kohn, T. 1988. Island involvement and the evolving tourist. An unpublished paper presented to the GAPP First British Conference on the Anthropology of Tourism.

Kuzaki 1939. *Kuzaki Kambeshi* (Records of the Sacred Guild of Kuzaki). Unpublished historical records of Kuzaki Ward, Toba City, Mie Province, Japan.

MacCannell, D. 1976. *The Tourist: New Theory of the Leisure Class.* Clinton, Mass: The Colonial Press.

Martinez, D. P. 1988a. The tourist as deity: ancient continuities in modern Japan. An unpublished paper presented to the GAPP First British Conference on the Anthropology of Tourism.

Martinez, D. P. 1988b. The *ama:* tradition and change in a Japanese diving community. Unpublished DPhil thesis submitted to Oxford University.

Meleghy, T. Preglau, M. and Tafershofer, A. 1985. Tourism development and value change. *Annals of Tourism Research* 12, 181–99.

Mendonsa, E. L. 1983. Tourism and income strategies in Nazare, Portugal. *Annals of Tourism Research* 10 213–38.

Mishima, Yukio 1956. *The Sound of Waves*, trans. M. Weatherby, drawings by Yoshinori Kinoshita. Tokyo: Charles E. Tuttle.

Moeran, B. 1983. The language of Japanese tourism. *Annals of Tourism Research* 10: 1, 93–108.

Moeran, B. 1984. *Lost Innocence: Folk Craft Potters of Onta, Japan.* Berkeley and Los Angeles: University of California Press.

Nash, D. 1977. Tourism as a form of imperialism. In *Hosts and Guests,* ed. V. Smith, pp. 33–48. Oxford: Basil Blackwell.

Passariello, P. 1983. Never on Sunday? Mexican tourists at the beach. *Annals of Tourism Research* 10: 1, 109–22.

Peck, J. G. and Lepie, A. S. 1977. Tourism and development in three North Carolina towns. In *Hosts and Guests,* ed. V. Smith, pp. 159–72. Oxford: Basil Blackwell.

Pierson, J. L. 1966. *Selection of Japanese Poems Taken from the Manyōsū.* Leiden: E. J. Brill.

Pi-Sunyer, O. 1977. Through native eyes: tourists and tourism in a Catalan maritime community. In *Hosts and Guests,* ed. V. Smith, pp. 149–155. Oxford: Basil Blackwell.

Said, E. W. 1978. *Orientalism.* Harmondsworth: Penguin.

Smith, V. L. (ed.). 1977. *Hosts and Guests, the Anthropology of Tourism.* Oxford: Basil Blackwell.

Tokuhisa, Tamao 1980. Tourism within, from and to Japan. *International Social Science Journal* 32, 128–50.

Yoshida, Teigo 1981. The stranger as god; the place of the outsider in Japanese folk religion. *Ethnology* 20 (2): 87–99.

Making an exhibition of oneself:
the anthropologist as potter in Japan

Introduction

The idea that I should hold my own exhibition started out as a kind of joke. Miyamoto Reisuke, a pottery dealer in Fukuoka City, had decided to take me into his confidence and help me out in what had until then been extremely difficult research into the production, marketing and aesthetic appraisal of the contemporary ceramic art world in Japan.[1] I had found out, to my cost, that this art world was an extremely closed-in category of department-store representatives, journalists, critics and eminent named potters. It seemed as if they were utterly respectable, but – if the gossip was to be believed – they were somewhat less so underneath the surface. It was becoming increasingly difficult for young and talented potters to make their way to the top of the ceramic art world unless they conformed to the demands and expectations of, what they themselves called, the 'mafia'. This meant that they had little choice but to tailor their work to suit the status quo of accepted taste. Innovation was becoming increasingly difficult and exhibition pottery correspondingly more stylised.

Miyamoto had suggested that I accompany him around the potteries of northern Kyushu and, during our trips, we discussed pottery at considerable length. I soon concluded that there was much that was very unsatisfactory about the quality of the pots being made. Miyamoto, however, encouraged me to be more objective, since he was not convinced that I really understood the potters' problems. As he put it:

It's easy to criticise from the outside, but what you really need to do as an anthropologist is experience what it's like being a potter yourself. I'm not saying you're wrong in your conclusions. But you need to understand things with your belly, not your head. Why don't you hold your own exhibition? That way you'd really begin to appreciate some of the paradoxes potters find themselves caught up in.[2]

I was intrigued by the idea. After all, I had learned to make pots in Sarayama (Onta) some years earlier,[3] and had more recently been making pottery in Koishiwara. It would be fun to see whether I could sell my work. At the same time, as I realised from the qualms that immediately assailed me, it would also be a challenge – and a nerve-wracking experience.

Establishing a frame

Nevertheless, I decided to pursue Miyamoto's idea by talking to a potter friend in Koishiwara, Kajiwara Jirō. Kajiwara had always helped me in my research and gladly offered to let me use the single kick-wheel in his workshop. He told me that I could fire my pots in his five-chambered climbing kiln when the time came, or I could use his oil-burning kiln if I preferred, depending on schedules. If the worse came to the worst, he continued, he could himself make some of the larger forms, which I could then decorate, glaze and exhibit in my show. After all, that was the way a number of famous Japanese potters produced their works, so why shouldn't I?

Regretfully, I declined Kajiwara's offer, even though I knew he was right. I had already seen for myself the work of one fourteenth-generation overglaze enamelware specialist, in which not just the forms, but the decorations too, were clearly the hand of several different craftsmen. Although there may have been a time in European art when this was accepted practice, my Western sense of 'creativity' somehow prevented me from going in for this atelier-style of production. The idea put forward by such potters as Bernard Leach, Hamada Shōji and Kawai Kanjirō that a potter should be responsible for all stages of his work was one to which I, at least, still clung. I felt that I should take responsibility for my work (however mediocre it might be), and not attempt to present a false image of my capabilities through the competence of my friend, Kajiwara Jirō.

In the meantime, Miyamoto had been talking to two acquaintances – one in the Fukuoka branch of the Tamaya department store, the other in the North Kyushu office of the *Mainichi* newspaper company. He wanted to find out from them whether there was any business mileage in the idea of my holding a one-man show and, if so, whether they would be intertested in getting involved in it. Both men reacted in a positive way and – later – the department store's Publicity Manager told me why he had accepted Miyamoto's proposal with such alacrity:

> For a start, we know Miyamoto. He's been doing business with us for several years now, putting on shows in our art gallery and acting as our agent in dealings with potters. We trust him. But there's something else. A department store like Tamaya spends most of its time and energy trying to find means of making money, and only money. So when an idea like this comes along, we tend to jump at it. After all, it's nice to enjoy ourselves occasionally. So far as we're concerned, it doesn't really matter whether your pots sell or not. The important thing is that people will come along and enjoy themselves and that'll be good for Tamaya's reputation.

Certainly, one of the most interesting aspects of Japanese business practices is that department stores are heavily involved in the sponsorship of cultural events which will bring in crowds of people.[4] The Publicity Manager's idea, therefore, was for Tamaya to *appear* to be putting on a fun show. This would encourage people to visit the store and indirectly persuade them to spend their money there, both then and in the future. My exhibition, like those of many other potters and artists, was to be used towards Tamaya's cultural capital. It was the *social* side of business, I realised, that was so effective in keeping the Japanese economy buoyant.

In the meantime, Miyamoto was playing a kind of spy-catcher game, in order to fix the show.

> With all shows, you have to have a *framework* in which to work, and it is this frame that's the most difficult thing of all to establish. So when I visited the Publicity Manager at Tamaya, I told him that the *Mainichi* newspaper was going to be the official sponsor of your show, even though that wasn't actually the case. And then, when I visited the Enterprise and Promotions Department at *Mainichi,* I told the manager there that Tamaya had agreed to let us hold the show in their Fukuoka store, even though that wasn't true either. The thing is that neither of the two men concerned knew this.
>
> Of course, in your case, things are quite simple. Both men have known you for some months now and want to help you out. Even so, *officially*, things aren't fixed yet. We're still working at the level of informal contacts. It's this, of course, that is the vital aspect of Japanese business. Formalities come much, much later – once the frame has been securely established.

There was a slight hiccup, however – one that revealed another strange element in the world of Japanese business. It was the Enterprise and Promotions Manager, who explained his difficulty to me one afternoon in a coffee shop located in Tenjin's underground shopping street.

> I haven't officially committed the paper to sponsoring your exhibition for two reasons. One is that I don't at the moment want personal connections to dictate a newspaper project, without first checking up on one or two alternatives. More importantly, if the *Mainichi* newspaper does decide to sponsor your show, it'll mean that we can get the RKB Broadcasting and TV station to help out, because they're part of the *Mainichi* network. But then there's a good chance that none of the other media organisations will write about the show. What I mean is, jealousy will prevent the *Nishi Nihon*, *Asahi* or *Yomiuri* newspapers from supporting your exhibition, and that would, of course, ultimately be detrimental to publicity both for Tamaya and for yourself.

He paused to allow the implications of this bombshell to sink into my shell-shocked head before continuing:

> Actually, I've another idea which I think would work very well, and which would allow us all more freedom when it comes to media publicity. There's an organisation known as the Anglo-Japanese Association (Nichi-ei Kyōkai), which is based in Kyushu University and whose members are primarily industrialists and intellectuals. What I'd like to do is get *it* to sponsor your show – in name only, of course. Then the *Mainichi* can take a back seat, while at the same time doing all the real promotion. In the meantime, Miyamoto can contact his friends in the *Nishi Nihon* newspaper and ask them to support your show, and they'll have no objections because we won't be acting as front-running sponsors.

I was fast realising that pottery exhibitions initially had very little to do with pottery *per se*. What was going on here was a very delicate juggling act, with a number of institutions eager to get in on an exhibition, but not willing to accept responsibility for anything should the act misfire. If the show was a failure, the only people to blame would be the official sponsors – an amorphous body which hardly ever met. If, on the other hand, the show was a success, both the department store and the newspaper company would certainly claim most of the credit.

It was the kind of politicking that intrigued me. I began to feel that I should not be outdone in this game, and suggested to Miyamoto that I get my own sponsorship from the British Council whose Director in Tokyo I happened to know. Permission was freely given ('As long as we don't have to finance you, or anything like that, old man!') and, of course, the Anglo-Japanese Association was prepared to support me as well.

All the same, a framework needed more than just verbal persuasion in the provision of sponsorship, and it was Miyamoto's wife who came up with the kind of idea needed to make the business fish bite and agree wholeheartedly to support my exhibition. One evening, as we sat over a very late dinner, she said:

What we really ought to do is hold your show at the same time as the Dentō Kōgeiten, the annual Traditional Crafts Exhibition, which is put on at Iwataya, Tamaya's rival department store down the road. Everybody goes to it – potters, patrons, collectors, critics, and the general public. Holding your show then would really appeal to the Publicity Manager, if we had the proper media backing, because that's the one week of the year when *nobody* visits Tamaya. If your show were to be properly advertised, all the potters visiting the Traditional Crafts Exhibition would drop by to see your pots. Just for the fun of it.

My immediate reaction was one of near panic. I protested that it would be extremely embarrassing to be showing my bad pots at the very time that one of the most prestigious ceramics exhibitions in Japan was being held. Miyamoto only laughed:

Believe it or not, we're not trying to be nasty to you. The thing about Japanese pottery is that it has a tradition of amateurism. Look at the *raku* wares so cherished by tea masters, but often made by people much less skilled than yourself. The way I see things, modern Japanese potters have become *too* skilled, *too* proficient technically. One or more of them even program computers to fire their work according to some traditional design or other. So far as I'm concerned, this leads to a paradox. On the one hand, they throw away pots that are bloated or aren't quite perfect because of some mishap during firing. On the other, they consciously copy old pots that are misshapen or overfired. They don't really know what it means to have *asobi*, 'play', in their work. Their work is too *kurushii*, too 'uptight'. And that, I think, is where you have the edge. After all, your pots are made to be used – rather than exhibited – and you have a certain *yutori,* a relaxed carefreeness in the way you work. And that's what we're missing in Japan today. The age of amateurs like Ishiguro, Rosanjin, or Tomimoto has gone. Nowadays everyone's a professional.

First pots

Miyamoto had come up with another good idea to help sell my work, and this was that I should exhibit both stoneware and porcelain (a medium in which I had never worked before). Almost all potters worked in one medium or the other, so it would be 'different' to have a one-man exhibition in which both were on show. I decided to start by making stoneware pots at Koishiwara – a couple of dozen slabware dishes; then half a dozen decorated tiles, followed by thirty dinner plates. Next, I decorated the plates with thick white slip over iron solution brushed on to the clay body. Not quite certain what design to fix on, I tried three or four patterns, before hitting upon what seemed to be a successful idea – combing through the slip in a criss-cross pattern.

Some of the iron solution was still left over, so I used it to decorate the dried slipped surface of the slabware dishes. I had in mind one or two Japanese-like floral designs, but, for some reason, I did not do any of these, but started madly brushing triangles all over their surfaces. By the time I had finished playing around, one dish had even ended up with a game of noughts and crosses on it.[5]

It was at this juncture that Kajiwara Jirō came across the drying yard to see what I was up to. He shook his head in a somewhat melancholy manner. 'I don't know, Boochan', he began, using the pet name that people had for me in the country,

> I just wouldn't dare do anything like that – however much I may want to. You see, here in Koishiwara, we're bound by tradition. People expect us to make our pots in a certain style and it's virtually impossible to ignore their expectations. If I went and did what you've just done here, you know what would happen, don't you? I wouldn't be able to sell a thing. Everybody'd complain that I wasn't producing 'proper', traditional Koishiwara ware. But you're free from pressures like that. You're not bound to copy our style, and you can see this lack of psychological restraint even in the way your brush moves as it makes these patterns.

He pointed to one or two designs that he liked, before suggesting that we go off and have a few drinks, but I said I wanted to do some more work while I was still in the mood. 'You *want* to make pots!' Kajiwara exclaimed in wonder. 'You know something? I haven't *wanted* to make pots for about a decade now. For me this is just a job. It's not a pleasure any more. That's the main difference between us two.'

What Kajiwara admitted to me then struck me as being true of a number of potters involved in both the folk craft movement and the ceramic art exhibition world. Very few potters in Japan seemed to be enthusiastic about their work. Pottery was a profession, a job – just as being a department-store elevator-girl or a bank clerk was a job – and a lot of potters found themselves being pressurised into meeting schedules, while at the same time entertaining casual visitors and dealing with mundane business matters. Potters were being obliged to market not just their wares but themselves into the bargain.

I began to learn all this first hand as I tried to settle down and produce work for my exhibition. I was always being disturbed – by phone calls and by visitors – and I found it difficult to get in more than an hour or two of concentrated work at any one time. A newspaper reporter came up to Koishiwara to watch me throwing pots, to take photographs and ask questions. And then, of course, I had to meet representatives of the Anglo-Japanese Association and get the final go-ahead for their sponsorship. Rarely was I left in peace to make pots.

Initial preparation

During such meetings, I found myself being obliged to talk about my pots – to create an ideology about my work which, although I was not fully conscious of the fact at the time, effectively clothed the *business* side of my show with an 'aesthetic aura'. By this I do not mean that I myself was interested in how much – if any – money I would make from the sale of my pots (as a scholar, I could afford not to worry); rather, that the dealer, newspaper and department store were all involved in the show for the direct or indirect profit that they would gain from it. The ideology of quality that I presented to the public through the media was, of course, vital to the show's success. But the actual quality of my pottery seemed to me to be of secondary importance.

One of the things that had to be prepared well in advance was the announcements of the show. There are various means by which potters in Japan introduce themselves, or have themselves introduced, to the general public. The simplest way is for them to write up what is known as a *tōreki*, a kind of 'potted history' of their career. In it, they usually cite where they studied pottery, to whom they were apprenticed, what exhibitions they have contributed to, and what prizes they have won. Alternatively, they can write up some sort of introductory note and talk about their work – about the traditions and history of their kiln, for example, or about the techniques they use and their origins.

A third method is to get somebody to write a *suisenbun*, or 'recommendation', on their behalf – their teacher, a member of the department store's art gallery staff, or, preferably, a pottery critic. Miyamoto, however, decided to approach a *potter* – Imaizumi Imaemon, the thirteenth-generation Nabeshima overglaze enamelware artist – mainly because Imaemon is a somewhat rare breed in the world of contemporary Japanese ceramics, in that he is respected by almost all potters in Kyushu.

With Imaemon's name signed at the bottom of the *suisenbun* printed on the announcements, I can send them off to every potter in Kyushu and know that a lot of them will come simply out of curiosity, because Imaemon has chosen to write about your work.

Miyamoto's aim was, he said, to sell my pots to potters, rather than simply to the casual passers-by who might drop in to see the show. This was not in itself that unusual an idea, since Japanese potters frequently do buy one another's work – partly out of *tsukiai* personal acquaintanceship, partly as a way of congratulating the potter who is holding a show.[6] People like to buy things as a means of remembering events which are, after all, fairly ephemeral. At the same time, however, a potter knows that by buying a pot at somebody else's exhibition, other potters will return the favour when he comes to put on his own show. Consumerism thus becomes both a form of memorialism and a matter of what the Japanese call '*gibu ando teki*' (give and take).[7]

Another of the little rituals essential for any potter working in Japan is the boxing of pots. The Japanese have been doing this for centuries as a means of safeguarding the provenance of a work, and some 'experts' now pay more attention to the box and to the calligraphy on its lid than they do to the actual pot inside the box.[8] A good box, with the right sort of calligraphy by the right person, can increase the value of a pot from £10 to £300, in the case of an unknown would-be artist potter. I did not like the system, but Miyamoto was adamant. All my pots would have to be boxed.[9]

Pricing

Miyamoto was by this time calculating costs. I would have to pay Kajiwara Jirō and Tanaka Hajime (the potter whose kiln I was using to fire my porcelain) for the use of their materials and kilns, and give them a little extra as a token of thanks for their allowing me to make such a nuisance of myself in their workshops. Then there were the costs of having the boxes made, as well as of the printing and mailing of the announcements. I was also having a number of decorated tiles framed as pictures or made into wooden trays. *In toto*, therefore, costs were likely to come to nearly £4000. And that was before I had sold a single pot.

And that was the next problem to be faced: what price were we to put on my work? Miyamoto always had one rule: aim for a *total* sales figure – in my case, somewhere between £8000 and £12000. In other words, he did not price individual pots on their respective merits, but according to the final sales total that he wanted to make from the show.[10] Of this Tamaya would get 30 per cent – the usual margin taken by a department store in commodity sales – while his own commission was the standard 20 per cent, which had to cover all his expenses.

I proceeded to work out what was – or was not – in this show for me as a potter, and discovered that I would have to sell about £8000 worth of pots just to break even. This brought me out into a cold sweat, and I began to understand why Japanese potters used to get so nervous and worried about their exhibitions. Miyamoto, however, told me not to worry, and assured me that I would not make a loss.

> In a way, things are easier for us than they are for other potters. There is, after all, no market price for your work. Instead, we have anarchy. A pot of yours can be priced at £30, £300, or even £3000. All we have to do is sell a couple of pots at the top price and our costs are covered!

He chuckled at the thought.

> At the same time, for an exhibition in a department store gallery like Tamaya's, there is an optimum number of pots that can be shown. I always think of seventy as being more or less the perfect number.

This information was even more shattering, for it meant that, if the show was not to make a loss, we are going to have to charge an average of more than £100 per pot. How could I dare talk of 'functional wares' (as I blithely had done to members of the Anglo-Japanese Association and press) if my own work was going to be so expensive? I began to appreciate the sort of paradoxes faced by such famous 'folk craft' (*mingei*) potters as Hamada Shōji and Bernard Leach. As far as any 'artistic sensibility' was concerned, the system was virtually out of the potter's control.[11]

Final pricing and display

And so I went back to work, with a certain feeling of desperation as I tried to make pots that might be worth their high price tags. And, of course, things began to go wrong – pots cracked during drying, were knocked over, or broken in firing. I began to wonder quite seriously if I would ever get anything together for a show, but in the second firing I was fortunate enough to get all of my big plates and sets of dishes out of the kiln both well-fired and unscathed. With only about a month to go, I had what seemed to be the kernel of an exhibition.

Eventually, for better or for worse, my pots were ready for the show, and I found myself sitting down in Miyamoto's store-room one bitterly cold evening trying to put price tags on what I had made. This we found extraordinarily difficult to do, mainly because Miyamoto knew that pricing was an arbitrary act which had little, if anything, to do with 'intrinsic' aesthetic values. Usually it was potters who set their own prices, in which case all Miyamoto had to do was add on his commission. In my case, however, pots were 'priceless'. There was no standard against which they could be measured, although if I were to charge high prices for my stoneware (which was, after all, not that different from other Koishiwara ware), it would probably upset other potters working in the village. Miyamoto felt, therefore, that people should not object to prices – thereby implying that the *artist* (as opposed to craftsman) potter in Japan was someone who ignored the market value of work similar to his own and created an arbitrary pricing scale. There was something else, too:

> You've suggested that we're pricing pots by size, rather than by quality, and that in this respect we're not that different from painters who charge so much per square inch of canvas. You're right, of course. After all, I've already told you what I think is the optimum number of pots for the Tamaya art gallery, and we know how much we've got to sell in order not to make a loss. But, at the same time, if you start suggesting that one pot is better than another, then you're setting a standard. A standard of quality. But in your case there's *no* objectively reliable standard – only your own. If you start pricing *one* pot higher than another one similar in size, then you're going to have to do the same right down the line for all your pots – even the small tea and sake cups. Instead, I suggest we stick to the idea of pricing by size. In other words, we decide what price is likely to attract a buyer and then leave the public to decide which pots they like at that particular price. That way, you'll learn which designs are popular, and which aren't. Let the public set a standard for any future exhibition you may hold.

And so we did as Miyamoto suggested. There were two pots on which we failed to agree on price and I hit on the idea of putting them up for auction, and of selling them to the person who submitted the highest written bid during the course of the show. In these two cases, we could allow members of the public to say what they thought of my work by giving in their own monetary values.[12] As for the rest, there were 294 pots in all (many of them forming sets of plates, dishes, cups and saucers) – giving a total sales potential of over £10000. Miyamoto said that he hoped to sell about 70 per cent of them.

The problem of quality emerged once more when we went down to Tamaya the next day to arrange the pots in the store's gallery. It was clear, to me at least, that there were far too many pots on display. The gallery looked more like a bargain sale than an 'artistic exhibition'. The store salesmen had decided to line up all the stoneware down one side of the gallery, and all the porcelain down the other.

Later, I asked Miyamoto whether we should not have mixed up Koishiwara and Ureshino pots, matching similar designs on stoneware and porcelain.

The trouble with your idea is that it is typically 'artistic'. If you mix up pots too much, the porcelain will reflect back on the stoneware, and the stoneware will reflect back on the porcelain. People will no doubt enjoy *looking* at the subtle differences, but they'd end up *buying* nothing at all, because they'd be too confused. They wouldn't know what to look for where, nor which they liked better.

Miyamoto was right. I was adopting a typical potter-cum-critic's attitude, more interested in the aesthetic side of the display, than in its ability to sell the objects on display. The interesting thing here was that Miyamoto's attitude towards selling pots was precisely the opposite to that of potters when they take their work to be judged at a large exhibition. There I had noticed one famous artist carefully place his celadon vase between two pure white porcelain vases, precisely in order to make it stand out for selection by the judges!

The crux of the matter was that Miyamoto was interested in display only in so far as it affected sales. Obviously, the shape and size of any gallery tended to affect the display, to set a limit on each show's potential, but Miyamoto had a plan which he followed as often as he could: start with teacups at the entrance; then sake cups; followed by small dishes and bowls; with larger pots at the further end of the gallery. There were reasons for this layout. First, people often stole sake cups, which are small but expensive, and so these needed to be near the sales counter where members of the store's staff could keep an eye on them. Second, a good way to attract people to the show was to place cheaper pots near the entrance of the gallery. In this way, they'd be drawn further and further into the gallery towards the more expensive pots.

Remember, the reason I first suggested you do a show was because we had both agreed that there was no 'relaxation' (*yutori*), no 'play' (*asobi*) in contemporary Japanese pottery. I wanted to put on a show by somebody who obviously enjoyed making pots. And that's the essence of your show. As merchandise, of course, your pots are close to 'zero'. I mean, you euphemistically call these dishes, plates and bowls 'sets'. But if you look at them carefully, you can see that their shapes are all different, their sizes don't exactly match, and the colour of their glazes differs from one pot to the next. When other potters come and see them, they're bound to laugh and criticise your techniques.

But it isn't technique that matters, so far as I'm concerned. I'm aiming at something beyond technique. The problem is whether anyone will recognise this extra 'something' that I can see in your work. If you were a Tomimoto or a Hamada, or even an Arakawa Toyozo perhaps, they'd most certainly see in your unmatched sets something more aesthetically pleasing than mere techniques. The question is, will they feel the same towards your work. I don't know. All we can do is wait and see. Wait and see.

The morning of the show I asked Miyamoto if he was worried about the outcome. He smiled reassuringly:

Not at all. It doesn't really matter to me how many of your pots sell. After all, either way I'm not going to make or lose a fortune out of your exhibition. What worries me is the fact that people are going to put aside any pretence to objectivity that they normally have. It's a question of getting them to see your pots as being more than just those of a foreigner playing around with clay.

He continued:

You can tell what's going to happen the rest of the week by the way pots sell on the first day of a show. And also by what sort of pots sell – large or small. Your research is just beginning. So far, you've been visiting other potters' shows and making detrimental remarks about their work. Now it's your turn to hear others being rude about you.

The exhibition begins

Eighteen hours later, I had given two newspaper interviews, appeared on a late-night television programme and sold just under £3000 worth of pots. I was astounded; Miyamoto moderately pleased. A number of potter friends and acquaintances had turned up, including Imaemon himself and Tanaka Hajime, and they had been kind enough to take me round and tell me freely what they liked and disliked about my work. For the first time, I had begun to feel a bond of sympathy with a group of people whom I had hitherto tended to regard merely as objects of research.

Just as I was thinking of going to bed, Miyamoto began talking:

So today was a success. But what made it so? A lot of small pots were sold. But then that is to be expected with a show like yours. What was important was that, fairly early on this morning, a plump middle-aged woman in a fur coat came into the gallery. She was a doctor's wife – the kind of person who has money to buy up art objects here in Japan.

So once she started buying pots, I got interested. Not in *how much* she would spend so much as in *which* of the pots on display she would buy. If she'd stuck to those between £10 and £75, that would've been that. But she didn't. She went for one of the four pots in the top price range of £400, and another at £300 just below that. As I see it, that doctor's wife was vital to the show because she helped create a mood among those visiting the gallery. Once people see somebody buying some of the more expensive works, they begin to want to do the same. It may sound ridiculous, but I can assure you it's true.

I'll have to admit that for a while I was worried. I thought I'd overpriced your pots. But now I feel there's hope.

Miyamoto leaned back in his chair and his eyes twinkled.

It's funny, but every time I've had a successful show, this 'mood creation' has come from a single stroke of chance. I did another exhibition a couple of years ago, where the department store concerned arranged for some of its better customers to go on a pre-show tour of the potter's kiln and get an advance view of the pots that would be displayed. That was the first time I came across the collector who rebuked you the other day for not selling him that pot you liked so much. Well, he suddenly ordered two pots worth £3000 each. Once he did that, the other nineteen people in the party began looking around for things to buy, too. They just couldn't bear to be left out. Before I knew where we were, we'd sold several tens of thousands of pounds' worth of pots. And it didn't stop there. Once the show opened, visitors saw all the red SOLD tabs and began buying anything they could lay their hands on. By the end of the week, we'd sold nearly £70000 worth of pots by a potter who, until then, had never made even one-third of that amount in a one-man show. It's all a matter of luck.

A very large percentage of pots sold that week were bought up by friends and acquaintances. Then there were Miyamoto's own private clients who ordered pots by phone, or who came over and bought things in the gallery. 'People is what business is all about', Miyamoto explained.

It's the network of relations between people that really accounts for so much in our Japanese version of industrial capitalism. There's a lot of give and take, you know. Precisely because I hold down shows here in Tamaya, I'm expected to attend their special functions and buy a suit for myself here, a fur coat or jewellery there for my wife. It's all part of the return for favours I've received from the store and its helps cement our business relationship. That's what *tsukiai* networks are all about!

. . .and ends

And the show went on. For the next four days, I went through various phases of pleasure, frustration, anxiety and joy – the typical gamut of emotions experienced by artists holding their own exhibitions. I learned to recognise potential buyers from non-buyers, to act the 'artist' for the benefit of the media (the Enterprise and Promotions Manager was right. Precisely because the *Mainichi* did not sponsor my show, all the major newspapers carried articles about it in their culture-section pages). I was labelled the 'second Leach' – the only way one journalist could fit me into the system. Approximately 80 per cent of all sales were made to people known to Miyamoto, Tamaya, or myself. But the gallery was almost always filled with people – thanks to two or three television news spots – and even if the visitors did not buy much, the department-store people were happy. At least one thousand people a day extra were being attracted to Tamaya to look around and spend their money elsewhere in the store. I learned a lot about my own work, too, as I overheard comments about this or that shape, glaze, or design. It was touching the way people would spend so much time considering pots that I regretted having done in such a slapdash manner. At the same time I learned by what people bought, or did not buy, which were the publicly 'successful' pots. It was interesting to take stock half-way through the show. A salad bowl that I had thought would be one of the first pots to be sold was still on the display shelf, as were some porcelain teacups with a fir-tree design that Tanaka Hajime himself had picked out as my best work! In general, my rather more 'Japanese' patterns did not sell as well as my more off-beat experiments. As for the porcelain ware in general, the transparent glaze had sold much better than the blue-white celadon, even though a lot of visitors had commented approvingly on the 'soft' nature of the celadon. It seems as though people somehow saw the celadon glaze as being more 'decorative', as providing a stimulus to 'aesthetic contemplation', rather than to a wish to purchase it for everyday use.

By Sunday morning, the last day of the show, a lot of the more expensive pots were still unsold and we went around mentally repricing them in the light of our experience that week. Miyamoto shook his head in obvious perplexity.

> You know, I can't understand why some of your pots have *not* been sold. This exhibition's been a real lesson for me, too. If you'd won a prize at some big national exhibition or other, all your work would've gone at the prices we've set. The thing is, people aren't really looking at your pots for what they are. They're looking at the fact that you're not a famous 'name' artist. This proves what I've always thought deep down inside: that there is absolutely *no* objective standard by which to judge pottery. A number of well-known potters have been into the gallery over the past four days and, because you don't belong to any faction or group, they've spoken fairly freely about what they think about your work. You know, they've all differed, too, in their opinions about what was good and what was bad.

Suddenly, the gallery filled with people and for the rest of the day I found myself caught up in a flood of friends and acquaintances, as the showed reached its finale. As for sales, it turned out that I need not have worried as much as I did, because Miyamoto's clients came and bought all my sets of plates, together with the remaining large vase and tile. By the time the day had come to an end, I had sold more than £7000 worth of pots. This was below our original 'break-even' total, but Miyamoto told me to relax. He would ensure that neither of us made a loss.

He was true to his word. I did not make a loss. Nor, of course, did I make a profit from sales. But I had made myself a 'name'. And that was the most important part of it all.

Conclusion

This essay is only one part of a story which would need further chapters from the dealer, potters, department-store managers, media promoters, and general public involved for it to begin to be complete. In other words, it is 'undertaken from a particular, historically and socially conditioned point of view . . . which form[s] a spiral and circle around the object which is being viewed' (Hauser 1982: xvii–xviii). Although I have tried to objectify the kinds of relations I encountered in the ceramic art world of contemporary Japan, I accept Bourdieu's warning that:

> There is no way out of the game of culture; and one's only chance of objectifying the true nature of the game is to objectify as fully as possible the very operations which one is obliged to use in order to achieve that objectification.
>
> (1984: 12)

This point is important, not only with regard to anthropologists' approaches to art, but also to the way in which they now discuss ethnographic writing (Clifford and Marcus 1986; Fardon 1989) – a comparison which should be of interest, given the way in which I have chosen to present this material. It seems to me that many of those promoting the new paradigm spend too much time discussing the *stylistic* ideals of 'post-modern' (Tyler 1986) ethnography, and too little the *social* definition thereof. In other words, they are concerned with what they *want* ethnographic writing to be, not with what it in fact *is*. True, to raise it to the Parnassian heights of 'literature' (Geertz 1988) is certainly more satisfying to some of us than to call it mere 'writing' (Clifford 1986: 26), but that does not alter the fact that ethnographic 'writing' will become 'literature' only when the *literary* world agrees to such a definition. Like unknown artists, anthropologists still have to prove themselves.

All this is merely to state the obvious: that art and anthropology are closely related in the way that they are defined by an 'art' or 'anthropological' world. Just as my own pottery was seen as 'art' because of the intricate web of relationships that existed between potter, dealer, department store, media, patrons and general public (a web that would have to include critics, museum curators, art-book publishers, and bureaucrats for it to be seen as 'Art', with a capital A), so is my ethnographic writing judged by colleagues who participate in a 'small world' (Lodge 1984) of academic departments, conferences, journals, university presses, prizes, honorary degrees, memorial lectures, research fellowships, funding organisations and so on. Here, then, we have the hidden 'rhetoric' (Barthes 1967: 89–92) of 'participant observation'.

This leads me to make one or two comments about 'aesthetics', particularly in view of the generally insidious and persistent idea that there is some kind of 'specificity' in art (Wolff 1983) – or, indeed, in anthropology. It will be clear from the account given here that art in Japan is by no means as 'pure' as some of its advocates might like us to believe (e.g. Warner 1958; Anesaki 1973). It will also be clear that I have grave doubts about the notion of 'aesthetic specificity', since what often passes for 'aesthetic' is, in fact, an amalgam of what the Japanese themselves refer to as 'aesthetic' (*biteki kachikan*), 'commodity' (*shōhin kachikan*), and 'social' (*shakai kachikan*) values. It is precisely this confusion – and its inexplicability, I suspect – that leads people to yearn for some 'inherent principle', some 'specificity' in art.

The relation between 'aesthetic' and 'commodity' values has already been discussed by a number of writers under the rubric of 'use' and 'exchange' (or 'barter') values. Hauser (1982: 506–17), for example, points out that it is meaningless to assume an analogy between value and price in art. Certainly, that was the way I felt about my own exhibition. I have no evidence to show that there was any clear-cut relation between quality and sales, on the one hand, or between prices and sales, on the other.[13] It is true that in the Japanese ceramic art world, people tend to equate the quality of an artist by the amount that s/he sells (Moeran 1987: 44–5), but, as a general rule, there is an inverse relation between quantity and quality (cf. Kato 1971: 34). The less an artist produces, the 'better' his or her work is seen to be, and vice versa. In other words, in Japan and other capitalist countries of the West, notions of quality tend to thrive on a concept of scarcity.

Thus, in spite of various attempts to resurrect the notion of the 'pure gaze', no art form can be seen for what it is 'in itself' (cf. Bourdieu 1984: 1–7; Moeran 1984: 25–7). According to Maquet (1979: 63):

> aesthetic phenomena disclose their immersion in the three cultural layers: processes of production, social networks, and ideational configurations. On each level they constitute a separate sub-system . . . but one which is closely connected to non-aesthetic cultural phenomena. The general impression is one of intricacy.

Such 'intricacy' is made the more intricate by the fact that art if but a particular part of 'the general system of symbolic forms we call culture'

(Geertz 1983: 109). In cultures that are bound by the parameters of industrial capitalism, we find that:

> the art aesthetic and the commercial aesthetic are not separate but are related via the art object. What is more, the relationship is not symmetrical: the commercial aesthetic contains the art aesthetic because the art object is contained within the entire range of communicable things.
>
> (Thompson 1979: 122)

I suspect that in such societies it is this 'wrapping' of the 'art aesthetic' by the 'commercial aesthetic' which helps define what we in the West actually mean by the word 'art'.

Of course, unless we happen to be in the business of marketing art, most of us do not *consciously* make the connection between aesthetic and commodity values. It is just that judgements which are made about other spheres of cultural life tend to slide across boundaries and affect those trying to value something on purely aesthetic grounds (Veblen 1925: 108). It is to these other spheres that I loosely refer when I talk about 'social' values. In particular, I am concerned with how *personalities* come to play an important part in the establishment of any 'aesthetic standard'.

The ways in which 'social' values affect the determination of what is, or is not, 'art', 'beauty', and so on are various. I have mentioned, for example, the importance of having a thirteenth-generation porcelain potter, Imaizumi Imaemon, write a *suisenbun* recommendation on my behalf, in order to smooth the path towards a favourable reception of my work by other potters. In this respect, Miyamoto merely followed time-honoured practice in the literary (and anthropological) world:

> As regards getting published, one fact has been observable since at least the eighteenth century – the fortunate situation of anyone who is in personal touch with writers who are well known and have their public and a certain prestige with the publishers. Their recommendation may carry sufficient weight to smooth away the main difficulties for the newcomer. Thus it is almost a rule that the beginner's work does not pass direct from him to the appropriate authority, but takes the indirect and often difficult course past the desk of an artist of repute.
>
> (Schucking 1974: 53)

Another way in which my own show exhibited the influence of social values can be seen in my 'choice' of Miyamoto Reisuke, rather than of any other dealer, as go-between. Here, the social influence was twofold. First, I gained prestige as an '*artist*' by having an agent who was prepared to take over my products. Second, Miyamoto himself – and then the department store, Tamaya – guaranteed a kind of 'pedigree' and offered the buyer a sense of security about my *work* that my name in itself could not afford (cf. Hauser 1982: 509). It is probably fair to say that none of my most expensive pots would have been sold without this personal 'guarantee'. It was only because they did sell that I can be referred to as an 'artist' potter (*tōgeika*).

A further point needs to be made concerning sales. It will be recalled that a lot of my work – particularly my expensive pottery – was sold to people whom either Tamaya department store, Miyamoto or I myself knew. This suggests that Marxists such as Sanchez Vasquez (1973: 168–80) are wrong to stress a historical progression from direct to indirect relations between the artist and his public, as the former increasingly comes to produce for an alien consumer. It is the fact that art works are *not* bought by 'alien consumers', but by known members of an art world, that helps define them as 'art' rather than as mere 'commodities'.

This brings me to the subject of patrons. One incident I have not related here concerns my brush with a collector to whom I refused to 'pre-sell' my 'best' work. In the end, annoyed by my obstinacy, he never came to my exhibition. Whether this affected my standing as an 'artist', I do not know, but it should be pointed out here that there has always been a very close relationship between artist and patron (or collector), which then affects the commodity value of the artist's work. In his historical account of the rise of the painter in fourteenth-century Florence, Antal (1970: 292) notes that:

> the more eminent the social position of the patron and the more the kind of work commissioned necessitated personal contact between the patron and artist, the more highly would the personal achievement of the artist be valued, and his own social standing, and his professional consciousness increase.

This mixture of social and aesthetic values brought on by the social intercourse between artist and patron could also include a daub of commodity value. Baxandall (1972: 81–5) shows how, in fifteenth-century Italian paintings, different pigments were differently priced and so applied to different personages. It was primarily social, or theological, rank – rather than aesthetic considerations – that influenced a painter's choice of colour in any composition (although, within these constraints, aesthetic considerations did take over).

I have commented in this essay on how potters are obliged to package (or 'wrap') *themselves* in order to sell their pots, and I have shown how the creation of a 'mood' is a vital aspect of an artist's success. In this respect, it is of interest to note that an exhibition of 'art' is in fact very similar to the general technique that emphasises 'entertainment' in the selling of commodities.

> The exhibition of commodities, their inspection, the act of purchase, and all the associated moments, are integrated into the concept of one theatrical total work of art which plays upon the public's willingness to buy. Thus the salesroom is designed as a stage, purpose-built to convey entertainment to its audience that will stimulate a heightened desire to spend.
>
> (Haug 1986: 69)

Another form of 'entertainment' – and a means by which such 'packaging' is achieved – consists of gossip. In the Japanese ceramic art world, having the inside story on a particular person or event indicated weighty connections, and hence reflected on one's own position as an artist potter. That this situation is by no means peculiar to Japan can be seen in Rosenberg (1970: 391):

> The Art Establishment subsists on words – much more, in fact, than it does on pictures. Talk there has more power than elsewhere because decisions are less sure and the consequences of acting on them more uncertain. In this sense, everyone in the art world has power, at least the power to pass the word along, mention names, repeat stock judgments, all of which produce an effect. The first qualification for entering the Art Establishment is to be familiar with its jargon and the people and things most often referred to.

Thus, on the one hand, those who gossip have a knowledge of certain conventions which define the art world concerned (Becker 1982: 46). On the other, by focusing on the personal affairs of participants in the art world, gossip prevents art works from being seen independently of such personalities (ibid. 48). Thus, the art work 'becomes a success only if . . . one gets talked about' (Schucking 1974: 71).

How much of what I have said here is applicable to the world of anthropology, I leave for my readers to judge. I suspect, however, that Camus's remarks about writers hold good for both artists and anthropologists alike:

> A writer writes to a great extent to be read (as for those who say they don't, let us admire them but not believe them). Yet more and more, in France, he writes in order to obtain that final consecration which lies in not being read . . . to make a name in literature, it is consequently no longer indispensable to write books. It is enough to be thought to have written one book, mentioned in the evening papers, and on which one can repose for the rest of one's life.
>
> (Camus 1967: 121)

Welcome, then, to a zen-like world whose sound and fury signifies no more perhaps than the anthropology of . . . nothing.

Notes

1 See Moeran 1987. I would like to take this opportunity to thank Michael Jackson, Anthony Forge, and my colleagues in the Department of Anthropology and Sociology at the School of Oriental and African Studies for their comments on this paper, and the Economic and Science Research Council and the School of Oriental and African Studies for funding the research upon which it is based (1981–2).

2 That Miyamoto should have even considered allowing an amateur such as myself to hold a one-man exhibition shows the fluid nature of the contemporary ceramic art world in Japan (cf. Rosenberg 1970: 388).

3 Where I spent two years doing research on the Japanese folk craft movement (see Moeran 1984).

4 See Havens 1982: 130–43; Moeran 1987.

5 In this respect, I could be classified as one of those 'naive' artists who produce work:

> without reference to the standards of any world outside its maker's personal life. Its makers work in isolation, free from the constraints of cooperation which inhibit art world participants, free to ignore the conventional categories of art works, to make things which do not fit any standard genre and cannot be described as examples of any class. Their works just are.
>
> (Becker 1982: 260)

Kajiwara Jiro's dissatisfaction stemmed from the fact that he had been obliged to shift from 'naive' to 'folk' artist, without ever having the social skills, conceptual apparatus, or understanding of art-world conventions as a whole to become an 'integrated professional', nor, perhaps, the necessary independence to opt out as a 'maverick' (ibid. 226–71).

6 This mode of celebrating one's own and others' successes is particularly common in rural Japanese society (cf. Moeran 1985: 84–5). Artists in general often buy one another's work (cf. Vollard 1978: 62).

7 For further discussion of 'goodwill marketing', see Dore (1983).

8 The separation of the pot from its box is part of the general aesthetic abstraction of commodities, whereby the packaging becomes 'disembodied' from the commodity itself and ends up as the focus of attention (Haug 1986: 49–50). Cf., for example, the Wilkinson Sword advertisement: 'I was so impressed I bought the bag'. (See Hendry's Chap. 2 in this volume for further discussion of wrapping.)

9 The crucial problem of how to establish the authenticity of art works, especially by the construction of a provenance, is discussed by Becker (1982: 114–5). I myself learned the importance of boxes when I once tried to sell a Bernard Leach 'Pilgrim' plate in Japan. Advised that I would be better not to put it on the market 'naked', I asked Janet Leach to sign the box that I had especially made for it. The net result was that I was able to raise my asking price from £2300 to £3800 (which suggests that the power of the artist's widow should not be ignored here, cf. Rosenberg 1970: 393–4). Terrorist attacks and

wars notwithstanding, there are still times when the pen would appear to be mightier than the sword.

10 Some dealers prefer different strategies – like pricing a pot at £60, but selling it at £50 in order to make the customer think s/he is getting a little more than the 'true value' of a pot. Others leave customers to name their own prices (Vollard 1978: 137; Moeran 1984: 208).

11 More pertinent, perhaps, is Thompson's comment (1979: 121) that 'whether we like it or not, the artist, simply by producing art objects, is both accepting the commercial aesthetic and reinforcing the power structure'.

12 In the end, these pots were auctioned for £216 and £53 apiece.

13 My readers will realise of course that, in order to conduct any kind of 'scientific' argument, I have been obliged to withhold all personal judgement about the quality of my own work. The net effect of this may have led to my over-emphasising the 'commodity' values of art in contemporary capitalist societies, but the experience of my own exhibition has led me to wonder whether there really is any such thing as a 'standard' in taste. I therefore question Miyamoto's theory that the public should be allowed to set a standard.

It would require further research to discover the extent to which Bourdieu's hypothesis that 'all cultural practices . . . and preferences . . . are closely linked to educational level (measured by qualifications or length of schooling) and secondarily to social origin' (1984: 1) is valid for Japan. For example, if the widespread belief, held by the Japanese themselves, that they belong to the middle class is true, then they *ought* to share a similar standard of taste. At the same time, Rohlen (1983: 307–14) has shown that a form of merit-based class consciousness has been created by the schools' and universities' examination system in post-war Japan. In which case, Bourdieu's argument about the parallel between social and taste hierarchies *ought* to be reinforced by the Japanese educational system. Unfortunately, there is little evidence in this paper to suggest that these *oughts* are anything other than theoretical expectations.

References

Anesaki, M. 1973. *Art, Life and Nature in Japan.* Tokyo: Tuttle.

Antal, F. 1970. Social position of the artists: contemporary views on art. In *The Sociology of Art and Literature*, ed. M. Albrecht, J. Barnett and M. Griff, pp. 288–97. London: Duckworth.

Barthes, R. 1967. *Elements of Semiology,* trans. A. Lavers and C. Smith. London: Jonathan Cape.

Baxandall, M. 1972. *Painting and Experience in Fifteenth Century Italy.* Oxford: Oxford University Press.

Becker, H. 1982. *Art Worlds.* Berkeley and Los Angeles: University of California Press.

Bourdieu, P. 1984. *Distinction: a Social Critique of the Judgement of Taste,* trans. R. Nice. London: Routledge & Kegan Paul.

Camus, A. 1967. *Lyrical and Critical,* trans. P. Thody. London: Hamish Hamilton.

Clifford, J. 1986. Introduction: partial truths. In *Writing Culture: the Poetics and Politics of Ethnography,* ed. J. Clifford and G. E. Marcus, pp. 1–26. Berkeley and Los Angeles: University of California Press.

Clifford, J. and Marcus, G. E. (eds) 1986. *Writing Culture: the Poetics and Politics of Ethnography.* Berkeley and Los Angeles: University of California Press.

Dore, R. 1983. Goodwill marketing and the spirit of market capitalism. *British Journal of Sociology* **34** (4), 459–82.

Fardon, R. (ed.) 1989. *Localising Strategies: Regional Traditions in Ethnographic Writing.* Edinburgh: Scottish Academic Press; Washington DC: Smithsonian Institution Press.

Geertz, C. 1983. Art as a cultural system. In *Local Knowledge: Further Essays in Interpretive Anthropology,* pp. 94–120. New York: Basic Books.

Geertz, C. 1988. *Works and Lives: the Anthropologist as Author.* Standford, Calif.: Stanford University Press.

Haug, W. 1986. *Critique of Commodity Aesthetics: Appearance, Sexuality and Advertising in Capitalist Society,* Trans. R. Bock. Cambridge: Polity Press.

Hauser, A. 1982. *The Sociology of Art,* trans. K. Northcott. London: Routledge & Kegan Paul.

Havens, T. 1982. *Artist and Patron in Postwar Japan.* Princeton, NJ: Princeton University Press.

Kato, S. 1971. *Form, Style, Tradition: Reflections on Japanese Art and Society.* Berkeley and Los Angeles: University of California Press.

Lodge, D. 1984. *Small World.* New York: Macmillan.

Maquet, J. 1979. *Introduction to Aesthetic Anthropology.* Malibu, Calif.: Undena.

Moeran, B. 1984. *Lost Innocence: Folk Craft Potters of Onta, Japan.* Berkeley and Los Angeles: University of California Press.

Moeran, B. 1985. *Ōkubo Diary: Portrait of a Japanese Valley.* Stanford, Calif.: Stanford University Press.

Moeran, B. 1987. The art world of contemporary Japanese ceramics. *Journal of Japanese Studies* **13** (1), 27–50.

Rohlen, T. 1983. *Japan's High Schools.* Berkeley and Los Angeles: University of California Press.

Rosenberg, H. 1970. The art establishment. In *The Sociology of Art and*

Literature, ed. M. Albrecht, J. Barnett and M. Griff, pp. 388–95. London: Duckworth.

Sanchez Vasquez, A. 1973. *Art and Society: Essays in Marxist Aesthetics*. London: Merlin Press.

Schucking, L. 1974. *The Sociology of Literary Taste*, trans. B. Battershaw. Chicago: University of Chicago Press.

Thompson, M. 1979. *Rubbish Theory: the Creation and Destruction of Value*. Oxford: Oxford University Press.

Tyler, S. A. 1986. Post-modern ethnography: from document of the occult to occult document. In *Writing Culture: the Poetics and Politics of Ethnography*, ed. J. Clifford and G. E. Marcus, pp. 122–40. Berkeley and Los Angeles: University of California Press.

Veblen, T. 1925. *The Theory of the Leisure Class*. London: Allen & Unwin.

Vollard, A. 1978. *Recollections of a Picture Dealer*. New York: Dover.

Warner, L. 1958. *The Enduring Art of Japan*. New York: Grove.

Wolff, J. 1983. *Aesthetics and the Sociology of Art*. London: Allen & Unwin.

Many voices, partial worlds:
on some conventions and innovations
in the ethnographic portrayal of Japan

Stanzas should be linked to each other through fragrance, reverberation, semblance, flow, fancy or some other indefinable quality.

Bashō (quoted in Ueda, 1985: 63)

Introduction

This paper examines some of the wider implications of three recently published ethnographies about Japan: Liza Dalby's (1985) *Geisha*, Brian Moeran's (1985) *Ōkubo Diary*, and Oliver Statler's (1983) *Japanese Pilgrimage*. Yet this is more than a review essay. This is because the paper's aim is to relate an examination of the aesthetic and literary dimensions of these ethnographies – that is, the ways in which they have been written and can be read – to the wider problems of both anthropological understanding and the portrayal of Japan.

The analysis commences from the rather general premiss that 'the arts must be taken no less seriously than the sciences as modes of discovery, creation, and enlargement of knowledge in the broad sense of the advancement of understanding' (Goodman 1978: 102). More specifically, it proceeds on the basis of a growing recognition within (and without) anthropology that in constructing ethnographic texts, ethnographers cannot avoid the use of literary devices: poetic and prose forms, characterisation, and figuration, or the use of allegories and metaphors for example. Yet this growing recognition of the literary dimensions of ethnographies involves more than a preoccupation with style or composition. For, as Clifford (1986: 4) notes, it is through the use of these devices that the cultural phenomena studied by anthropologists are created and constructed in ways that 'make sense' to professional and other types of readerships.[1] Literary aspects in other words, are integral to,

> any kind of written expression, inseparably bonded to the substantive content of the narrative, interpretation, or analysis presented. Just as the logic of argument of a text is abstractable for a certain purpose such as theoretical discussion, so the [literary] dimension of a text and its argument are abstractable for a certain purpose such as a critical discussion of how a text persuades and effectively communicates its meanings.
>
> (Marcus and Cushman 1982: 58–9)

The present analysis, however, does not form part of the recent spate of studies which have sought to demystify the dominant conventions of representation in 'classic' ethnographies (Boon 1982; Marcus and Fischer 1986: Chap. 2; Stoddart 1986); nor is it just another polemical work aimed at encouraging an experimentation with new literary options in anthropological research and writing (Marcus and Cushman 1982; Marcus 1986; Tyler 1986). Rather, it offers what I hope is an interesting exploration of some issues which have to do with ethnographic portrayal in general and the portrayal of Japan in particular.

The ethnographic portrayal of Japan by Western anthropologists goes back to Embree's (1939) pre-war work and the studies published in the 1950s (Cornell and Smith 1956; Dore 1958; Beardsley *et al.* 1959). A full-blown overview of the ethnographic writing about Japan since that period is beyond the scope of this paper. What is interesting to note, however, is that during the 1980s a host of studies of this society experimenting with new forms of textual presentations and devices have been steadily published.[2] One may cite as examples of these works – each of which seeks through its innovative literary presentation to illuminate previously untouched or problematic aspects of Japan – the following: Kelly's (1985) efforts at relating local 'Shrine Talk' to wider problems of modernisation and a nostalgia for a newly created past; Hamabata's (1986) use of his fieldwork 'character' in order to explore the problematics of ethnographic boundaries; Bernstein's (1983) portrayal of rural women through the eyes of her book's principal character, Haruko; or Plath's (1980) evocative placement of personal and fictional narratives side by side in order to uncover processes of maturing and ageing.

Yet these works, like most of the newer anthropological pieces guided by the new 'literary consciousness', rarely deal with an issue which is only recently receiving any measure of professional attention: the literary and aesthetic possibilities for ethnographic construction which are emerging from the non-Western experience (Clifford 1986: 19). More specifically, this issue concerns the potential use that can be made of indigenous genres, styles and forms (in both the strict literary and wider artistic senses) within ethnographic texts in order to further the understanding of the societies being studied.[3] In effect, however, this issue actually involves two interrelated problems. The first has to do with the more 'technical' aspects of integrating indigenous genres within an anthropological work. Here the problem is one of delineating the kinds of local literary and artistic devices which can be used in anthropological works and their fit (or lack of it) within the overall forms of these works. The second problem entails the more basic consideration of the type of anthropological 'understanding' facilitated by the use of such genres. This problem touches upon the very nature of anthropology – as indeed of all of the humanities – and upon the kinds of appreciations and perceptions that it engenders.

The Japanese case seems especially useful for an examination of these problems. This is because Japan has not only a great literary tradition of both poetic and prose forms, it also has a long-standing tradition of graphic and plastic arts. All three works which form the object of this study – *Geisha*, *Ōkubo Diary* and *Japanese Pilgrimage* – make explicit attempts at utilising certain aesthetic forms taken from Japan's traditions in order to construct their ethnographic accounts. Hence a focus on these compositions may facilitate an exploration of the issues involved.

In what follows, I begin with a short consideration of each ethnography in order to highlight the place of Japanese aesthetic forms in its formulation. I then go on to treat some of the wider implications of this examination.

Geisha productions

Of all three works, Liza Dalby's *Geisha* comes closest in its aims to those of more conventional interpretive ethnographies. It represents an attempt at describing and illuminating the worlds populated by geisha. As Dalby (1985: xvi) herself acknowledges:

> This book could be called an ethnography, a descriptive study of the customs of a particular people. My goal, however, has not been to compile a catalog of customs of geisha ... I think of this study as an interpretive ethnography; my goal is to explain the cultural meaning of persons, objects, and situations in the geisha world.

Yet the literary means that she employs in order to achieve this goal differ radically from those utilised in 'classic' ethnographies. This is because Dalby's work, like many of the newer 'experimental ethnographies' (Marcus and Cushman 1982: 61), specifically seeks to make problematic both the construction of her descriptions and interpretations, and the writing conventions through which they are expressed. As Dalby (1985: xv) is careful to warn the reader,

> this remains a personal book, and I have included large parts of unabashedly personal material. In particular, I have written as much about my own experience as the geisha Ichigiku as I have about the more orthodox geisha whom I went to study. I cannot pretend that I was the invisible observer, seeing but not seen, simply reporting what appeared before my eyes, and it would be disingenuous of me to say that my presence had no influence on the interactions I sought to record.

Indeed, a page later she again returns to this theme: 'the reader here will not be permitted to forget that his understanding is being shaped by Ichigiku'.

Along these lines, Dalby utilises descriptions and reports of her experiences as devices for uncovering many of the meetings and sensibilities involved in being a geisha. Her attempts at mastering the *shamisen*, at wearing a kimono, or handling customers and other geisha are all used in order to make intelligible what this world involves. Her accounts of interactions with certain characters introduced also serve to highlight more general points: for example, Dalby's relations with her *okasan* (mother) and its illumination of the ties binding geisha, or her interchanges with the 'old auntie' and its uncovering of the criteria by which professional approval is given or withheld.

It is as part of the process of uncovering meanings that Dalby – not unlike other anthropologists who have used fictional pieces as documents for cultural analysis – utilises a whole host of examples and excerpts taken from Japanese works. Thus for example, *kouta* (short lyrical pieces whose performance is not limited to geisha) are used as epigraphs to many chapters. Chosen by the author as her *gei* – a geisha's chief artistic specialisation performed at parties – the inclusion of these short pieces in the text serves a number of textual functions: to provide the reader with a sense of their form and texture (they are transliterated and translated); to exemplify the type of performative genre Dalby decided to undertake; and to foreshadow or suggest the theme of the chapter which follows them. It is in a similar way that Dalby wields excerpts taken from such diverse compositions as Buddhist sutras, classics like the Tales of Ise, *shamisen* ditties, geisha sayings, or even polemical works of the Meiji period. Other indigenous forms which are directly integrated into the text are metaphors: for instance an elderly geisha's likening of the sudden ripping of a brain during a stroke to the tearing of a *shamisen*; proverbs: like the one about the pride of an impoverished samurai who uses a toothpick although he has not eaten; or the use of Japanese idiomatic expressions like *iki, zashiki* or *Setsubun*.

Of no less importance is her utilisation of a rich array of graphic and photographic designs throughout the work. Dalby carefully places a host of paintings, prints, etchings, sketches, drawings and crests to illustrate both the tenor and the importance of aesthetic sensibilities to the geisha world. These elements depict such themes as kimono styles and patterns, geisha activities and interests, or classic poses and posturing. The overall effect is thus one in which the indigenous elements – the songs and poems, the pieces of classical and modern literature, and the graphics and art forms – all echo one another, and grant the text an unmistakable flavour of Japanese aesthetics.

Yet for all this, these indigenous elements are all subject to, and integrated within, the overall textual logic of a professional treatise: a systematic study of geisha. Dalby does not utilise Japanese genres in order to fashion the framework or structure of her book, but rather uses them as devices which illustrate, amplify and reflect the discussions found in the text. This is evident in the general structure of the work which is governed by the exploration of different types of geisha and their activities, as well as by the integration into the text of more 'standard' tools of anthropological reportage: answers to questionnaires, graphs, tables, maps and photos (which depict historical figures, scenery, advertisements and the work's main characters). Although the table of contents is arranged in a refreshing format it still functions in a 'conventional' way that informs the reader about the book's subject matter. Finally, the book contains an array of notes, glossary, bibliography and index, which guide and instruct the reader.

The result is thus a work which at one and the same time evinces a closeness and intimacy to its subjects and subject matter and a distance and analysis of them. It is a professional exposition yet one which depends heavily on the use of Japanese genres and the descriptions of personal experiences in order to achieve its ethnographic aims. A short vignette related by Dalby (1985: 252) may encapsulate these impressions. She tells us about a *shamisen* she brought to Japan but left in her room in order to practise with another instrument. Then, during one of the *tsuyu*'s dank, misty days she hears something snap but goes back to her other activities.

> Several days passed, and I decided to take out my *shamisen* . . . it was – completely split down the middle. I was taken by surpirse and felt a pang of guilt. Even though I know full well about *tsuyu*, it seemed to me that my *shamisen* had burst with jealousy . . . while I carried on with another instrument. *O-shami* is the affectionate term geisha use for the *shamisens*, and though I was shamelessly anthropomorphizing I realized how much I had absorbed of the geisha's attitude toward the instrument.

The valley of disenchantment

Brian Moeran's *Ōkubo Diary* is a fictionalised account (see Moeran, Chap. 7) of his four-year stay in a Japanese country valley. As its subtitle suggests, the volume is a portrait, that is, a sketch or drawing of life in this Kyushu area. More than Dalby's *Geisha*, it is a personal account, and we learn of the valley and of its people primarily through Moeran's characterisation and depiction. Yet it is the explicit use of Japanese literary genres in the actual construction of the *Diary* that is of significance for our analysis. As Moeran (1985: 4) is clear to note,

> I am becoming steadily more convinced . . . that the only way to write sensitive interpretations of other cultures is to write in the style of the people we study. . . . In the case of a literate culture like that of Japan, the chosen artistic style should perhaps be influenced by an accepted literary genre.

The two major kinds of genres Moeran chooses to adopt are the *zuihitsu* essay style, and the innovative usage of classical poetry rendered into prose within the text.

Zuihitsu essays consist of 'stray notes, expressing random thoughts in a casual manner' (Ueda 1985: 90). While this genre originated in Japan's middle ages, it still has a strong influence on such diverse forms of writing as modern Japanese novels which tend to break up into weakly related parts (Keene 1955: 10), or the notebooks kept by patients undergoing Morita psycho-therapy (Reynolds 1980: 118).

The adoption of this literary genre makes it possible for Moeran to construct his account in a fascinating way. He places side-by-side – and at first sight without apparent order – 103 passages of different textures and diverse forms: impressionistic depictions of scenes and scenery, more systematic reflections about local customs and relations, descriptions of characters, allusions to literary classics, thoughts about changing seasons, and mixed throughout all of these the interlinked episodes of a sad, melancholy story about the author's son.

The employment of a host of allusions from classical Japanese literature is the other major device through which Moeran taps into indigenous genres in order to construct his ethnography. These allusions are taken from a variety of sources such as Basho's *Haiku*, Tales of Ise, Essays in Idleness, *kayōkyoku* songs, traditional *bon odori* pieces, and various collections of classical poetry.[4] At the end of his book, Moeran provides a list of the sources from which he draws his quotations and allusions. This list, which includes translations and transliterations of the cited works, appears to have been constructed in order to enhance a Westerner's appreciation of the volume: of the ways in which by adding to these classical excerpts and by placing them in novel contexts they gain new accents and nuances. In the use of this device Moeran not only adopts the classical pieces themselves, but no less importantly seems to borrow from the Japanese literary convention of mixing lyrical and prose sections within the same work (Keene 1955: 10; Cranston 1969: 98).

Yet despite the adoption of a *zuihitsu*-like format and the mix of lyrical and prose sections, the book differs from some of the classical and modern compositions written in these styles. As May (1981: 191) notes, these latter types of works seem to be constructed by adding one episode after another, rather than along the lines of a complex story with a climax and a definite end. *Ōkubo Diary*, by contrast, proceeds along a shifting and diverging but nevertheless constant trajectory (but not story-line or plot): the arrival, fascination, and ultimate disillusionment of the author. It is a book of 'lost innocence' (to use the author's own metaphor), but the innocence lost is that of an anthropologist.

We learn of this disillusionment however, not through a detached analysis, nor through a distanced reflection – as in Dalby's work – but rather through a surrender to the feelings and experiences of the author. There is no specification of truth here, no determination or appraisal (although Moeran can write in these ways – cf. his *Lost Innocence*, 1984). Rather, we readers are invited to dwell, in ways so characteristic of Japanese literature (Miner 1985), on what is left implicit, on what is left unstated in the text.[5]

Yet for all this, whether he intends it or not, Moeran remains equivocal regarding how one is to reach an understanding of the work:

> The discourse that you read is no longer one between the people of Oni valley and myself. It is a discourse between them and you, and between myself and you. In these creative interstices between the words, perhaps, lies the meaning of anthropology.
>
> (Moeran 1985: 5)

Encased within these three short sentences – and admittedly this is my own reading of the paragraph – is a tension. This is a tension between the active, operating effectual discourse of anthropology, and the unstated, passive (and ineffectual?) understanding of Japanese literary communication.

A journey of wanderings and wonderings

Of all three works, Oliver Statler's *Japanese Pilgrimage* is least explicit about its aims and about the logic which underlies its construction. In essence, this is an account of the famous Shikoku pilgrimage which follows the 88 stops that a holy man, Kōbō Daishi, is supposed to have hallowed. At times it is reminiscent of Basho's sensitive and reflective work written during the somewhat isolated interludes of an otherwise busy life.

The general contours of the book are constructed on the basis of two exemplars. The division into three main parts – 'Master', 'Savior' and 'Pilgrims' – was suggested to Statler (1985: 337) by an earlier essay of the historian of religion Joseph M. Kitagawa (1967). At the same time, the book's apportionment into 22 chapters is related – this number being a submultiple of 88 – to the number of pilgrimage stops in the Shikoku pilgrimage itself.

Beyond these rather general constraints *Japanese Pilgrimage* seems to be constructed along the lines of three closely related classical genres: the diary, the travel account and the *zuihitsu* (Putzar 1973: 81; Plutschow 1981: 2). All three genres, according to Keene (1955: 11–12) are 'relatively formless, although not artless' in the way they organise their authors' impressions and perceptions.[6] This mix of genres turns the work into an elaborate, at times wandering, tableau of different literary forms and devices of both Japanese and non-Japanese derivation. Like Moeran, Statler too masterfully plays – often cutting up and through the division into chapters – a medley of impressions, portrayals, recollections, speculations and musings. But the historical depth of his subject matter allows him to undertake other literary operations: for example, the construction of historical figures; or the movement between pilgrimages carried out by the same people years apart, or by different people at the same time.

Furthermore, in fashioning his account Statler utilises literary devices drawn not only from Japan's classical high culture but also from other sources. Thus one finds that integrated into the text are not only classic Buddhist invocations and songs, but also a host of folk tales, parables and myths, proverbs and maxims, folk songs and hymns. All of these elements are set one against the other in the manner of the ancient Japanese poem-tales in which prose and verse sections functioned to both explicate and amplify each other.

In ways resembling Dalby's *Geisha*, the graphic dimensions of the volume are also rather pronounced. Statler employs such graphic illstrations as drawings and paintings, cloth and woodblock prints, calligraphy and etchings, and photographs of sculptures and *henro* (pilgrimage) stone markers. These depict such themes as holy men, scenery, talismen, or entertainers, but above all they depict the temples which have been erected along the pilgrimage route and the pilgrims themselves – walking, supplicating, resting.

For all of its meandering and at times formless quality, *Japanese Pilgrimage* does seem to evince an essential unity. What does this consist of? Clearly it is not the unity – as is *Geisha's* – of a professional treatise aimed at a systematic uncovering of systems of meanings. It is more akin to the unity of Moeran's *Ōkubo Diary* in terms of setting forth a portrait of a Japanese phenomenon through what is an intensely personal – and one might well add transformative (Turner 1978: Chap. 1) – experience. It is this experience, I would suggest, that grants the book its essential unity, and that draws it closest to many of Japan's classic literary works.

Ueda (1985) has, following Kenneth Burke (1953: 124–5), used the term 'qualitative progression' in order to characterise much of Japan's classic literary tradition. Qualitative progression, according to him 'is a structural method in which the quality of personal mental experience is the central principle unifying different parts of a literary work . . . since it integrates different parts of a literary work through the association of the author or a main character' (Ueda 1985: 98). This kind of sequencing is contrasted to a plot in which a 'law of causality' unites all the parts of a whole. It is this qualitative progression then, that provides *Japanese Pilgrimage* – as well as the *Ōkubo Diary* – with an overall artistic unity. The integrity of both works, then, consists not of a technical uniformity which governs the types of format chosen, but of a basic identity centred on the experiences of Moeran and Statler. This unity, to put this differently, is not one that is based just on an association of the work with a specific author, but one that is related to an internal or intimate route followed by them.

That it is Statler's experience of the pilgrimage which forms the core of his narrative is perhaps most evident in the words with which he chooses to close his work. At the end of his travels, he recalls the words uttered long ago by the abbot who saw him off to his first pilgrimage:

> he sent me off by saying 'You will see all aspects of man, some pure, some impure. You should see both without misunderstanding.' Pure and impure: I have seen both aspects in myself. He also said 'If you are earnest, you will to some degree be transformed.' This I know to be true. [Yet] of one thing I am certain: the transformation I yearn for is incomplete. I do not know whether I am any closer to enlightenment – I do not really expect to achieve it – but I know that the attempt is worth the effort. . . . It is a striving, and that goes on. What is important is not the destination but the act of getting there, not the goal but the going.
>
> (Statler 1985: 377)

Experiments and experience

All three works, I would suggest, belong to what Marcus and Fischer (1986: vii) have termed the 'experimental moment' in the human sciences: a period in which many of the humanities – including anthropology – are grappling with the problem of representing an increasingly complex modern world. In order to 'isolate' the special peculiarities of our three compositions – in terms of their use of indigenous genres and aesthetics – it may first be useful to trace out their similarities to many of the ethnographic texts now being published. Indeed, even a cursory review of *Geisha*, *Ōkubo Diary* and *Japanese Pilgrimage* reveals how they all share a number of basic features with many of the 'experimental ethnographies' now being written within and adjoining anthropology.

One such feature is the authors' – at times implicit – recognition of how the domains or objects of their concern are no longer independent of the means used in order to make them 'visible': that is, examined, researched, documented, represented. Rather than making these domains visible as though they exist in a 'natural state' divorced from the observer (Stoddart 1986: 114), their materialisation and representation is effected through the utilisation of the ethnographer: either as an instrument (to use a mechanical image) or as a character (to use a literary one). The authors use themselves and their own experiences, in other words, as the means through which the cultures examined are illuminated. Yet as all three works well attest to, making the ethnographer's place within the text problematic need not regress into a fruitless self-absorption which has been characterised by someone as navel anthropology.

A related property which marks these compositions is their active incorporation of what in many of the more conventional ethnographies were 'irrelevant topics': violence and desire, confusions and struggles, or economic transactions with locals (Clifford 1986: 14). Examples of such matters include Dalby's disquiet at having to withstand the subtle gibes of geisha from other (competing) communities, Moeran's anger and confusion during the dealings with the school authorities, or Statler's impatience with the modern 'motorised' pilgrims and their mockery of the journey's aims. All of these references to the ostensibly 'personal' realm of attitudes and feelings, nevertheless contain the potential of suggesting the centrality of certain cultural elements: Dalby's disquiet hints at the status hierarchy between geisha communities, Moeran's anger at the bureaucratic problems of undertaking responsibility, and Statler's impatience at the standards by which 'true' pilgrims are appraised.

In terms of the present analysis, however, perhaps the most important characteristic of these works is their recognition of the need to capture and to convey both the richness and drama and the complexities of meaning which unfold during the field experience. In these accounts then, illustrative accounts of pesonal narrative, bits of biography, or vivid passages from field notes are not introduced as 'embellishments' on the ethnographic texts, as 'decorations' designed to somehow make them more real or alive (E. M. Bruner 1986: 7–9). Rather than being byproducts, these elements are made of central concern to the construction of the texts.[7] From the point of view of the literary construction of such texts the problem thus becomes one of how to *frame* and *articulate* the unfolding experiences through which the culture being studied is understood.

It is as part of this question about the literary processes of framing and articulation that my analysis of the adoption of local indigenous genres and devices should be seen. One, rather trivial, conclusion from our examination is that the adoption of such local conventions may aid in the construction of composite anthropological texts in which the 'standard' modes of ethnographic reportage are but a few components among others (Marcus and Cushman 1982: 63).

A related implication – popular with many of our American colleagues – is that the use of indigenous genres and devices may contribute to what Tedlock (1979) terms 'dialogic' and Tyler (1986) calls 'polyphonic' texts. Put somewhat simply, these terms refer to the efforts to represent multiple voices within a text and to encourage readings from diverse perspectives (Marcus and Fischer 1986: 68).[8] Thus, for example, Statler's introduction of letters written by pilgrims who have visited temples along the pilgrimage route suggests how the journey may be instigated by motives different from his. Dalby's bringing in of excerpts from a geisha reader hints at the discrepancies between geisha's self-perceptions and the perceptions of them by other groups. Moeran, in providing the explanations given to him by a rather exceptional local individual (belonging to the Communist Party), achieves the creation of a different critical perspective on the valley's goings-on.

Yet polyphony or the use of multiple voices does not consist merely in the juxtaposition of different comments, versions, or perspectives within a text. To carry the image of voice further, the pitch, the tone, or the beat through which the voice expresses things may in themselves determine the meanings of what is said. In other words the very forms of the indigenous literary genres and devices which are employed in the construction of a text may carry their own potentials and constraints for expression.[9] It is thus to the specific possibilities and limits of the Japanese forms which are used in our three works that we now turn.

Aesthetics and appreciations

Three major considerations merit stressing in this regard: the role of visual aesthetics in the appreciation of ethnographic texts, the potential of certain indigenous Japanese literary genres for encouraging the participation of readers, and the kinds of understandings which the use of such textual devices may facilitate. Let us begin with the first point.

The importance of graphic displays in the construction of ethnographic accounts is exemplified in the contributions of Dalby and Statler in which a wealth of pictures, etchings, prints, calligraphy and images of plastic works are offered. Because the role of such visual devices within anthropological texts is a relatively unexplored area, what I offer here are a number of suggestions rather than a full-bodied analysis. In the first place, the graphic parts of a book may simply function as illustrations for a text. In this capacity these displays may provide concrete examples of the matters being discussed: what does a turn-of-the-century geisha look like? How have kimono fashions changed over the years? What kind of temple structures are found along the pilgrimage route? What does a leaf from a pilgrim's album look like? In this role of 'example of', the graphic displays are *subordinated* to the other parts of a text.

A second possibility, especially suggested by Dalby's and Statler's works, is that these displays may form, along with the other textual passages (lyrical and prose) one integral organisational whole. Thus for example, the etchings, paintings, prints and photos of kimono which are found in Dalby's volume do not only illustrate the ongoing discourse about these pieces of clothing. They form part of the comments through which the symbolic system of kimono – the set of interrelated categories of shades, colours, designs, seasons and occasions involved – are uncovered for the reader. Similarly, the various depictions of temples and temple buildings which are provided by Statler serve to enrich his account of the pilgrimage experience. In this respect the graphic displays offer a *complement* to the other sections of a text. By commenting upon these other sections and by being commented upon by them they contribute to the overall construction of the account.

A third possibility is that the graphic works which are depicted in ethnographic accounts may be experienced through their *detachment* from the text. This experiencing does not involve, for example, the process of perceiving systems of meaning, nor does it entail the process of identifying with a certain character or mood. Rather, the peculiar attitude referred to is that of the non-discursive, disinterested, concentration of attention on a visual object, that is, aesthetic contemplation (Bachelard 1964: xxvii; Maquet 1986: 33). It is in this light that the use of such devices as prints or paintings by Statler and Dalby should also be seen. These means may be designed to spark an attitude of contemplation which is not directly related to the ongoing discourse of the text.

Given the centrality of aesthetic considerations in Japanese society – and even more so in the geisha world – the experience of 'immersion' in a certain picture or print, or even a particular arrangement of furniture is an integral part of the understanding of this culture. But while this may be an especially salient point in regard to Japan, it holds for any culture. The portrayals or depictions found in ethnographies, in other words, may be greatly enhanced by including visual devices designed to trigger aesthetic contemplation. To sum up then, in this capacity the graphic displays found in an ethnographic text serve not so much to comment on it, as to add another aspect of appreciation to it and to the culture it seeks to portray.

Formlessness, suggestion and understanding

The textual construction of *Ōkubo Diary* and *Japanese Pilgrimage* is governed, as I have tried to show, both by a set of closely related genres which are marked by a certain formlessness, and by a tendency to leave the conclusions and implications of their accounts unstated. These features may be related, it could be suggested, to the more general Japanese aesthetic preference for irregularity and asymmetry in such diverse fields as poetry, flower arranging, gardening, painting, or even dance (Valentine 1986: 117). Of importance in terms of the present analysis, however, are three points. The first is that the use of such conventions may allow the inclusion *within one ethnographic text,* of a diverse mixture of literary forms which are usually not combined together: reflections, discussions, impressions, depictions, characterisations, or evocations, for example.

The second point is related to the kind of invitation that these literary peculiarities may extend to a reader of the text. Readers, to put this rather strongly, are invited, are encouraged by the use of such devices to participate in the completion of the text: to use their imaginations, in Jerome Bruner's (1986: 35) words, to rewrite it. Given the utilisation of these genres, then, much is left for readers to trace out connections, find underlying thematics, draw inferences, or compare the text with other stories and ethnographies.[10]

The third point is related to how both peculiarities of such texts – their formlessness and suggestiveness – appear to be highly appropriate devices for drawing attention to the fragility of the text's authority. This is because the text's apparent disorder, when coupled with its lack of expressed conclusions, alludes to the problematic nature of any attempt at representing another culture. While we shall return to this point presently, suffice it to note here that this seems an especially important point in regard to the portrayal of Japan which has often been marked by works seeking to offer one certain key, one sure-fire formula for understanding this society.

At the same time, however, the invitation or suggestion which may result from the skilful use of such devices may actually involve more than a richer grasp of the meanings of a text: other dimensions of experience may be expressed through such genres. The peculiar emotional mix of resignation and wistfulness created by the use of certain suggestive poetic forms as the haiku, may be one example of this point. This is because in its evocation of a transient moment, a well-constructed haiku may not only trigger a reflection on how ephemeral human life is, but also an accompanying (albeit subtle) sensation of sadness at this thought.[11] Similar examples are, of course, Moeran's intimations to the confused web of feelings which accompanied his last days in the valley, or Statler's allusions to the complex mix of sentiments of fulfilment yet unfulfilment which marked the completion of his journey.

These realisations lead us to the last point of this section, and one that is related to what I have referred to as the artistic unity of apparently formless works such as *Ōkubo Diary* and *Japanese Pilgrimage*. Keene (1955: 11) in discussing the similar formlessness of many modern Japanese novels nevertheless notes that,

> their intrinsic beauty is such that our enjoyment of the whole work is not lessened by the disunity. In retrospect it is as brilliantly colored bits somehow merging into a indefinite whole that we remember the novel . . . [they] leave us with an imprecise understanding of their life.

If there is one central element that has been – perhaps relentlessly – underscored in recent anthropological thought it is that our versions of other cultures are always partial, they are always incomplete (Clifford 1986: 18): there is no absolute comprehension of another cultural experience, only degrees (Marcus and Fischer 1986: 64). The contribution of such accounts as Moeran's and Statler's then, lies not only in their facilitating an ever more sophisticated translation of Japanese culture so that we can 'co-experience' it with them (Marcus and Fischer 1986: 64). The import of their compositions can also be seen in an exemplification of how the actual textual means used in the construction of an ethnography, may be employed in order to portray the very open-endedness and the uncertain order of the cultures anthropologists study.[12]

Power and textual experimentation

A discussion of the ethnographic portrayal of Japan raises questions about the political dimensions of anthropology. It may be worthwhile to go beyond the confines of the present analysis towards a number of wider – and perhaps also speculative – suggestions about the issues it raises in regard to a sociology of anthropological knowledge. One set of themes has to do with the manner by which ethnographic texts translate meanings and enact power relations between cultural systems (Asad 1986; Clifford 1986: 9). In today's international context of economic competition the place of the social sciences in constructing an understandable – and therefore manageable and manipulable – image of this society seems especially pertinent[13] (Bix 1980; Schiffrin 1986; Steenstrup 1986). In this sense, anthropological compositions figure as part of the means by which Japan is continually presented and represented to a variety of readerships in Western countries.

I would rather focus, however, on another respect (which has received very little serious scholarly attention within anthropology) in which poetics and politics are inseparable: the complex interrelationships between intra-academic power formations and the construction of ethnographic texts. One basic question in this regard involves the power of gatekeepers – publishers, editors, academic committees, or consultants, for instance – to directly influence the aesthetic dimensions of ethnographies. Take for example the issue of saleability which figures as a prime consideration for publishers. Ironically, it was this consideration which led Stanford University Press to decide against the inclusion of graphic displays in Ōkubo Diary. These displays, it was reasoned, would somehow 'defile the scholarly text and therefore possibly compromise the press's image as a scholarly publisher (as opposed to a popular one where the chief emphasis is on marketing and sales)' (Moeran, personal communication). Given the importance of the aesthetic dimensions of ethnographies this kind of decision – or related ones about the quality and quantity of displays – bears directly upon the kinds of understandings engendered by these texts.

Rabinow (1986: 253) touches upon a related issue in observing that tenured professionals are allowed greater leeway to experiment with textual innovations. On one level this observation is related to the manner by which a greater array of aesthetic options are now being opened for legitimate exploration in anthropology (Marcus 1986: 265).

On another level this comment calls attention to the intriguing possibility of including in ethnographies an exploration of how the social relations within the profession influence the kind of knowledge being produced. Let me get at this point by way of a literary device shared by many (if not all) of what are termed the 'experimental ethnographies'. All of these works attempt to integrate into their texts an exploration of the *social context* of research. By focusing on the interactions of the ethnographer with other people, and by utilising the author as a character in the text, they attempt to portray different aspects of the cultures being examined. Interestingly, however, the *only* type of social context which appears in these experimental works is the fieldwork situation. We hear nothing – or next to nothing – about another social context which is no less crucial for understanding the way the 'ethnographic knowledge' found in the text was produced: the interactions and discussions, and the constraints and possibilities afforded by the academic milieu in which the work was written. These social contexts – which include for example supervisors and mentors, as well as colleagues and competitors – seem to be as important as field situations in influencing the ways anthropological texts are fashioned and produced.

At the same time, however, because such issues bear directly upon professional careers, one would expect few direct allusions to them in published works, even if they are experimental: one could hardly expect anthropologists (even tenured ones) to discuss matters which could jeopardise their professional lives. Indeed, if an allusion to these intra-professional matters does appear, it is in marginal and relatively unintegrated passages like appendices, prefaces, forewords, footnotes, or acknowledgements (Ben-Ari 1987). What is implied by these remarks is not, of course, a call for unwittingly including descriptions and analyses of power relations within newer ethnographies. Rather, they imply a clear-sighted appreciation of the limits of experimentation in ethnographic writing.

And the portrayal of Japan?

It may be appropriate to conclude with a few words about the import of my analysis for the portrayal of Japan. The main line of my analysis should not, of course, be seen as a simple endorsement of a process by which anthropologists should all start composing haiku or collaborating in the creation of linked verse. It should be viewed more along the lines of an attempt at showing how through the integration of Japanese literary genres into our ethnographic texts we may be able more fully to capture the experiences of that culture. Through the use of pieces created by other people, or through constructing our own accounts along the lines of classical or folk conventions, we may be able to express things which lie beyond the more standard means of anthropological reportage.

Moreoever, this short essay can also be seen as an attempt to show how issues of representation and construction are not only intra-textual but also inter-textual. For it is only through the comparison – and contrast – of our three works that one can fully appreciate how each carries its own voices, evokes its own images, conveys its own experiences, and constructs its own worlds. Juxtaposed in this essay, *Geisha, Ōkubo Diary* and *Japanese Pilgrimage* seem to suggest a polyphony, but a polyphony on an inter-textual level. Japanese culture appears through this juxtaposition of ethnographic works to be a giant cyclorama: one that is never fully apprehended from any one angle, nor by any one viewing instrument. Like any other society then, the ethnographic voices portraying Japan can only capture partial worlds.

Notes

1 Put this way, ethnographies may be termed fictions. This term, however, should not connote something which is opposed to truth, a falsehood, but rather suggest that ethnographic writing can be called fiction in the sense of something made or fashioned. As I will try to show throughout the text, such a term suggests the 'plurality of cultural and historical truths' which are conveyed through such writings (Clifford 1986: 6).

2 A related development is the emergence of what Clifford (1986: 9) calls the 'indigenous ethnographer'. For lack of space I cannot go into an analysis of such Japanese exemplars as the writings of Takie S. Lebra (1984) or E. Ohnuki-Tierney (1982).

3 Among the few works which have been devoted to this issue are the compositions of Chernoff (1979) and Feld (1982).

4 These are coupled with Moeran's own short lyrical passages about such things as children in the snow, or the scent of mothballs.

5 As Keene (1955: 29) eloquently puts it:

A really good poem . . . must be completed by the reader. It is for this reason that many of their poems seem curiously passive to us; for the writer does not specify the truth taught him by an experience, nor even in what way it affected him.

6 A small number of travel diaries – out of seventy known works – have been translated into English: Reischauer (1951), Miner (1969), Kato (1979) and Plutschow and Fukuda (1981).

7 All of this implies, of course, that one uses different criteria in appraising such new ethnographies. The quest, as Jerome Bruner (1986: 10) puts it, 'is not to prove or disprove a theory, but to explore the world of a particular literary work'. Indeed,

157

> Believability in a story is of a different order than the believability of even the speculative parts of physical theory. If we apply Popper's criterion of falsifiability to a story as a test of its goodness, we are guilty of misplaced verification. (J. Bruner 1986: 14)

8 It may be suggested that since the ethnographer is ultimately the one to author the text these are not true dialogues being represented. For my purpose I follow Marcus and Fischer (1986:68–9) in trying to delineate just what a dialogic mode of *textuality* can achieve.

9 I believe this is Bachnik's (1987) main thesis, although she develops it in a direction different from mine.

10 Keene (1981: 20) exemplifies this point through contrasting two kinds of attitudes engendered by different visual constructions:

> The Sistine Chapel is magnificent, but it asks our admiration rather than our participation; the stones of Ryoanji, irregular in shape and position, by allowing us to participate in the creation of the garden, may move us even more.

11 Barthes (1982: 72; see also Bachelard 1964: 15) illuminates this point by showing how

> the ways of interpretation, intended in the West to pierce meaning ... cannot help failing the *haiku:* for the work of reading which is attached to it is to suspend language, not to provoke it; an enterprise whose difficulty and necessity Basho himself, the master of *haiku,* seemed to recognize:

> How admirable he is
> Who does not think 'life is ephemeral'
> When he sees a flash of lightning

12 This should not imply an indiscriminate blurring of genres and literary tropes. But rather, as Strathern (1987) cautions us, it means being aware of the constraints and rules which govern textual representation as well as the freedom they allow us.

13 Thus for example, Sugimoto and Mouer (1980: 12) note how Japan's foreign office or its National Commission for UNESCO have encouraged the translation of many *nihonjinron* classics while deliberately not supporting works which document conflict in this society.

References

Asad, T. 1986. The concept of cultural translation in British social anthropology. In *Writing Culture; the Poetics and Politics of Ethnography,* ed. J. Clifford and G. E. Marcus, pp. 141–64, Los Angeles and Berkeley: University of California Press.

Bachelard, G. 1964. *The Poetics of Space.* Boston: Beacon Press.

Backnik, J. M. 1987. Native perspectives of distance and anthropological perspectives of culture. *Anthropological Quarterly* 60 (1), 25-34.

Barthes, R. 1982. *Empire of Signs*. New York: Hill & Wang.

Beardsley, R. K., Hall, J. W. and Ward, R. E. 1959. *Village Japan*. Chicago: University of Chicago Press.

Ben-Ari, E. 1987. On acknowledgements in ethnographies. *Journal of Anthropological Research* 43 (1) 63-84.

Bernstein, G. L. 1983. *Haruko's World: a Japanese Farm Woman and her Community*. Standord, Calif.: Stanford University Press.

Bix, H. 1980. Japan at the end of the seventies: the treatment of the political in recent Japanology. *Bulletin of Concerned Asian Scholars* 12, 53-60.

Boon, J. 1982. *Other Tribes, Other Scribes*. Ithaca, NY: Cornell University Press.

Bruner, E. M. 1986. Experience and its expressions. In *The Anthropology of Experience*, ed. V. W. Turner and E. M. Bruner, pp. 3-30. Urbana: University of Illiniois Press.

Bruner, J. 1986. *Actual Minds, Possible Worlds*. Cambridge, Mass.: Harvard University Press.

Burke, K. 1953. *Counter-Statement*. Los Altos, Calif.: Hermes.

Chernoff, J. 1979. *African Rhythm and African Sensibility*. Chicago: University of Chicago Press.

Clifford, J. 1986. Introduction: partial truths. In *Writing Culture: the Poetics and Politics of Ethnography*, ed. J. Clifford and G. E. Marcus, pp. 1-26, Los Angeles and Berkeley: University of California Press.

Cornell, J. B. and Smith, R. J. 1956. *Two Japanese Villages*. Ann Arbor: University of Michigan Center for Japanese Studies.

Cranston, E. A. 1969. Introduction to *The Izumi Shikibu Diary: a Romance of the Heian Court*, pp. 1-127. Cambridge, Mass.: Harvard University Press.

Dalby, L. C. 1985. *Geisha*. New York: Vintage.

Dore, R. P. 1958. *City Life in Japan*. Berkeley: University of California Press.

Embree, J. F. 1939. *Suye Mura: a Japanese Village*. Chicago: University of Chicago Press.

Feld, S. 1982. *Sound and Sentiment: Birds, Weeping, Poetics, and Song in Kaluli Expression*. Chicago: University of Chicago Press.

Goodman, N. 1978. *Ways of Worldmaking*. Indianapolis: Hackett.

Hamabata, M. M. 1986. Ethnographic boundaries: culture, class, and sexuality in Tokyo. *Qualitative Sociology* 9 (4), 354–71.

Kato, E. (trans.) 1979. Pilgrimage to Dazaifu: Sogi's *Tsukushi Michi no ki*. *Monumenta Nipponica* 34 (3).

Keene, D. 1955. *Japanese Literature: an Introduction for Western Readers*. Tokyo: Tuttle.

Keene, R. 1981. *Appreciations of Japanese Culture*. Tokyo: Kodansha.

Kelly, W. W., 1985. Rationalization and nostalgia: cultural dynamics of new middle-class Japan. *American Ethnologist* 13 (4), 603–18.

Kitagawa, J. M. 1967. Three types of pilgrimage in Japan. In *Studies in Mysticism and Religion*, ed. E. E. Urbach *et al.*, pp. 155–64. Jerusalem: The Magnes Press.

Lebra, T. S. 1984. *Japanese Women: Constraint and Fulfillment*. Honolulu: University of Hawaii Press.

Maquet, J. 1986. *The Aesthetic Experience: an Anthropologist Looks at the Visual Arts*. New Haven, Conn.: Yale University Press.

Marcus, G. E. 1986. Afterword: Ethnographic writing and anthropological careers. In *Writing Culture: the Poetics and Politics of Ethnography*, ed. J. Clifford and G. E. Marcus, pp. 262–6. Los Angeles and Berkeley: University of California Press.

Marcus, G. E. and Cushman, D. 1982. Ethnographies as texts. *Annual Review of Anthropology* 11, 25–69.

Marcus, G. E. and Fischer, M. M. J. 1986. *Anthropology as Cultural Critique: an Experimental Moment in the Social Sciences*. Chicago: University of Chicago Press.

May, E. 1981. The 'other' tradition – modern Japanese literature and the structure of literary life in Tokugawa Japan. In *Tradition and Modern Japan*, ed. P. G. O'Neill, pp. 191–5. Tenterden: Paul Norbury.

Miner, E. (trans.) 1969. *The Tosa Diary*. In *Japanese Poetic Diaries*. Berkeley: University of California Press.

Miner, E. 1985. The collective and the individual: literary practice and its social implications. In *Principles of Classical Japanese Literature*, ed. E. Miner, pp. 17–62. Princeton, NJ: Princeton University Press.

Moeran, B. 1984. *Lost Innocence: Folk Craft Potters of Onta, Japan*. Loss Angeles and Berkeley: University of California Press.

Moeran, B. 1985. *Ōkubo Diary: Portrait of a Japanese Valley*. Stanford, Calif.: Stanford University Press.

Ohnuki-Tierney, E. 1982. *Illness and Culture in Contemporary Japan: an Anthropological View*. Cambridge: Cambridge University Press.

Plath, D. W. 1980. *Long Engagements: Maturity in Modern Japan*.

Stanford, Calif.: Stanford University Press.

Plutschow, H. 1981. Introduction. In *Four Japanese Travel Diaries of the Middle Ages*, trans. H. Plutschow and H. Fukuda. Ithaca, NY: Cornell University East Asia Papers Number 25.

Plutschow, H. and Fukuda, H. (trans.) 1981. *Four Japanese Travel Diaries of the Middle Ages*. Ithaca, NY: Cornell University East Asia Papers Number 25.

Putzar, E. 1973. *Japanese Literature: a Historical Outline*. Tucson: The University of Arizona Press.

Rabinow, P. 1986. Representations are social facts: modernity and post-modernity in anthropology. In *Writing Culture: the Poetics and Politics of Ethnography*, ed. J. Clifford and G. E. Marcus, pp. 234–61. Los Angeles and Berkeley: University of California Press.

Reischauer, E. O. (trans.) 1951. Izayoi Nikki. In *Translations from Early Japanese Literature*. Cambridge, Mass.: Harvard University Press.

Reynolds, D. K. 1980. *The Quiet Therapies: Japanese Pathways to Personal Growth*. Honolulu: University of Hawaii Press.

Schiffrin, H. Z. 1986. The response and reaction of east Asia to its scholarly study by the west. *Comparative Civilizations Review* 13/14, 253–65.

Statler, O. 1985. *Japanese Pilgrimage*. London: Picador.

Steenstrup, C. 1986. Reflections on 'orientalism' from the angle of Japan related research. *Comparative Civilizations Review* 13/14, 233–52.

Stoddart, K. 1986. The presentation of everyday life: some textual strategies for 'adequate ethnography'. *Urban Life* 15 (1), 103–21.

Strathern, M. 1987. Out of context: the persuasive fictions of anthropology. *Current Anthropology* 28 (3), 251–81.

Sugimoto, Y. and Mouer, R. 1980. Reappraising images of Japanese society. *Social Analysis* 5/6, 5–19.

Tedlock, D. 1979. The analogical tradition and the emergence of a dialogical anthropology. *Journal of Anthropological Research* 35 (4), 387–400.

Turner, V. 1978. *Image and Pilgrimage in Christian Culture*. New York: Columbia University Press.

Tyler, S. A. 1986. Post-modern ethnography: from document of the occult to occult document. In *Writing Culture: the Poetics and Politics of Ethnography*, ed. J. Clifford and G. E. Marcus, pp. 122–40. Los Angeles and Berkeley: University of California Press.

Ueda, M. 1985. The taxonomy of sequence: basic patterns of structure in premodern Japanese literature. In *Principles of Classical Japanese Literature,* ed. E. Miner, pp. 63–105. Princeton, NJ Princeton University Press.

Valentine, J. 1986. Dance space, time, and organization: aspects of Japanese cultural performance. In *Interpreting Japanese Society,* ed. J. Hendry and J. Webber. Oxford: JASO Occasional Papers, no. 5, 111–28.

Deconstructing an anthropological text: a 'moving' account of returnee schoolchildren in contemporary Japan

Introduction

This article[1] complements one I wrote as I was starting my fieldwork in Japan in 1984 (Goodman 1984). In that paper I suggested that, since fieldwork is a very subjective experience, it is important to give the reader some background against which to judge the validity of any anthropological account. As the educational ethnographer Peter Woods, in a somewhat extended metaphor puts it: 'We need to know something . . . of how these neat accounts were arrived at, something of the journey, of the time spent at sea, how the storms, icebergs and monsters were negotiated, means of navigation devised, changes of course mapped out' (1986:114). I am particularly keen to sail this course in the case of my experience of writing up my fieldwork, since I was surprised to discover that I ended up taking a position almost completely opposite to that which I had presented in the first articles I produced after my return from Japan.

I am interested as to why my own position changed so drastically, but I am also worried about the ethical implications of holding these different positions. The analysis of my fieldwork was, in practice, something of a theoretical exercise but it was also undertaken in an area which has seen a large amount of applied work and this has had important results for the children, families and schools concerned. Had my reports been commissioned by an educational authority as the basis for positive action, then entirely different decisions could have been made depending on which draft of the report had been read.

Roger Goodman

Historical background of *kikokushijo in Japanese society*

In this paper I want to give a very brief chronological account of the three basic phases my thinking went through, before I settled on a final position. First, however, I need to introduce some background to the subject of the research itself. I will start with a brief definition of the word *kikokushijo*.

It is doubtful whether the word *kikokushijo* was used in daily conversation in Japan before the early 1970s. Despite such recent coinage, though, it has now become a common element of the Japanese language and frequently appears in newspaper headlines and book titles. The exact definition of this word is both complicated and slightly controversial (see Goodman 1987a: 16–25), but for the purposes of this paper it can be taken as referring to any Japanese schoolchildren who, because of a parent's (99% of the time a father's) job, have spent a period of time (at least three months) attending a school outside Japan before returning to the mainstream Japanese educational system.

Although the Japanese have a long history of travel overseas, it was not until colonial expansion began, in the last quarter of the nineteenth century, that children were taken abroad in any number and that overseas Japanese schools were constructed. Little was officially instituted for the education of such children on their return to Japan, though a few private individuals did set up schools to help the returning children of diplomats and other elite groups. Keimei Gakuen, founded in 1940 by a member of the Mitsui family, was one such school and is the oldest extant school for *kikokushijo* (see Roberts 1973: 337, 386, 411).

The real impetus for returnee education, however, can be traced to the middle of the 1970s. The reason for this is easy to find. Paralleling a similar increase in Japanese investment overseas[2] the number of Japanese children living and attending schools outside Japan quadrupled between 1971 and 1982 and has continued to rise (see Figure 1). In many cases, as traditionally, men continue to go overseas leaving their families at home. Increasingly, though, due to a shift away from such personal sacrifice for the sake of companies, and the fact that more employees are now expected to spend longer overseas, the trend has changed towards whole families moving abroad (Hirano 1984: 13).

Throughout the late 1970s, the number of Japanese children returning from a period of education overseas increased (see Table 1), as did the

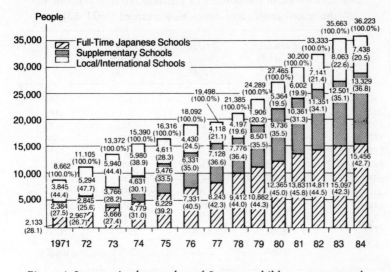

Figure 1 Increase in the number of Japanese children overseas and
the educational facilities they attend
Sources: Ōgiya 1977: 17; Monbushō 1985: 4.

length of time which they had spent abroad. The complaints of parents
about the treatment their returnee children were receiving in Japan grew
correspondingly louder (Kitsuse *et al.* 1984). It was argued that, because
of the monolithic, uniform and conformist nature of the Japanese
education system and society, these children were finding it very difficult
to reassimilate. In particular, they were being bullied for their poor
Japanese and their lack of understanding of Japanese society. Moreover,
they were falling behind in the education system in Japan – a system
which is based on exams that test the amount of effort expended on
accumulating facts rather than intellectual ability.[3] The results were
twofold. The children were doing poorly in their examinations and
thereby were able only to enter lower-prestige universities. Their job
prospects were badly hit as a result and the status of their families looked
liable to decline. Not surprisingly, the parents felt poorly rewarded for
their overseas service to country and company. Even worse, though, were
newspaper reports of cases of reverse culture shock and inability to adapt

165

Table 1: Increase in the number of Japanese returnee children and the school grades into which they returned (1971–83)

	Elementary school (ages 6–11)	Middle school (12–15)	Senior school (16–18)	Total
1971	896	435	212	1543
1972	1423	515	242	2180
1973	2241	685	203	3129
1976	3225	1000	373	4598
1977	3963	1168	628	5759
1978	4545	1301	672	6518
1979	4563	1420	581	6564
1980	5137	1500	867	7504
1981	5723	1874	873	8740
1982	6215	2275	1073	9563
1983	6304	2258	1224	9786
	(64.4%)	(23.1%)	(12.5%)	(100.0%)

Source: Monbushō 1985: 55

so severe that individual children suffered mental breakdowns which drove them to the extremes of suicide or homicide.[4]

The government responded to these complaints, in part, by setting up research projects. Several of these (significantly) were undertaken by returnee researchers who had been members of the original pressure group. Research began from a whole variety of angles. The most influential research project, mainly because it was the first and largest, was carried out by an educationist in Kyoto who uncovered basic patterns of, and average times needed for, readaptation to Japan. He coined a word, which means literally 'non-adaptation disease' (futekiōbyō), that had crucial significance for the way these returnee children came to be perceived (for a summary of this research, see Kobayashi 1982).

The image of the 'returnee child with problems' was picked up and widely disseminated in Japan. Many personal accounts were published to support it and one student, who had never been outside Japan in his life, wrote a 'true-life account' of what it was like to be a returnee. This forgery was only discovered when the author's former school friends saw his photograph in a national newspaper (see Kubota Etsurō 1985). In certain areas of Tokyo and Osaka where the head offices of many of

Japan's major overseas trading offices are housed, special sections can be found in bookshops labelled 'The returnee children problem' *(Kikokushijo Mondai)*.

It was, moreover, on the basis of the view of *kikokushijo* as having problems that the Japanese government, and specifically its Ministry of Education (Monbushō) took action. It set up the Kaigai Shijo Kyōiku Shinkō Zaidan (known in English as Japan Overseas Education Services) to co-ordinate overseas and returnee education for Japanese children, as well as providing more money for research into the problems of the children both overseas and on their return.

Most significant was the money provided for 'schools which would accept returnees' *(ukeirekō)*. Three large schools were established (each connected with a private Christian university) of which two-thirds of the intake was to be reserved for returnees. Eleven of the so-called 'laboratory schools' attached to the national universities were given extra funding to set up separate grades or classes for returnees. Another sixty or so establishments (more if one counts the separate senior and junior sections of the same schools) were given the status of 'schools co-operating in research on the education of returnees' *(kyōryokukō)* and in recognition rewarded financially. The school in which I undertook my main fieldwork was of this last category. Although I shall use some examples from this particular school in my account, I intend to present more of a macro-analysis showing how these schools as a type operate in the context of, primarily, the Japanese education system and, more broadly, Japanese society.

Attempts at analysis

I

My first attempts at analysing the position of *kikokushijo* in Japan were based on my belief after a few weeks of fieldwork that there was nothing actually 'wrong' with the children themselves. It was 'society' which labelled them as having problems and in need of help rather than having the tolerance to accept them as they were. I began to examine closely the work which declared that returnees had problems. Kobayashi's work on non-adaptation disease was paralleled and expanded, for example, by that of a well-known psychiatrist who, by documenting cases of extreme behaviour of Japanese overseas and on their return, appeared to suggest that non-adaptation was a peculiar problem caused by the Japanese social system (Inamura 1982). In similar vein, a psychologist suggested that the whole experience of biculturalism was inherently unstable, liable to lead not only to culture shock for the individual involved, but even possibly to severe identity crisis or neuroses (Hoshino 1983).

Anthropologists (implicit, for example, in Nakane 1972) posited a zero-sum formula whereby the acquisition of foreign cultural traits is perceived by the Japanese as reducing native ones, and linguists offered a similar model in which competence in a foreign language detracts from native language ability (Nomoto 1985). This idea was probably pushed to its extreme in the well-known and widely espoused thesis of a researcher in neurophysiology (Tsunoda 1985) who claimed that the Japanese brain has been so affected by the Japanese language that the functions of the cerebral hemispheres are the reverse of those of any other people (except Polynesians who also have a vowel-based language like Japanese). Tsunoda claimed that this gives rise to a unique Japanese logic and emotion which cannot be duplicated by non-Japanese. More importantly for returnees (whom he had examined), Tsunoda asserted that this unique Japanese brain pattern is severely hampered by interference from foreign languages and, most seriously, is developed before the age of 8. The corollary was that any Japanese child who lives overseas before that age will never be able to develop a Japanese brain pattern; and those who go overseas after the eighth year will be seriously impaired in their ability to think in a Japanese fashion (*ibid.* 103–8).

It was quite clear to me that almost all of this research suffered from the same major methodological and theoretical problems. It was essentially pseudo-scientific, using scientific jargon and statistics which were in fact nothing more than reflections of the researcher's own *a priori* assumptions. The main assumption (or brief) was that *kikokushijo* did actually have problems and each researcher was actually doing nothing more than 'measuring' those problems. Therefore, every 'problem' which a returnee had had since his or her return was directly related by the researchers to the fact that the child was a returnee. The major trouble with the research, though, was the complete lack of any control group so that it was not possible to tell whether the problems from which the returnees were said to be suffering were problems caused by being a returnee, by the Japanese educational system, by adolescence, or simply by Japan itself. As a result, the research was limited very much to the individual child and his, or her, experience of having lived overseas.

Indeed, three surveys which compared the anxieties and problems of returnees with those of so-called 'regular students' (*ippansei*) in Japan suggest that, although *kikokushijo* do have problems *qua kikokushijo*, the sum of these problems are no greater, may even be less, than those experienced by other youngsters in the Japanese educational system (see Takahagi 1982; Matsubara and Itō 1982; Murase 1983).

The question which I sought to answer in my early analysis, therefore, was why was such work being carried out and the results so widely disseminated? Moreover, in the light of this work, how could one interpret the significance of the special schools for *kikokushijo*? It seemed clear to me that Japan as a society and certain groups within that society felt threatened by the different ways of thinking and acting of the *kikokushijo*; and as such wanted protection against them. I had little trouble finding data in my fieldwork notes to support this argument. In what areas of life, after all, would the perceived individuality and non-Japanese value orientation of *kikokushijo* not constitute a threat? If they had been fully assimilated into a different society (as, regardless of reality, they were generally perceived to have been) then there would always be the fear that they were importing different world views which could upset the concepts of homogeneity and Japaneseness which are so earnestly taught in Japanese schools and which have permeated the society so thoroughly.

I examined the workplace and the traditional family structure as obvious candidates for the threat posed by returnee children to traditional Japanese values. Education was another area. Teachers, in particular, often found it hard to like these children. Returnee children, particularly those who had been to the west,[5] were a new kind of student of whom Japanese teachers had had no experience. Such students knew that the teacher was not always right; they knew that the Japanese style of teacher-centred lesson was not the only way of learning; and their foreign-language ability was often far superior to that of many Japanese foreign-language teachers. Japanese teachers were poorly trained to deal with such children. Not only did they have to deal with up to fifty students in a single class, but they had generally only had two weeks' teaching practice, of which the first week was devoted to observation and the second to a mere eight practice lessons. Hence when teachers had problems dealing with *kikokushijo* they sometimes preferred to project these problems on to the children themselves, insisting that they were in need of not only educational, but even psychological help (eg. Kubota Morihiro 1983).

169

Hence it was that I applied something of a functionalist analysis in interpreting the significance of the special schools for returnees. I saw them in terms of their ability to reintegrate the children into the mainstream society (Goodman 1988a, 1988b). In doing so, I found myself in broad agreement with the models proposed by Befu (1983) and White (1980). The language of functionalism, with its view of society being like a biological organism, demands the removal, or rectification, of pathological elements that threaten the social equilibrium. Hence, I argued that, whether they felt threatened by them or really felt they needed help, the proponents of the attitude that these children should be decontaminated or reassimilated all looked to the same end: a period of repurification. It was the setting up of a special system of schools for returnees which provided the site for this purification process through which the children had to pass before they were allowed to re-enter the mainstream society.

II

For several reasons, which I shall discuss later, I began to realise that this model did not tell the whole story; indeed it was directly contradicted by much of my data. Why, for example, did so many non-*kikokushijo* want to enter schools which took *kikokushijo*? Why, indeed, was there the apparently strange, recent phenomenon of Japanese children going overseas in order to become *kikokushijo*? Such questions led me to move from the teachers, employers and researchers on whom I had thus far focused all my attention, and to consider the *kikokushijo* and their families.

If, for example, one looked at the schools for returnees from the viewpoint of the Japanese education system, then what was extraordinary about them was the fact that they existed at all. Even more extraordinary was the special quota system for the entrance of returnees into most major and many minor universities, a system which avoided the normal exams, and which 94% of 18–19 year-old overseas Japanese hoped to make use of on their return to Japan (Monbushō 1982: 15). Furthermore, the percentage of returnees in the attached senior high schools of the national universities (the most elite schools in Japan) was 35 times the national average (Hasebe 1985: 85). These facts were extraordinary because the idea of any separate education within the mainstream system is, supposedly, anathema in Japan. Even children who are mentally handicapped are, as far as possible, integrated into the mainstream education system and, where this is impossible, go to special schools which endeavour to reflect and copy the mainstream style.

In recent years there have been calls for the greater liberalisation of the education system, but there still remains a strong belief that educational opportunities should be equal to all. This is largely for the sake of maintaining what most perceive as a genuine educational meritocracy which functions as the primary status-sorting system in Japan (Tanaka 1984). How was it then that this separate, and apparently elitist, education system for returnees came to be created? I argued that, as with most social problems, it could be said that the returnee children issue had been 'constructed' (Spector and Kitsuse 1977). The parents of these children were an elite group in Japanese society of whom a large proportion were diplomats, businessmen, journalists and professors. A survey of the average educational level of the parents overseas showed that 85% of fathers were university graduates and 60% of mothers had received tertiary education (Kawabata and Suzuki 1981: 31). Both these figures were well above the national average for their age bands. We have seen how these parents felt that they were being unfairly discriminated against on their return to Japan, and how they brought pressure to bear on the government to rectify this situation by setting up special schools and a special university entrance system for their children. They appear to have been very successful. The Ministry of Education spent over £50 million on education for overseas/returnee children in 1985 with the Foreign Ministry providing a further £5.5 million (Monbushō 1985: 22).

There was, of course, some variety among the schools for returnees (ukeirekō) which I studied. This variety was largely dependent on the proportion of kikokushijo among the total school population, though there were no schools which had only kikokushijo. It is important, however, to note that no teachers were specially trained in how to handle or teach kikokushijo.[6] Mainly as a result of this, there was virtually no difference – apart from the employment of foreign teachers in a few schools – between the academic curricula in ukeirekō and any other school in Japan. Where there were differences, these related to non-curricular elements: special uniforms, rituals, ceremonies, boarding facilities and vocabularies (examples I encountered included 'house-master', 'common space', 'blazer coat style', 'table manner'.)[7] These differences were highlighted and emphasised to differentiate ukeirekō from other Japanese schools.

In all schools catering for kikokushijo there appeared to be a search for

171

some kind of balance between the education of Japaneseness and the retention of skills learnt overseas. The idea was for a pay-off between *kikokushijo* and non-*kikokushijo*, a process described by one journalist as 'chasing two hares' (*nito o ou*) (*Mainichi Shinbun* 1985). The *kikokushijo* would become more assimilated into Japanese culture through contact with the non-*kikokushijo* who in turn would pick up something of the 'internationalism' of the former, a knowledge of overseas countries, an interest in languages, perhaps even a glimpse of different ways of thinking. In the case of both groups, the idea was to create a 'Japanese-plus', that is to say, a Japanese who could be called truly Japanese but had something a little extra to offer in the line of 'internationalism' – a person often referred to in Japan as a '*kokusaijin*'.

Many examples of such a superficial coating of 'internationalness' could be seen at the school where I undertook my main fieldwork. Children there could retain, or, if they were new to the subject, pick up a smattering of English, French, Spanish, Chinese, or Italian from native speakers. There was a heavy concentration on western classical music, and the school had surely one of the few authentic harpsichords in Japan, shipped in from Europe and for which was composed a Latin inscription. Western art was practised to the exclusion of Japanese. The school's two dramatic outings of the year were to a concert given by the world's only remaining full-time baroque dance group (visiting from Europe) and a performance of *Oedipus Rex*. Rugby football was chosen as the school's main sport and every student had to attend lessons in western table manners. Ikeda Kiyoshi's description of British public-school life in the 1940s, *Jiyū to Kiritsu*, was compulsory reading for all students (Ikeda 1983).[8] Indeed the school had pretensions to a British public school and in its fees at least certainly managed this. One of the most expensive schools in Japan, boarders for their first year would have to pay over £2700 basic fees. Foreigners were occasionally invited to give talks to the pupils and before one such lecture the teacher in charge of international affairs told the speaker in front of his audience: 'The purpose of inviting you here is to broaden the students' points of view because within ten or twenty years they will probably be some kind of leader in Japan'. This kind of superficial westernisation among the elite has a tradition in Japan at least as far back as the Meiji period, when those in important positions were famous for learning to ballroom-dance and wearing western clothes (Sansom 1950: 395–467; Barr 1965). Such values, in the case of *kikokushijo* constituted, I began to think, what

172

Bourdieu (1977) would describe as the elite's 'cultural' or 'symbolic capital' – a system of values which differentiate the elite from the rest of the population.

The desire to gain entry into this special group of *kikokushijo* could be seen most clearly in the recent phenomenon of parents taking or sending their children overseas specifically so as to qualify as *kikokushijo* on their return to Japan (see Ichi 1983; Kinoshita *et al.* 1985: 9, 61). Only those with considerable financial resources, however, could resort to such unorthodox methods. In short, this special network and the special schools for the returnees could be seen as a way for those from an 'upper-class', in a generally self-perceived 'classless' Japan,[9] to maintain and reproduce their status in society. By originally using the guise of special needs for their children, they avoided upsetting the ideology of equality in education which has been so important for the Japanese view of themselves as homogeneous and egalitarian and so effective in mobilising an efficient Japanese workforce. Rohlen's excellent 1983 examination of the role of class in Japanese education gave me the confidence that this radical interpretation was along the right lines and it was in the light of this analysis that I proposed (Goodman 1987b) the theory that, through access to dominant symbols in Japanese society, *kikokushijo* had had the power to manipulate their marked nature in Japanese society in their own favour.

III

By this time, I found myself with two very different explanations for the significance of the *ukeireko*, one taken from the viewpoint of the mainstream society, one from the returnees themselves. At that point, however, I turned to the analysis of two large questionnaire surveys I had carried out on *kikokushijo*, non-*kikokushijo* children and their teachers. I expected the conclusions from these surveys to confirm my two models. They did not. All the way through there were clear divisions: teachers who felt that *kikokushijo* should be 're-Japanised' and teachers who felt their special characteristics should be encouraged: non-*kikokushijo* who despised the returnees, and non-*kikokushijo* who set returnees up as models to be emulated; and finally among returnees themselves those who wanted desperately to be no different from their non-*kikokushijo* peers and those who wanted to flaunt and develop their overseas experience.

If anything was clear from these surveys, it was that there were a variety of role models and positions for *kikokushijo* in Japanese society. I began also to consider other points which had puzzled me for some time. Why was there such enormous public interest in what was, in relative terms, such a small group of children? Why was so much money spent on them? Why were so many researchers examining and holding conferences about them? Why were so many books published concerning them? Why did discussions about them so often become so heated, even acrimonious? It seemed to me that I was in danger of presenting a too-homogeneous view of Japanese society and that the prevalence of debates about returnees might be a reflection of a deeper social dynamic. I was interested to discover that, in fact, much of my data confirmed that this was so.

Not all Japanese companies wanted the compliant, group-oriented workforce to which *kikokushijo* might seem threatening. In fact the more long-sighted had realised the need for more creativity, individuality and flexibility in the Japanese workforce as the flow of ideas from the west started to dry up. Not even all members of the notoriously conservative Japanese Ministry of Education had the same ideas about the importance of Japanese values in education. Similarly, not all overseas and returnee parents believed that their children should become a new breed of international Japanese. Suzuki (1984), for example, had identified two groups of overseas parents, those he called '*genchi shikō no kokusaiha*' (an international faction which tends towards the local culture) and '*kikokugo no kyōiku jūshi no kokunaiha*' (a parochial faction which attaches great importance to their children's education after their return to Japan). In the United States, the Japanese were sometimes described as the most assimilated of all Asian communities (Cheung 1976: 49–66), whereas the new communities created by short-stay businessmen had to be among the least assimilated. In Britain, also, there were several close-knit Japanese communities, whereas other Japanese expressly tried to assimilate into the society; the same phenomenon had been noted in Thailand (Musikasinthorn and Ressler 1980). The divisions between those who follow one or other line, moreover, was not always clear. Indeed, the same individuals sometimes made statements which appeared to reflect both attitudes.

The views of the main *ukeireko* I studied were also divided. One quality newspaper described the school as a model for all other schools in Japan to follow, while another, a 'tabloid', a few months later, saw it as selective and elitist. These articles in turn were a 'reflection' of the wider debate over the significance of returnee schools in Japanese society. While these schools were officially described as institutions to help facilitate smooth re-entry to the Japanese educational and social systems (Monbushō 1985: 92–106), they were also characterised as a process of 're-dying' (*somenaoshi*) or 'peeling off the foreignness' (*gaikoku hagashi*) of returnee children (Inui and Sono 1977: 143–4; Befu 1983: 247). A cursory survey of three major newspapers for a month in 1984 turned up seven articles about *kikokushijo* demonstrating not only the depth of interest in the subject, but also the variety of viewpoints stretching from them being '*bunka taishi*' (cultural ambassadors) to '*okure wa hōkago cover*' (slow students in need of extra lessons).[10]

What was I to make of these 'debates'? Social attitudes, I realised, always retain the potential for change and the direction in which they move is a matter of negotiation between different interest groups within the society as well as their relations *vis-à-vis* the outside world. In Japan, it seemed to me, the tension between competing viewpoints had been at a fairly high point recently. Demands from outside for Japan to open up and internationalise were increasingly vociferous; on the other hand, Japan was becoming increasingly self-confident in its own identity rediscovered since defeat in the war. This tension appeared to be at the heart of many of the contemporary debates in Japan such as the role of women, the nature of individuality, loyalty to the company, and so on. The 'traditional' picture was seen as 'Japanese'; the opposite as 'foreign', by which was generally implied 'western'. Japanese values (conformity, loyalty, harmony, homogeneity) had been vital for modernisation; western values (individuality, creativity, heterogeneity) were necessary for internationalisation and, some thought, the continued success of modernisation. *Kikokushijo*, it seemed, constituted an important symbol in this 'internal cultural debate' (Parkin 1978: 286–311; Moeran 1984), and hence their position on the periphery of society was both a powerful and a precarious one. The terms of the debate reflected social themes which were far more important than the interest in *kikokushijo* as individuals. Indeed, the debate over *kikokushijo* perhaps expressed one of the most important underlying dynamics of contemporary Japan.

Finally, I attempted to incorporate all three above analyses of the significance of *kikokushijo* and their schools into one coherent historical account (Goodman 1987a). Hence, while originally the schools and the special university entrance network may have served to protect the homogeneity of mainstream society, as the national political rhetoric shifted from *kindaika* (modernisation) to *kokusaika* (internationalisation), the status of the parents of the *kikokushijo* led to them being represented, and representing themselves, as a new elite, 'international' Japanese youth. This historical process is, of course, neither complete nor necessarily uni-directional; it is perhaps only a short-lived trend – the first complaints that *kikokushijo* are in fact too privileged are now beginning to be heard (Zadankai 1987: 289–90) – though the investment in the special schools suggests otherwise.

Attempts at self-analysis

Although I did not realise it at the time, there was, throughout the period I was writing, a close correlation between the line I was taking and my own views of Japanese society. At the time I left the field, I had a very negative view of Japanese society. I saw it as a totally conformist society which discriminated against minority groups and the individual alike, and I was angered at what I saw as palpable attempts to stigmatise or label children who had lived overseas. In some ways I saw myself as a champion of the *kikokushijo*, and this anger came through clearly in my writing. Increasingly, I found myself drawn to books which described this negative view of Japan (eg. Woronoff 1983; Minority Rights Group 1983; Hidaka 1984; Taylor 1985).

My anger was tempered in part by the comments of my academic supervisors, but also, ironically, by the very literature I was now reading. It soon became clear that while *kikokushijo* might be a minority group in terms of numbers, they were not a minority group like other minority groups I was reading about such as the *burakumin*, Ainu, Japanese-Koreans, or Okinawans.[11]

All the statistics I looked at showed very clearly that *kikokushijo* had managed to secure for themselves a very strong political position. The minority schools that had been set up for them enabled direct access to top universities; the amount of money spent on each returnee child was far more than the average spent on other Japanese children; concern over their position was acknowledged and spread throughout the society (*kawaisō* – 'how pitiful' – remains the most common response to the word *kikokushijo*). Furthermore, there was increasing evidence of the successes of *kikokushijo*, not despite, but because of, being returnees; evidence that far from being a put-upon minority, they were in fact rapidly becoming a new, fashionable, international Japanese elite (see Goodman 1987a: 347–52, 387–90).

It was in the area of education that the treatment afforded to *kikokushijo* was so different from that given to other minority groups in Japan. There were, for example, more than 150 schools for children of North Korean residents in Japan (Rohlen 1981: 186), but like international schools and other foreign schools, they were classified as *kakushu gakkō* (miscellaneous schools) and hence the children who graduated from them could not enter Japanese universities. As a result, over 75% of the more than 125,000 school-age children of Korean residents in Japan attended Japanese state schools (Rohlen 1981: 185). The eleven schools run by the South Korean organisation in Japan (*Mindan*) followed a policy of assuming continued residence in Japan and, therefore, stuck closely to the Japanese Ministry of Education curriculum which allowed students to enter Japanese universities. Whichever track they took, though, children of Korean residents fared much worse than their Japanese counterparts in the educational, and thereby employment, stakes. As Rohlen pointed out, while 45.8% of all Hyogo Prefecture high-school graduates went on to university, only 26.3% of the Korean graduates did so (1981: 197).

Similar statistics could be found in the case of the Ainu. Only 78.4% of Ainu of the relevant age group proceeded to senior high school, some 15.8% lower than the national average; and only 8.1% went on to tertiary education, as opposed to the national average of well over 30% (Mizuno 1987: 146–7). As with the Japanese-Koreans, the Japanese government has always refused calls for affirmative action to support the Ainu case.

The *burakumin,* of whom it is estimated there are some two to three million in Japan, was one minority group which has, after a hundred years of political mobilisation, begun to make improvements in its level of social mobility and educational attainment. The number of *burakumin* receiving welfare payments, however, remained eleven times the national average and there were significant differences in educational attainment between *burakumin* and the majority of Japanese youth, especially at the post-secondary level (Shimahara 1984).

Although the islands, on which the million or so Okinawans live, finally reverted from American to Japanese control in 1971, their average salary remained at around 71% of that of mainland Japanese and unemployment, officially put at 5%, was double the national average (Katayama 1985).

There was, finally, one other minority group I came across who seemed in many ways to offer the most interesting contrast to the case of *kikokushijo*. These were the war-displaced orphans who had been left in China at the end of the Second World War (*chūgoku zairyū koji*). In many ways, one might have thought that treatment of the 2300 children of these returnee Japanese who had been completely brought up in China would have paralleled the special help given to the *kikokushijo*. In actual fact, they were dispersed among a thousand schools in Japan of which only 70 (6.8%) had anything approaching a special programme for such children. Perhaps most symbolic of their poor treatment, though, might be found in the fact that responsibility for the children of the 'orphans' fell not to the Ministry of Education but to the Health and Welfare Ministry, from which families received in 1987 a mere ¥30,000 (about £120) a month (*Japan Times Weekly*, 9 May 1987). This was highly symbolic because, as in many societies, the concept of receiving welfare benefits has very negative connotations in contrast with the prime status given to education.

Having looked at these other minority groups, I could no longer support the idea of *kikokushijo* as a genuinely stigmatised minority. It was true that they were a minority, in terms of numbers, but they clearly were in a totally different relationship *vis-à-vis* the mainstream society and were anything but marginal to the power centres of the society. In short, I began to feel that it was invidious to include returnees with other minority groups as an example of the suppression of minority groups in a suffocatingly conformist Japan. This realisation led me very rapidly from championing the cause of *kikokushijo* to actively attacking their elitist position and their manipulation of the egalitarian education system. Similarly, my views of the education system changed from being critical of it as stifling to recognising its social justice. I began to see conspiracies and manipulation in whole areas of Japanese society with which *kikokushijo* were concerned.

The final position I took can, in some ways, be seen as the realisation that while there may have been great efforts made on behalf of their children by the parents of *kikokushijo*, similar efforts have been made by other minority groups in Japan and there must have been wider social reasons which allowed the position of *kikokushijo* to change so radically. My analysis, therefore, moved entirely away from cultural explanations which relied on the idea that there were certain elements in Japanese society which tended towards discrimination against external and minority influences. Such explanations led to a static, normative picture which I had already realised to be far from the truth. Moreover, I could not sustain an argument that suggested that the families of *kikokushijo* could successfully abuse the main status-sorting system in Japan without anybody else being aware of what was being done.

It was both more realistic and, in the long term, more useful to discuss the position of returnees, and the general view of outside influences in Japan, in terms of a confluence of political, economic and historical (what might be termed 'social') forces. Moreover, the same analysis could be applied to any minority group in any society. Should a group at one time have been in a position of relative deprivation, there was nothing innate in that position: indeed, it retained within it the seeds of a totally different status. I found this position useful in examining the position of returnees in another supposedly 'closed' country (South Korea) and in one which is thought of as very 'open' (Thailand). In both these societies, the position of returnees could be much more closely related to internal and external social forces than national characteristics. This approach also allowed me to distinguish between the different minority groups within Japanese society.

The foregoing self-analysis has, of course, been an essentially intellectual rationalisation of the process of developing an approach to explaining the significance of *kikokushijo* in contemporary Japanese society. There was concurrently, of course, an emotional response that has hardly been touched upon. As Ben-Ari discusses in Chapter 8, the anthropologist does not only need to be aware of his or her position *vis-à-vis* the host society while undertaking fieldwork, but he or she should also take into account the influence of social contexts both before and after the fieldwork experience. This certainly was relevant to my own emotional response.

The negativism with which I left the field could be related to the immediacy of a whole variety of experiences while undertaking fieldwork. I certainly projected some of the frustration I felt at trying to combine full-time fieldwork with teaching and undertaking other school duties on to Japanese society as a whole. I have also described elsewhere an example of how I came to believe other researchers of *kikokushijo* were fabricating evidence to 'prove' their own hypotheses (Goodman 1988b: 110–11). I clashed with several teachers and researchers who I felt were more interested in their own positions than they were in working for the benefits of the children. I had even been told (à la Miller – 1982) that as a foreigner I could never understand Japan. In a way, I was taking on all these incidents, individuals and irritations when I started the writing-up process.

It was difficult to sustain this righteous anger in the sober seminar rooms of Oxford, although I discovered that anger conveyed a conviction and focus to my work which was difficult to introduce from a more rounded perspective. Distance – chronological, geographical, emotional – from the subject continually reduced my determination to take on the Japanese establishment in my writing and forced me to examine the further complexities of the situation.

That I moved from championing the 'impoverished situation' to attacking the 'elite status' of returnees so swiftly could doubtless, in part, be put down to a feeling of annoyance that I, too, had been duped by their manipulation of the system. Neither view – both of which were divorced from their proper social and historical contexts – was, of course, tenable. It was only when I finally stepped back from the whole situation – helped enormously by spending several weeks analysing comparative material I had collected on the status of returnees in South Korea and Thailand – that the significance of *kikokushijo* took on more reasonable proportions and became simply one element of change in contemporary Japan.

Conclusion

The implications of a personal account such as I have just offered are, as I suggested in my Introduction, perhaps most significant in the field of applied anthropology. As more and more anthropologists are asked to undertake work for health, development, education and other public agencies, so they need to express clearly the backgrounds to their final supposedly objective accounts. The case of *kikokushijo* in Japan presents a very good example of this issue. An enormous amount of research has been undertaken in this field. Three conferences I attended in 1985 which discussed *kikokushijo* had, in chronological order, two hundred, sixty and one hundred participants.[12] I estimated that somewhere in the region of a hundred individuals were, at that time, actively engaged in the study of *kikokushijo*. So many people were involved in the research, the advice centres, the government bureaucracy, the schools, and the pressure groups, that the issue had spawned an industry and become much larger than the number and position of the children themselves could ever have merited. Yet, almost all the research on *kikokushijo* produced by this industry presented itself as purely objective data regarding the problems of these few children. Nobody has stood back and examined their own position *vis-à-vis* their research.

Perhaps, it was only because I approached the subject of *kikokushijo* with no personal stake that I was allowed to take a broader viewpoint. Nevertheless, as I have shown, even the detached view I believed I was taking was, in fact, very largely determined by my personal – intellectual and emotional – position *vis-à-vis* Japan. If this paper can make only a single contribution to anthropology, it is, therefore, to suggest that the recent trend for anthropologists to analyse how they fit into their own accounts when 'writing culture' (see Clifford and Marcus 1986; Fardon, 1989) is neither unscientific nor self-indulgent, but both ethically and morally responsible.

Notes

1 The research on which this paper is based was funded by the Economic and Social Research Council and the Japan Foundation Endowment Committee.
2 Direct Japanese overseas investment increased from US$1,000,000,000 to US$9,000,000,000 between 1970 and 1981 (*Economist Rinji Zokan* 1984: 207). Minoura shows how closely the growth curve of Japanese–US trade has been paralleled by the growth in the size of the Japanese supplementary school in Los Angeles (Minoura 1984: 15).
3 The best descriptions of the Japanese education system in English are: Rohlen (1983), Cummings (1980), Kobayashi (1976), Singleton (1967).
4 There has been a spate of articles over the past few years describing extreme actions by *kikokushijo* which appear to link those actions to the fact of returnee experience, e.g. *Asahi Shinbun* (1982), Satō (1985) *Daily Yomiuri* (1983).
5 Since I am particularly keen to avoid the idea of a 'western' culture – an artificial creation based on ideas of politics, history and education that is often directly compared with Japan – I have decided always to write the words 'west' and 'western' without a capital 'W'. While recognising that it is also impossible to talk about a specifically Asian or European culture, or even dangerous to talk about a Japanese or American one, I have decided to leave such words with a capital letter since they also represent recognisable geographical areas.
6 The Tokyo Gakugei University Overseas Children's Education Centre is attempting to introduce some training for teaching *kikokushijo* into teachers' training colleges, as well as offering training for teachers in overseas supplementary schools (Interview with Nakanishi Akira, 15 February 1985).
7 Throughout this paper, I have not followed the standard romanisation of words in Japanese which have been taken from western language, eg. *manyuaru* (for manual) or *karuchā shokku* (for culture shock). This is to avoid unnecessarily confusing people who cannot read Japanese who might well also be interested in the number and form of such western loan-words in the discussions that follow.

8 It may be important for the argument here to give some comparative context with other schools in Japan. While private schools constitute only 5% of junior high schools (for those aged 12-15) and about 24% of senior high schools (ages 15-18) in Japan as a whole, in urban areas like Tokyo the latter constitute closer to 50% of all senior high schools. In the state system, children generally wear the same style of uniforms throughout the country; school outings tend to be seen as a release from the normal school routine and not as educational; boarding facilities are extremely rare; only English is taught as a foreign language; and Rugby football is played in less than 1% of Japanese junior high schools.

9 Every year around 80-90% of Japanese declare themselves to be members of the upper middle class (*Daily Yomiuri*, 17 January 1985) or 'middle-income' (*Daily Yomiuri*, 1 October 1984). Class here is not used with the hereditary connotation of European class systems, but in the sense of the self-perpetuation of higher income groups in a society where income and status are closely related.

10 The full list of articles is: Fujiwara Kietsu, 'Kaigaishijo: Kyuzo suru, Bunka Taishi ni, Kichona Seikatsu Taiken (Overseas children: rapid increase, cultural ambassadors, valuable life experience)', *Yomiuri Shinbun*, 12 June 1984; *Nihon Keizai Shinbun*, 'Kikokushijo ni Kibishii Shiren (Severe ordeals for returnee children)', 19 June 1984; *Mainichi Shinbun*, 'Kikokushijo wa "Ima" (Returnee children "now")', 22 June 1984; Nakatsu Ryoko, 'Kikokushijo no Kurushimi (The sufferings of returnee children)', *Mainichi Shinbun*, 26 June 1984; *Nihon Keizai Shinbun*, 'Shiren Nori-Koeyo Kikokushijo: Shui no Rikai ga Hitsuyo (Returnees surmounting ordeals: need for those around to understand them)', 5 July 1984; Nakadate Satoru, 'Kikokusei to Tomo ni: Okure wa Hokago Cover (Together with returnee children: extra lessons for slow students)', *Mainichi Shinbun*, 6 July 1984; Nakadate Satoru, 'Kaigai no Taiken Ikaseru (It's possible to make use of overseas experience)', *Mainichi Shinbun*, 8 July 1984.

11 The Japanese-Koreans, many of whom are third-generation members of Japanese society, often only know and speak Japanese, but are still considered a foreign population, forced to carry identification cards for which they are fingerprinted. The *burakumin*, sometimes known as Japan's untouchables, are a legacy of the feudal class system and are still strongly discriminated against in marriage and work. The Okinawans, the inhabitants of Japan's southernmost islands that were long independent and once possessed an empire of their own, are still often considered inferior by mainland Japanese. The Ainu were the earliest inhabitants of northern Japan who were pushed back into Hokkaido as the Japanese took over the island of Honshu. They have in recent years been gradually assimilated into Japanese society and discriminated against at the same time. Perhaps the clearest indication of the way in which all these minorities are discriminated against in contemporary Japan is the fact that the government still refuses to accept that there are any minorities.

12 The Showa 59 Nendo Kikokushijo Kyoiku Kenkyu Kyogikai held in Tokyo in June 1984; the Showa 59 Nendo Kokusai Kyoiku Kenshukai held in Nagoya in November 1984; the Ibunkakan Kyoiku Gakkai Dai Rokkai Taikai held in Fukuoka in May 1985.

References

Asahi Shinbun 1982. Rōnin Shōnen, Oji Fūfu Sasshō: 'Baka ni Sare' Naguri-Korosu; Beikoku Gaeri Nihongo Nigate (Young retake student murders uncle and aunt: beat them to death for 'calling him a fool'; returnee from America with poor Japanese ability), 12 December.

Barr, P. 1965. *The Deer Cry Pavilion: a Story of Westerners in Japan 1868–1905*. London: Macmillan.

Befu, H. 1983. Internationalization of Japan and Nihon Bunkaron. In *The Challenge of Japan's Internationalization: Organization and Culture*, ed. H. Mannari and H. Befu, pp. 232–66. Tokyo: Kwansei Gakuin University and Kodansha International.

Bourdieu, P. 1977. *Outline of a Theory of Practice*, Cambridge: Cambridge University Press.

Cheung, L.M.Y. 1976. A study of the ignored variables in the traditional paradigm of assimilation. Unpublished M.A. thesis, University of Maryland.

Clifford, J. and Marcus, G.E. (eds.) 1986. *Writing Culture: the Poetics and Politics of Ethnography*. Berkeley and Los Angeles: University of California Press.

Cummings, W.K. 1980. *Education and Equality in Japan*, Princeton, NJ: Princeton University Press.

Daily Yomiuri 1983. Repatriate student leaps from high rise. 13 December.

Economist Rinji Zōkan (Economist Special Edition) 1984. 59 Nenji Keizai Hōkoku Yori: Waga Kuni Kaigai Chokusetsu Tōshi no Sui-i (1984 Annual Economic Report: The Change in the Country's Direct Overseas Investment), Vol. 8, No. 27.

Fardon, R. (ed.) 1989. *Localising Strategies: Regional Traditions in Ethnographic Writing*, Edinburgh: Scottish University Press.

Goodman, R. 1984. Is there an 'I' in anthropology? Thoughts on starting fieldwork in Japan. *Journal of the Anthropological Society of Oxford* 15 (2), 157–68.

Goodman, R. 1987a. A study of the *kikokushijo* phenomenon: returnee schoolchildren in contemporary Japan. Unpublished D.Phil. thesis, University of Oxford.

Goodman, R. 1987b. A comment on Mihashi's 'The symbolism of social discrimination'. *Current Anthropology*, 28 (4), S25–6.

Goodman, R. 1988a. Japan's returnee children: some initial observations, In *Contemporary European Writing on Japan: Scholarly Views from Eastern and Western Europe*, ed. I. Nish, pp. 153–9, 268–9. Tenterden: Paul Norbury.

Goodman, R. 1988b. The problem of the problem of Japan's returnee schoolchildren (*Kikokushijo Mondai*), pp. 105–17 and 185–90. In *Proceedings of the British Association for Japanese Studies 1986*, Vol. 9, University of Sheffield, ed. J. Chapman and D. Steeds, pp. 105–17.

Hasebe, Shōji (ed.) 1985. *Kaigaishijo Kyōiku Manual* (Manual for Educating Children Overseas), Tokyo: Kaigai Shijo Kyōiku Shinkō Zaidan.

Hidaka, Rokurō 1984. *The Price of Affluence: Dilemmas of Contemporary Japan*, Tokyo: Kodansha International.

Hirano, Kichizō 1984. *Kokusai Jinji Kanri Jidai: Kaigai Chūzaiin no Shitei no Kyōiku Mondai no Mirai* (The Era of International Personnel Affairs: the Future of the Education of the Children of Overseas Employees), Tokyo: Eiko Shuppansha.

Hoshino, Akira 1983. Kodomotachi no Ibunka Taiken to Identity (Children's experience of different cultures and identity). In *Ibunka ni Sodatsu Kodomotachi* (Children Brought up in a Different Culture), ed. Kobayashi Tetsuya, pp. 29–61. Tokyo: Yūhikaku.

Ichi, Yūki 1983. Gaikoku no Kōkō o Dete Tokubetsu Waku de Kyōdai ni Hairō?! (Let's enter Kyoto University through the special network by going to an overseas senior high school?!), *Shūkan Asahi*, 11 April, pp. 167–9.

Ikeda, Kiyoshi 1983. *Jiyū to Kiritsu: Igirisu no Gakkō* (Freedom and Discipline: School in England), (first published in 1949). Tokyo: Iwanami Shoten.

Inamura, Hiroshi 1982. *Nihonjin no Kaigai Futekiō* (The Non-Adaptation of Japanese Overseas), Tokyo: NHK Books.

Inui, Susumu and Sono, Kazuhiko 1977. *Kaigai Chūzaiin no Shijo Kyōiku: Kage o Otosu Shingakkō Kyōso* (Education for the Children of Overseas Employees: under the Shadow of the Education Rat-Race), Tokyo: Nihon Keizai Shinbunsha.

Katayama, F. 1985. It's not all sun and fun in Okinawa, *The Japan Times*, 21 July, 8.

Kawabata, Matsundo and Suzuki, Masayuki 1981. Kaigai Nihonjin no Jidō, Seito no tame no Kyōiku ni kansuru Kisoteki Kenkyū (Towards a general theory of education for children overseas) *Kōbe Daigaku*

Kyōiku Gakubu Kenkyū Shūroku, Part I, no. 68, pp. 29–39.

Kinoshita, Tomio (ed.) 1985. *Kyōto Daigaku ni okeru Tokubetsu Senbatsu Seido no Keika to Hyōron* (The Progress and Criticism of the Special Selection System at Kyoto University). Kyoto Daigaku Kyōiku Yōbu.

Kitsuse, J.I., Murase, A. E. and Yamamura, Yoshiaki 1984. *Kikokushijo*: the emergence and institutionalization of an education problem in Japan. In *Studies in the Sociology of Social Problems*, ed. J.W. Schneider and J.I. Kitsuse, pp. 162–79. Norwood, NJ: Ablex.

Kobayashi, Tetsuya 1976. *Schools, Society and Progress in Japan*, Oxford: Pergamon Press.

Kobayashi, Tetsuya 1982. Kaigai Kikokushijo no Tekiō (Overseas and returnee children's adaptation). In *Gendai no Esprit: Culture Shock (L'esprit d'aujourd'hui: Culture Shock)*, No. 1161, ed. Hoshino Akira, pp. 83–101.

Kubota, Etsurō 1985. Tōdaisei no Nise 'Kaigai Kyōiku Taikenki' no Hakushindo (The verisimulitude of the fake 'diary of overseas educational experience' of a Tokyo University student), *Shūkan Asahi*, 1 February, pp. 24–7.

Kubota, Morihiro 1983. Kikokushijo no Seishin Kōzō (The psychological structure of returnees), *Nihon Hikaku Kyōikukai Kiyō*, no. 8, March, 59–64.

Mainichi Shinbun 1985. Nito o Ou: Shingakuryoku Kōjō mo (Chasing two hares: rise in school advancement rate, too), 16 July.

Matsubara, Tatsuya and Itō Sakiko 1982. Kaigai Kikokushijo no Minzokuteki Kizoku Ishiki. Shūdan Dōchōsei. Kojin Shikōsei no Kenkyū (A study of overseas returnees' ethnic identity, group conformity and individual directivity). In *Tōkyō Gakugei Daigaku Kaigaishijo Kyōiku Centre Kenyū Kiyō, Dai I Shū*, pp. 5–24.

Miller, R.A. 1982. *Japan's Modern Myth: the Language and Beyond*, New York and Tokyo (1983): Weatherhill.

Minority Rights Group 1983. *Japan's Minorities (Burakumin, Koreans, Ainu, Okinawans)*, Report No. 3.

Minoura, Yasuko 1984. *Kodomo no Ibunka Taiken: Jinkaku Keisei Katei no Shinri Jinruigakuteki Kenkyū* (Children's Experience of Different Cultures: a Psycho-Anthropological Study of the Process of Personality Formation), Tokyo: Shisakusha.

Mizuno Takaaki 1987. Ainu: the invisible minority. *Japan Quarterly*, **34** (2), April–June, 143–8.

Moeran, B. 1984. Individual, group and *seishin*: Japan's internal cultural debate. *Man* 19 (2), June, 252–66.

Monbushō 1982. *Kaigai Kinmusha Shijo Kyōiku ni kansuru Sōgōteki Jittai Chōsa Hōkokusho* (Comprehensive Survey Concerning the Education of the Children of Japanese Working Overseas). Tokyo.

Monbushō 1985. *Kaigai Shijo Kyōiku no Genjō* (The Current State of Overseas Children's Education). Tokyo: Monbushō Kyōiku Joseikyoku Zaimuka Kaigai Shijo Kyōikushitsu.

Murase, A. 1983. Kikokushita Kodomotachi no Fuan (Anxiety levels among Japanese returnees). In *Ibunka ni Sodatsu Kodomotachi* (Children Brought Up in a Different Culture), ed. Kobayashi Tetsuya, pp. 152–73. Tokyo: Yūhikaku.

Musikasinthorn, R. and Ressler, P. 1980. The Japanese community in Bangkok, *Sawaddi*, July–August, pp. 16–19.

Nakane, Chie 1972. *Tekiō no Jōken: Nihonteki Renzoku no Shikō* (The Conditions of Adaptation: the Contemplation of Japanese Continuity) Tokyo: Kōdansha Gendai Shinsho.

Nomoto, Kikuo 1985. *Kikokushijo* no 'Tekiō' dō Toraeru ka? Gengogaku no Tachiba kara (How should the 'adaptation' of *kikokushijo* be approached? From the viewpoint of linguistics). Unpublished paper presented to the 6th Ibunkakan Kyōiku Gakkai, Fukuoka, 11 May.

Ōgiya, Shōzō (ed.) 1977. *Zaigai Shitei no Kyōiku: Genjō to sono taisaku* (The Education of Overseas Children: a Counterplan of the Present Situation) Tokyo: Aoba Shuppan.

Parkin, D. 1978. *The Cultural Definition of Political Response: Lineal Destiny among the Luo*, London: Academic Press.

Roberts, J.G. 1973. *Mitsui: Three Generations of Japanese Business*, New York and Tokyo: Weatherhill.

Rohlen, T.P. 1981. Education: policies and prospects. In *Koreans in Japan: Ethnic Conflict and Accommodation*, ed. C. Lee and G. De Vos, pp. 181–222. Berkeley and Los Angeles: University of California Press.

Rohlen, T.P. 1983. *Japan's High Schools*. Berkeley and Los Angeles: University of California Press.

Sansom, G.B. 1950. *The Western World and Japan*. London: The Cresset Press.

Satō, Yōko 1985. Kaigai Ijū, Tenkō, Chichi no Tanshin Funin . . . Haha o Kotoshita Ichi Rōsei no 'Fukugō Gen'in' (Migration overseas, change of school, father living away for work . . . the 'composite causes' for a first-year exam retake student who killed his mother), *Sunday Maini-chi*, 31 March, p. 201.

Shimahara, Nobuo 1984. Towards the equality of a Japanese minority: the case of *Burakumin*. *Comparative Education* 20 (3), 339–53.

Singleton, J. (1967). *Nichū: a Japanese School*, New York: Holt, Rinehart & Winston.

Spector, M. and Kitsuse, J.I. 1977. *Constructing Social Problems*. Menlo Park, Calif: Cummings.

Suzuki, Masayuki 1984. Kaigai Kikokushijo no Kyōiku (The education of overseas and returnee children) *Kyōikugaku Kenkyū* 51 (3), September, 38–47.

Takahagi, Yasuji (ed.) 1982. *Kaigai Kikokushijo ni okeru Culture Shock no Yōin Bunseki to Tekiō Programme no Kaihatsu Shikō* (The Trial and Development of a Programme for Adaptation and Fundamental Analysis of Culture Shock among Overseas and Returnee Children), Tokyo: Tōkyō Gakugei Daigaku Kaigaishijo Kyōiku Centre.

Tanaka, Toshiyuki 1984. Kyōiku wa Kuni no Ishizue (Education: the cornerstone of the country) *Mainichi Shinbun*, 21 April.

Taylor, J. 1985. *Shadows of the Rising Sun: a Critical View of the 'Japanese Miracle'*, Tokyo: Tuttle.

Tsunoda, Tadanobu 1985. *The Japanese Brain: Uniqueness and Universality*, trans. Ōiwa, Yoshinori, Tokyo: Taishūkan.

White, M. 1980. Stranger in his native land: group boundaries and the Japanese international returnee. Unpublished Ph.D. thesis, Harvard University.

Woods, P. 1986. *Inside Schools: Ethnography in Educational Research*, London and New York: Routledge & Kegan Paul.

Woronoff, J. 1983. *Japan: The Coming Social Crisis*, Tokyo: Lotus Press.

Zadankai (General Discussion) 1987. 'Sayōnara Eigo Complex (Good-bye English Language Complex)', in *Chūō Kōron*, No. 6, July, 286–95.

Arne Kalland

Sea tenure and the Japanese experience: resource management in coastal fisheries

Introduction

With annual catches of about 12 million tonnes, Japan is the leading fishing nation in the world. More than 400,000 people are directly engaged in fishing and many others receive their income from processing and marketing fish products. Few people in the world can match the Japanese who, on the average, consume between 65 and 70 kilograms of fish a year. For these reasons alone Japan's fisheries deserve attention from social scientists. But there are more urgent reasons to study Japan's fisheries. Foremost of these is the Japanese management structure which until recently has received scant notice abroad, despite the fact that Japanese scholars have written extensively on the subject (for example, Habara 1954; Arai 1970; Hara 1977; Ninohei 1978).

One reason for this sad situation is, of course, the language barrier. But more importantly, Western scholars have long been blinded by a Western conception of the sea. It was taken for granted that the sea and its resources were commons open to everybody to exploit and few scholars have had the vision to question this widely shared notion. Social scientists, with few exceptions, did not look for indigenous ways of managing the marine resources either in Japan or in other countries. Until recently it was the exception rather than the rule that monographs on fishing people discussed the relationship between population and marine resources. On the other hand it is hard to imagine a monograph dealing with the economic life of hunter–gatherers, pastoralists, or peasants which did not discuss in detail concepts of hunting territories, migration routes, or land distribution.

This situation has far-reaching consequences for many a fisherman today. With the new ocean regime the coastal states have been forced to design new laws and regulations. In this process small-scale fishermen are often the losers. Indigenous fishing populations are usually far from the national centres where decisions are made, and they frequently constitute ethnic minorities. Their pleas are seldom heard, not necessarily because of ill intent from the authorities, but because of ignorance. They often lack knowledge of the proper ways to articulate their views to the law makers who have very little information on traditional fishing regulations. It is therefore urgent for social anthropologists in particular to study such institutions so that indigenous concepts of fishing rights can be modified (if necessary) and incorporated into the new emerging management systems.

Yet a beginning has been made. During the last decade or so social anthropologists, marine biologists and other scholars have uncovered a number of indigenous systems of management (Ruddle and Akimichi 1984; Ruddle and Johannes 1985; Cordell, in press). Gradually we have come to understand that open access to the sea is not an obvious or taken-for-granted matter, but is itself a concept which is a function of historical, cultural, economic and political processes. It is only one way of management, among many others. It is an extreme form of *laissez-faire* policy, while at the other extreme we find the 'closed sea' where access to the marine resources is strictly regulated.

Japan provides us with an example of the latter type of resource management and her experience is important to social anthropology for a number of theoretical reasons. In order to construct theories and models of sea-tenure systems – and human territorial behaviour in general – comparative studies are needed, and in so doing the Japanese experience is highly revealing.

Sea tenure is a matrix of institutions defined and enforced on many levels; from the formal rights and licences issued by the state and local authorities and enforced by the police, to more informal regulations made by the villagers and sanctioned through gossip or social ostracism. What makes the Japanese system invaluable for any anthropologist interested in comparative maritime anthropology and model building in general – apart from being based on the concept of closed access – is both the richness and complexity of her institutions and the fact that in no other country do we find such a blend of customary and formal laws as in Japan.

Rich historical records where fishing rights and licences are spelled out in great detail (frequently in connection with disputes) make it possible for anthropologists to take the historical dimension into account and to analyse sea-tenure systems as processes linked to social, ecological, demographic and technological changes. This fact coupled with the apparent success of the Japanese to regulate their fisheries (at least when compared to the situation in Western Europe, North America and many developing countries) has made many decision makers ask whether the Japanese model is applicable in other cultural settings.

An understanding of Japanese sea-tenure systems can thus contribute both theoretically and methodologically to social anthropology in general and to applied anthropology in particular. The main purpose of this paper is to improve our understanding of the sea-tenure system in Japan by describing its development and workings. Finally some contributions to applied and theoretical anthropology will be suggested.

The Japanese system of sea tenure

The Japanese system of sea tenure – which can briefly be defined as 'the ways in which fishermen perceive, define, delimit, "own" and defend their rights to inshore fishing grounds' (Ruddle and Akimichi 1984: 1; Cordell 1984) – is based on the two principles of fishing rights and licences. Fishing rights define access to a particular space of water while licences give the holders permission to conduct a certain fishery. Whereas fishing rights are limited to the inshore coastal waters, licences are issued for coastal, off shore and pelagic fisheries.[1] Both rights and licences developed over the centuries and it will be illuminating to take a look at how these institutions evolved.

The emergence of fishing rights
The foundation for the present territorial arrangements were made earlier, but it was during the Tokugawa period (1603–1868) that fishing rights were firmly defined and allocated to fishing communities. Coastal waters were regarded as an extension of the land and thus an integral part of the feudal domains. As the sea could therefore be disposed of as feudal lords saw fit, important differences between domains emerged. It is nevertheless possible to outline some basic features which were common to most domains.

Many fiefs separated the fishermen from the farmers. Certain villages were classified as coastal villages (*ura*). These were given fishing territories in return for payment of taxes in kind, money and corvée. Such territories were defined by village borders or easily recognisable topographic features like capes, rocks, estuaries, or shallows.[2]

One of the main problems with small exclusive fishing territories based on a village is that frequently they are ill suited to the fishing industry. In the first place, fish are capricious. Except perhaps for some benthos one seldom knows where the fish will appear. Secondly, many territories cannot support year-round fisheries. Finally, small territories make it difficult for the fishermen to speciálise in certain fisheries. Though this may help conservation it must be regarded as poor management when the fishermen are idle in one place while their neighbours have too much to do. For these reasons many fishing villages tried to obtain access (*iriai* rights) to the territories of their neighbours. Some paid fees for access, while others tried to obtain the same by strategic poaching.[3]

Another important process during the Tokugawa period was the continuous tug-of-war between private and communal interests regarding sea tenure. While many of the fishing rights in the medieval period were allocated to individuals, the general pattern during the Tokugawa period was to allocate the rights to whole villages or groups of villages. Individual households, however, managed to retain some of their old privileges. There was, furthermore, a marked tendency towards privatisation of fishing grounds in the more capital-intensive fisheries (Habara 1954). This was particularly the case with large stationary nets which monopolised whole tracts of a territory. When influential households got control over some of the rights, they employed other fishermen to work their nets.

The position of the absentee net-owners was challenged towards the end of the Tokugawa period (Arai 1970; Kalland 1984) and it was further undermined during the Meiji era (1868–1912). Four kinds of rights were defined in the first national fishery law of 1901.

(1) Exclusive fishing rights (*senyō gyogyōken*) and joint exclusive fishing rights (*kyōyū senyō gyogyōken*). The first of these gave the fishermen of the village exclusive access to the territory while the latter implied a codification of the old *iriai* rights and that they thus had to share the territory with a few other villages.

(2) Set-net fishery rights (*teichi gyogyōken*) gave the holders rights to certain areas for fixed equipment like set nets.

191

(3) Sectional fishery rights (*kukaku gyogyōken*) gave the holder lots to cultivate seaweeds, shells and fish.

(4) Special fishery rights (*tokubetsu gyogyōken*) allowed the holders to operate large nets in coastal waters as well as to construct artifical shallows in order to attract fish.

One important difference from the Tokugawa system was that the exclusive fishing rights were not allocated to the fishing villages, but to newly established fishing associations. The village leaders who often had been absentee net-owners lost, in theory at least, the access to these corporate estates. Individual fishermen could, however, acquire rights of the last three categories permanently as the rights could be inherited, leased and even sold (Ninohei 1981).

The new fishery law of 1949 sought to remedy this situation. Special fishery rights were replaced by licences and community fishery rights (now called *kyōdō gyogyōken*) are now exclusively given to reorganised fishing co-operative associations (FCAs). These rights allow the members of an FCA to operate within the exclusive territory of the FCA provided that they keep the regulations stipulated in the rights and hold the necessary licences. Sectional fishery rights and set-net fishery rights can no longer be transferred to other persons, and individuals and private enterprises will only obtain such rights as long as the FCA or a group of fishermen do not want to make use of their privileges.

Licences

While licences have come to play an increasingly important role in Japanese fisheries, they have ancient roots. Many villages and individuals were given privileges (often monopolies) to use certain gear as far back as in the Heian period (794–1185) if not before (Kada 1984). It was thus an alternative to bestowing exclusive fishing territories (rights) on loyal followers.

During the Tokugawa period several kinds of licences were in use. Time-honoured privileges were recognised. For example, in Fukuoka Domain four (later three) fishing villages were licensed by the feudal lord to dive for the valuable abalone in return for payments of fees (Kalland 1988). Large nets were usually also licensed by the authorities. In Fukuoka Domain licences for tuna and whale nets were issued for periods of three or five years and neighbouring villages were consulted before any village was given a permit for such nets (Kalland 1984). The authorities in this domain were also more inclined to give licences to a group of fishermen or to a whole village than to an influential entrepreneur. This is in sharp contrast to Uwajima Domain where licences for large nets were issued to village headmen who also received fishing spots (*ajiro*) from the lord (Arai 1970: 22–23; Ruddle 1985: 166). There were thus important differences in policy between the domains.

Finally, the operators of the same gear often formed guilds (*nakama*) in order to protect their interests. Their number as well as the conduct of fishing were laid down in the guild regulations. Although these guilds were seldom supported by the feudal authorities, they were often strongly supported by the village leadership, thus barring newcomers from entering the fisheries. The struggles between the licence-holders and those outside the guilds often lasted for years and became very bitter (Kalland 1984).

The licences during the Tokugawa period were designed to regulate coastal fisheries, usually inside the exclusive village territories. With the development of offshore and pelagic fisheries during the Meiji era it soon became apparent that regulations were also necessary in these fisheries. The central government introduced licences for several fisheries after 1909. Since 1945 licences have begun to cover almost all kinds of Japanese fisheries (Oka *et al.* 1962: 178).

Licences for small-scale coastal fisheries were issued by the prefectural government either to the FCAs (in which case they allocate the licences to their members) or to individuals and private enterprises. The central government issues licences for large-scale pelagic fisheries, while licences for medium-scale offshore operations are issued by the central government although their number is decided by the local governments. Licences for large- and medium-scale fishing were mainly issued to individuals and enterprises for a period of five years (Akimichi and Ruddle 1984).

The exploitation of both fishery rights and licences are restricted by a number of regulations. The fishery rights cover only certain species and gear and also have seasonal limitations. Licences are restricted by regulations pertaining to the size of the vessel, the power of its engine, the number and design of gear, seasons, areas, quotas and so on. Each licence-holder receives a certificate which is endorsed if he is found fishing against these regulations, and the licence can be confiscated with repeated violations. Many regulations, however, are not imposed by the authorities, but have their basis in customary law administered by an FCA or a group of fishermen within an FCA, the fishermen being much less inclined to break such regulations (Short, in press).

An appraisal

Fishery rights and licences are designed in such a way as to meet a number of objectives. The Tokugawa authorities wanted to secure supplies of food, taxes and corvée, as well as the physical survival of the fishermen and tranquility in the fishing villages. The villagers had to do corvée in connection with the coastguard and marine transport, and some villages had to send seafood to the daimio's table. Later the need to provide marine products for export to China and whale oil as insecticide also became important considerations for the feudal authorities. The duties levied on the fishing villages and the operators of the fisheries were directly related to the productivity of the fishery rights and the licences issued by the authorities.

The objectives have changed over the years and today they primarily involve preserving order on the fishing grounds, securing the livelihood of fishermen and their families, securing food for the population, and conservation. It will be clear that the sea-tenure system has been a qualified success in meeting these objectives, at least when compared to what other leading fishing nations have achieved.

Production and income

The desires to increase the production on the one hand, and to improve the income of the fishermen on the other, are often at odds, particularly in pre-industrial societies. Landing more fish may cause lower prices, and an individual fisherman will get lower returns for his efforts unless his efficiency is improved correspondingly. Many developing countries have shown interest in developing fisheries both to solve the problem of unemployment and to feed the hungry masses. Consideration for the fishermen's standard of living has usually come last.

In Japan this conflict of interests has been less severe due to her tenure system. Except for an aborted attempt made by the Meiji government to open up the sea, increases in production have been possible only through improving the efficiency of already existing units.[4]

Not much is known about the total catches in Tokugawa Japan, but with the exception of some benthos, production was probably well below the maximum sustainable yield for most of the species. It is likely that the sea-tenure system at that time inhibited food production, both by closing the sea for all but the fishing villages and by restrictive licensing policies. Nevertheless, most fishermen were poor even by the standards of the day, and poverty was one of the most potent arguments used by fishermen in order to procure rights and licences and to keep outsiders out. The authorities had also the livelihood of the fishermen in mind when it was decided that the fishermen should be allowed to work a net even though a net-owner had mortgaged or sold it (Fukuoka-ken 1963). The establishment of credit institutions for the development of fisheries can be seen as a policy aimed at both increasing food production and securing the fishermen a minimum standard of living (Kalland 1983).

The Meiji government embarked on a vigorous promotion of the fishing industry, and total catches rose rapidly. From a total production of less than 1 million tonnes at the turn of the century this increased steadily and reached a pre-war peak of 5 million tonnes in 1933 when Japan caught twice as much fish as any other country in the world. After a drop during the war years it again reached 5 million tonnes in 1955, before it passed 10 million tonnes in 1975 and 12 million in 1984. The Japanese have been able to double their per capita intake of marine products between 1950 and 1975.

This increase has been possible only by going further out, which has been one purpose behind the licensing system. One of the important objectives for the management system in modern Japan is that the high productivity fishing grounds along the coast, where 80 per cent of the Japanese fishermen work, should be left entirely to low efficiency boats (Oka *et al.* 1962: 196). The more efficient vessels have therefore been forced to enter the offshore and pelagic fisheries. This policy has been a major factor behind the rapid opening of new fishing grounds (which has occasionally caused international disputes) and thus increasing total catches. While the coastal fisheries have produced between 2.5 and 3 million tonnes since 1925 (with a slight increase to more than 3 million tonnes in recent years due to aquaculture), pelagic and offshore fisheries have increased manifold since 1925.

This policy has nevertheless not prevented a dramatic reduction in the number of fishermen in Japan. In 1984 about 440,000 people were directly engaged in fishing. This is a far cry from the peak of about 1,250,000 in the 1920s and 1930s. The fishermen have become more productive, but their catches are still small compared to the fishermen in other industrialised countries. Though the value of fish is high, it is only due to secondary incomes that fishing households today can show incomes comparable to the Japanese average.[5] The management system has only managed to arrest the exodus from the fisheries in a very limited way, which leaves the coastal fisheries in the hands of elderly fishermen.[6] This may have serious consequences for the resource policy in the future as there are clear indications that old fishermen without heirs in the trade generally prefer short term profits to long-term resource management (Kalland 1981; Short, in press).

Ideally the management system ought also to prevent capitalist firms or individuals from 'usurping the access rights or means of production from the indigenous fishermen' (Short, in press). Though it has not always been the case in the past, the law has, from this point of view, to a large extent been a success. The FCAs are open only to active fishermen and the coastal waters are closed to the more capital-intensive technologies. The great majority of the management units are owner-operated and small-scale.

Preserving order on the fishing grounds

Order was the motive behind many of the regulations of the Tokugawa period and this objective was also very important in the 1901 and 1949 fishery laws. The authorities tried to limit conflicts between villages by defining exclusive territories. Allocation of areas is, moreover, made for technologies that monopolise sea space for an extended period of time, as is the case with large stationary nets and aquaculture.

Success as a Japanese fisherman is not measured so much in terms of economic gains as in terms of relative catches. The competition between fishermen is a zero-sum game: my success implies your failure (in prestige). Competition is therefore endemic to this industry and is an important motivational force.[7] Yet it can also be destructive because many people invest in more efficient equipment which leads to overfishing and overcapitalisation.

Another effect is the intense competition for the best fishing spots. To avoid a situation where the fishermen are forced to leave earlier and earlier in order to capture the best places, many fishing communities have imposed rules about departure time from the harbour. Some fishermen have consequently invested in more powerful and faster boats, and regulations limiting horse-power have proved unenforceable.[8]

It is often assumed that regulations are introduced to limit competition and avoid conflicts. It is obvious that regulations can also cause conflicts.[9] Even in Japan, where the fisheries are regulated in more detail than in any other country, conflicts are a daily occurrence. They can grow to considerable proportions as when prefectures are involved (Kaneda 1979; Matsuda and Kaneda 1984), or they may be fought out between individuals.

Fishing rights, licences and other regulations can be seen as the outcome of processes linked to social, ecological and technological changes (Akimichi 1984: 90). Illegal fishing (for instance poaching in other villages' territories, fishing in closed areas, and using more powerful engines and finer meshes than permitted) form part of these processes.[10] and probably no management regime will ever be able to eliminate such conflict entirely.

Conservation

In the West it was overfishing that forced the authorities to give up the 'open sea' policy and introduce limited entry to many of the fisheries, usually against the wishes of the fishermen.[11] Limited entry has, on the other hand, long been taken for granted in Japan and her *fishermen* occasionally argued in favour of conservation as early as the Tokugawa period. Conservation has nevertheless been a minor consideration in Japanese management until recently. There can be no doubt, however, that conservation has become more important in recent years and is now the expressed purpose of many of the restrictions on fishing efforts. Moreover, as we shall see, many of the regulations which were aimed at order and secure livelihood also have direct consequences for conservation.

By closing the sea in the early Tokugawa period 90 per cent or more of the population was excluded from exploiting marine resources. Access to the resources was further limited when the territories became estates for fishing co-operatives with the enactment of the Meiji Fishery Law in 1901. Finally, absentee net-owners were excluded by the Fishery Law of 1949. On top of this, customary prohibitions against women in most fisheries further limited the number of potential fishermen to a small fraction of the country's population.[12] A number of other taboos have further restricted the fishing efforts. Menstruation still places some restrictions on female fishermen and deaths are followed by long periods of defilement for the bereaved households. Annual festivals also stop fishing for several days at a time.

The coastal fisheries were, until 1949, mainly regulated by fishing rights. The authorities chose to limit the number of fishing spots, and this is in many cases a more efficient way to limit fishing effort than licensing.

Frequently there are more nets than fishing spots, in which case it is common for the net-owners to take turns in using the spots (cf. Alexander 1977). New nets will in this situation not increase the fishing efforts and not be a threat to the resources, although they will cause overcapitalisation and reduced profits.

As the link between the central and local governments and the individual fishermen, the FCAs have important roles to play in conservation, not only by restricting the number of potential fishermen, but also by adopting internal regulations that are both stricter than those made by the authorities and easier to enforce. This is particularly true for fisheries of stationary species (benthos) where they do not have to compete with fishermen from other FCAs.

Many cases of overfishing have occurred despite the rigid Japanese regulations. Introduction of engines and synthetic nets increased the efficiency of existing gear and have caused overfishing (Befu 1980). The development of new markets may have the same effect. Often more licences are issued than advisable due to political, economic, social, or other considerations. Much of the implementation is delegated to the local FCA which may have different priorities than the central government. The struggle for a living and the intense competition are both incentives to install stronger engines, use smaller meshes, and use more nets than permitted. None the less, stable coastal catches since the 1920s testify to a remarkably successful management.

Conclusion

In this paper an attempt has been made to analyse the development and workings of the Japanese sea-tenure system, which in many ways stands in sharp contrast to such systems in the West. Being based on the concept of the 'closed sea', a concept shared by many other fishing societies around the world, the coastal waters have been divided into territories exclusively exploited by the fishermen from one or a few fishing villages. The territory forms an estate for a local FCA to which all fishermen must belong. The FCA also serves as an important link between the fishermen and the authorities, facilitating an endless flow of information and exchanges of opinion and interpretations (Ruddle 1987). Within the FCA, formal laws and customary laws are allowed to interact and the implementation is to a great extent left to the FCA. This kind of system is thus extremely sensitive to local needs and is very flexible.

Though the roots of the present sea tenure can be traced several centuries back into the past, this does not mean that the system has not changed. With bigger and more powerful boats the territorial rights along the coast may seem anachronistic to many, but it is premature to come to such a conclusion. There are in particular two fields where fishing rights may have increasing importance. One is in the regulation of fish, shellfish and seaweed culture. The FCAs and the sectional fishing rights are useful tools in securing this industry to the local fishermen. The other field where the FCAs and the fishing rights can be useful is to protect the fishing grounds against environmental deterioration. Many FCAs have done much to improve coastal fishing grounds by constructing artificial shallows and so on. The FCAs are more inclined to carry on this work within exclusive territories where they know that their efforts will not be 'harvested' by outsiders.

The exclusive territories resemble in several ways the new economic zones which give the coastal nations exclusive property rights over both the marine life and the mineral resources on the sea-bed and beneath. The FCAs are thus in a position to negotiate compensation for loss of fishing grounds due to reclamation and pollution of their waters. Few other countries give these fundamental rights to fishermen.[13]

The Japanese system has thus been a qualified success. Although more comparative research needs to be done it seems that fishermen's organisations tend to be less powerful with a management regime which is based on the 'open-access' concept; that it is more difficult to integrate customary and formal laws; that the distance between the fishermen and the decision makers in the administration tends to be longer; and that decisions are made more centrally while giving less considerations to local needs, with the possible effect that the fishermen will ignore or try to circumvent regulations they find unreasonable. Decision makers and anthropologists working in planning and policy formulation would therefore do well to study the Japanese experience.

The Japanese experience has great theoretical value as well. It warns us that much of the anthropological literature on fishing societies has been based on a narrow Western conception of the sea. It is hoped that new conceptual tools will emerge from studies of Japanese (and similar) systems of sea tenure and that these will find their way into anthropology and challenge the ethnocentrism in much maritime anthropological writing. In a comparative perspective the Japanese material is invaluable in order to build models of sea tenure and of human territorial behaviour in general.

Maritime institutions are still poorly understood and more research is needed to answer a number of interrelated questions. First, is there any correlation between sea-tenure systems on the one hand and the complexity of the ecosystem, the behaviour of the various species, the cost of defending fishing regulations, and technologies on the other? Secondly, to what extent do indigenous management systems have any impact (intended or unintended) on conservation, and how do people legitimise the institutions involved? How are these institutions embedded in wider social and cultural configurations and how do they evolve over time? Japanese studies will make an important contribution in answering such questions and thus make maritime institutions more intelligible to decision makers and social anthropologists alike.

Notes

1 The Japanese fisheries are divided into three categories: (a) Coastal fisheries (including aquaculture) which are conducted by small boats, often family-operated, of less than 10 gross tons within 12 miles from the shore. (b) Offshore fisheries which consist of operations between 12 and 200 miles from the shore, and in which a voyage may last up to a week. Most of the enterprises are medium or small in scale. (c) Pelagic or distant-water fisheries which are operated by large efficient vessels far from Japan, often within the 200-mile zones of other nations.

2 It has been claimed that the territories were defined by the seaward projection of terrestrial boundaries of villages (Ruddle 1985), but this was probably more the exception than the rule. Since many of the villages along the coast were defined as farming villages and thus did not hold fishing rights, the water space in front of these villages was incorporated into the territories of the fishing villages in the area.

3 The process suggested here is very different from the three-stage development model suggested by the Meiji government (Hirasawa 1980, quoted by Ruddle 1985: 166). The stages are: (1) village A got exclusive fishing rights outside farming villages B and C; (2) B and C started to fish and A lost its rights but for a few *iriai* rights; (3) B and C got exclusive rights and A was expelled. I do not deny that this model can in some cases describe the actual development, but it is by no means universally applicable. Arai (1970: 17–21), among others, further suggests that the exclusive fishing territories developed in response to commercialisation of the fisheries since only then did the rights acquire any value. However, fishing rights serve other functions than regulating access to a commercial product, as the many intricate forms of sea tenure among indigenous Pacific populations clearly tell us (Johannes n.d.; Sudo 1984). Fishing rights in Japan are probably much older than commercial fishing.

4 Improved efficiency does not, however, necessarily lead to higher returns to the

fishermen (cf. Emmerson 1980).

5 But even where the income from the fisheries compares favourably with the income of wage workers, the number of fishermen has continued to decline. There are thus other reasons to give up fishing than the level of income (Kalland 1981).

6 With a less restrictive management regime it is on the other hand likely that the number of fishermen would have decreased even more, leaving many coastal settlements impoverished or deserted.

7 Competition lies behind much of the behaviour of commercial fishermen all over the world. The operations are often covered by secrecy and misinformation (Andersen 1972; Stuster 1978; Byron 1980; Palsson 1982; Gatewood 1984). Yet secrecy and misinformation may have an important positive impact on conservation.

8 This dilemma has been solved by the Itoman fishermen (Ryukyu Islands) where the fisherman claims fishing spots for the next day by placing marks on the desired spots on the way home the previous day, thus forcing the fishermen to return early (Akimichi 1984). The effect of competition in this case might be a reduction in the overall fishing effort.

9 Regulations do not in themselves necessarily prevent conflicts but they are often institutional ways to solve them. The FCAs mediate in a number of conflicts both between villages and within them. For examples of conflict resolution at higher levels, see Matsuda and Kaneda (1984).

10 It should be added that violations of regulations laid down by one's own FCA seem to be rather rare, probably due to the social stigma such behaviour leads to (Short, in press). The FCA-controlled territories are thus an important stabilising factor in the management of coastal fisheries.

11 Fishery economists and law-makers have therefore accused the fishermen of being unable to regulate their own fishing. The fishermen should have been victims of 'the tragedy of the commons' (Hardin 1968), a concept that in recent years has come under severe criticism by anthropologists (Berkes 1983; McCay and Acheson, 1987).

12 This taboo has never been completely observed. The female divers in Japan are rightly famous. Since World War II more women have entered this industry as many skippers take their wives on board, and with the development of aquaculture. Today women occupy about 17 per cent of the labour force in the fisheries. See Segawa (1973) and Yoshida (Chap. 4) for analyses of the ritual impurity of women.

13 However, the fishermen have not been able to prevent pollution disasters like those in Minamata and the Inland Sea. Moreover, the pressure from industry and the authorities on leaders of the FCAs has led to cases of corruption (Okada 1979; Befu 1980), and severe internal conflicts between those who want to sell out to the industrialists and those who do not. The outcome is usually the same; the FCA gives up some of its rights. In the short run the fishermen benefit financially (and many return in fact to fisheries in order to get part of the compensation money) but these outcomes are detrimental to the development of coastal fisheries.

References

Akimichi, Tomoya 1984. Territorial regulation in the small-scale fisheries of Itoman, Okinawa. In *Maritime Institutions in the Western*

Pacific, ed. K. Ruddle and T. Akimichi, pp. 89–120. Senri Ethnological Studies No. 17, National Museum of Ethnology, Osaka.

Akimichi, Tomoya and Ruddle, K., 1984. The historical development of territorial rights and fishery regulations in Okinawa inshore waters. In *Maritime Institutions in the Western Pacific*, ed. K. Ruddle and T. Akimichi, pp. 37–88. Senri Ethnological Studies No. 17, National Museum of Ethnology, Osaka.

Alexander, P. 1977. Sea tenure in southern Sri Lanka. *Ethnology* 16 (3), 231–51.

Andersen, R. 1972. Hunt and deceive: information management in Newfoundland deep-sea trawler fishing. In *North Atlantic Fishermen*, ed. R. Andersen and C. Wadel. St. John's: Memorial University of Newfoundland.

Arai, Eiji. 1970. *Kinsei no gyoson* (Fishing villages of the Early Modern Period). Tokyo: Yoshikawa Kobunkan.

Befu, Harumi. 1980. Political ecology of fishing in Japan: techno-environmental impact of industrialization in the Inland Sea. *Research in Economic Anthropology* 3, 323–47.

Berkes, F. 1983. A critique of the 'tragedy of commons' paradigm. Paper read at the XIth ICAES, Quebec.

Byron, R. 1980. Skippers and strategies: leadership and innovation in Shetland fishing crews. *Human Organization* 39 (3), 227–32.

Cordell, J. C. 1984. Defending customary inshore sea rights. In *Maritime Institutions in the Western Pacific*, ed. K. Ruddle and T. Akimichi, pp. 301–26. Senri Ethnological Studies No. 17, National Museum of Ethnology, Osaka.

Cordell, J.C. (ed.) (in press) *A Sea of Small Boats: Customary Law and Territoriality in the World of Inshore Fishing*. Cambridge, Mass: Cultural Survival.

Emmerson, D. K. 1980. *Rethinking Artisanal Fisheries Development: Western Concepts, Asian Experiences*. Washington DC: World Bank Staff Working Paper No. 423.

Fukuoka-ken 1963. *Fukuoka kenshi* (History of Fukuoka Prefecture), Vol. 2, Part 2. Fukuoka: Fukuoka-ken.

Gatewood, J. B. 1984. Corporation, competition, and synergy: information sharing groups among Southeast Alaska salmon seiners. *American Ethnologist* 11 (2), 350–70.

Habara, Yūkichi 1954. *Nihon gyogyō keizaishi* (The Economic History of Japanese Fisheries). Tokyo: Iwanami Shoten.

Hara, Teruzō 1977. *Nihon gyogyōken seido shiron* (On the History of Institutions in Japanese Fisheries Rights). Tokyo: Kokushokan Kokai.

Hardin, G. 1968. The tragedy of the commons. *Science* 162, 1243–8.

Johannes, R. E. (n.d.) The role of Marine Resource Tenure Systems (TURFs) in sustainable nearshore marine resource development and management in US-affiliated tropical Pacific islands. Ms submitted at request of Office of Technology Assessment of US Congress.

Kada, Yukiko 1984. The evolution of joint fisheries rights and village community structure on Lake Biwa, Japan. In *Maritime Institutions in the Western Pacific*, ed. K. Ruddle and T. Akimichi, pp. 137–58. Senri Ethnological Studies No. 17, National Museum of Ethnology, Osaka.

Kalland, A. 1981. *Shingū: a Study of a Japanese Fishing Community*. London: Curzon Press.

Kalland, A. 1983. A credit institution in Tokugawa Japan: the *Uratamegin* fund of Chikuzen Province. In *Europe Interprets Japan*, ed. G. Daniels. Tenterden: Paul Norbury.

Kalland, A. 1984. Sea tenure in Tokugawa Japan: the case of Fukuoka Domain. In *Maritime Institutions in the Western Pacific*, ed. K. Ruddle and T. Akimichi, pp. 11–36. Senri Ethnological Studies No. 17, National Museum of Ethnology, Osaka.

Kalland, A. 1986. Pre-modern whaling in northern Kyushu. In *Silkworms, Oil, and Chips . . .* , ed. E. Pauer, pp. 29–50. Bonner Zeitschrift für Japanologie, Vol. 8. Bonn: Förderverein.

Kalland, A. 1988. In search of the abalone: the history of the *ama* of northern Kyushu, Japan. In *Seinan chiiki shiteki tenkai*, pp. 588–617. Kyoto: Shibunkaku Shuppan.

Kaneda, Yoshiyuki 1979. *Gyogyō funsō no sengoshi* (A History of Postwar Fisheries Disputes). Tokyo: Seizando Shoten.

McCay, B. J. and Acheson, J. M. 1987. Tragedies and comedies of the commons. In *The Question of the Commons: Culture and Ecology of Communal Resources*, ed. B. J. McCay and J. M. Acheson. Arizona Studies in Human Ecology. Tucson: University of Arizona Press.

Matsuda, Yoshiaki and Kaneda, Yoshiyuki 1984. The seven greatest fisheries incidents in Japan. In *Maritime Institutions in the Western Pacific*, ed. K. Ruddle and T. Akimichi, pp. 159–81. Senri Ethnological Studies No. 17, National Museum of Ethnology, Osaka.

Ninohei, Tokuo 1978. *Gyogyō Kōzō no shiteki tenkai* (The Historical Development of the Structure of Fisheries). Tokyo: Ochanomizu Shobō.

Ninohei, Tokuo 1981. *Meiji gyogyō kaitakushi* (Fisheries Exploitation in the Meiji Era). Tokyo: Heibonsha.

Oka, N., Watanabe, H., and Kasegawa, A. 1962. The economic effects of the regulation of the trawl fisheries of Japan. In *Economic Effects of Fishery Regulations*, ed. R. Hamlisch, pp. 171–208. FAO Fisheries Report No. 5.

Okada, Osamu 1979. Japanese Fisherpeople's fight against nuclear power plants. *AMPO* 11 (1), 38–45.

Palsson, G. 1982. Territoriality among Icelandic fishermen. *Acta Sociologica* 25, 5–13.

Ruddle, K. 1985. The continuity of traditional practices: the case of Japanese coastal fisheries. In *The Traditional Management in Coastal Systems in Asia and the Pacific*, ed. K. Ruddle and R. E. Johannes, pp. 158–79. Jakarta: UNESCO.

Ruddle, K. 1987. The management of coral reef fish resources in the Yaeyama Archipelago, Southwestern Okinawa. *Galaxea* 6, 209–35.

Ruddle, K. and Akimichi, T. (eds.) 1984. *Maritime Institutions in the Western Pacific*. Senri Ethnological Studies No. 17, National Museum of Ethnology, Osaka.

Ruddle, K. and Johannes, R.E. (eds) 1985. *The Traditional Knowledge and Management of Coastal Systems in Asia and the Pacific*. Jakarta: UNESCO.

Segawa, Kiyoko 1973. Menstrual taboos imposed upon women. In *Studies of Japanese Folklore*, ed. R. M. Dorson. Bloomington: Indiana Press.

Short, K. (in press). Territoriality in a modern Hokkaido fishing community. In *A Sea of Small Boats: Customary Law and Territoriality in the World of Inshore Fishing*, ed. J. C. Cordell, Cambridge, Mass.: Cultural Survival.

Stuster, J. 1978. Where 'Mabel' may mean 'Sea Bass'. *Natural History* 87 (9), 65–71.

Sudo, Kenichi 1984. Social organization and types of sea tenure in Micronesia. In *Maritime Institutions in the Western Pacific*, ed. K. Ruddle and T. Akimichi, pp. 203–30. Senri Ethnological Studies No. 17, National Museum of Ethnology, Osaka.

Festival management and the corporate analysis of Japanese society

Introduction

Festivals are performed in most Japanese communities with varying frequencies. They are organised by members of the communities in which they take place. Various organisational forms required to carry out the festival reflect the social organisation and management practices of the given community. In a broader more general view they reflect general organisational forms common in Japanese society. Festivals are loci in which we can identify different social forms in Japan. The central event of most festivals is a shrine ritual. In the ritual the major participants in managing and running the festival take part. Using the data from my own fieldwork in Yuzawa-shi, Akita Prefecture, and comparing it to other data, I suggest a mode of analysis whose results have broader theoretical implications for the understanding of Japanese society.[1]

Atago-jinja's festival: organisation and management in the festival ritual

The following description of a major festival ritual is intended to focus the discussion on a concrete event. The ritual described is representative, albeit somewhat more elaborate than the majority of rituals in Shinto shrines. I am, however, not interested in the ritual's progress so much as in the *personae* and their social relationships.

The participants, all men, are arrayed in groups along the sides of the assembly hall of Atago-jinja. They sit on their knees facing inwards. The groups, or rather units, are separated by two obvious differences. Between each unit there is a space, and each is dressed differently. Clockwise from the entrance we have the neighbourhood representatives (*toban*), a group of fifteen men. Following them, on a slightly raised platform is the festival head (*sai-cho*), a young boy dressed in white. On the other side of the aisle, in a semi-enclosed alcove, sits the chief priest (*guji*) in red robes. Beside him sits a group of priests (*kannushi*) dressed in brocade robes. Near the entrance sit the four former-owner representatives (*jigannushi*) in wide-shouldered surcoats.

The ritual starts with an orchestral piece played by the priests. One of them performs an invocation before the altar. Two others then purify the assembly with salt and with water. Offerings are passed to the main hall by the priests headed by the *guji*. The *guji* then reads a prayer. A priest offers a flax-and-paper-decorated sprig of evergreen (*tamagushi*) to an individual from each of the units mentioned above. These approach the altar, offer the sprig, bow and clap their hands. The priests play their instruments again. The *guji* thanks the assembly. Wine and rice cooked with red beans are offered.

Atago-jinga's ritual described above is fairly representative of most shrine rituals in Japan. Many rituals are less elaborate, others, particularly in famous and large shrines, are more elaborate. The general structure of the rituals remains, however, the same, with modifications of elaboration, rules and attendance. The ritual of Atago-jinja serves as a locus in which several different corporate units interact. The autonomy of each unit is symbolised graphically by the central element of the ritual. In this element, called *tamagushi hoten*, a representative of each of the units offers an evergreen sprig before the altar. As he makes the required bows and claps his hands, the members of his group bow and clap with him though no others do so.

The *toban* present at the ritual include two representatives from each of seven neighbourhoods in the town. They are all members of the Young Men's Association (*wakamono-kai*) which in many Japanese communities takes responsibility for certain civic functions. Each *wakamono-kai* can be identified clearly in terms of its membership: several generations of residence in the neighbourhood, and age between 17 and 42 in most cases are prerequisites for membership. The four formal characteristics of a corporate unit are quite evident. Members of the *wakamono-kai* in any given neighbourhood in Yuzawa perform certain functions within the community. In one, at least, they maintain several festivals in two shrines. In most neighbourhoods they lead clean-up campaigns. Each of the neighbourhood *wakamono-kai* has procedures to run its affairs, whether these be modes of decision making or recruitment of new members. Finally, in each we can distinguish different organisational forms. There are associations in which there are only a few officers, while in others elaborate organisational structures include general councils, sub-committees and *ad hoc* commissions can be found.

As part of its affairs, each of these neighbourhood units performs duties within the *toban* system. The *toban* system is composed of seven corporate members. Five of these take it upon themselves to manage the Atago-jinja yearly festival in rotation. The *toban* are responsible to other social units: the Festival Preservation Committee (which is not formally represented in the ritual), the *guji*, and the town in general, for the festival. The internal arrangements of the *toban* as a whole, as well as the procedures by which matters are settled, and details of their organisation, are internal matters. It is necessary to distinguish between the affairs of the *toban* whose members are constituent neighbourhood groups and the internal affairs of these constituent groups themselves.

The intricacies of the arrangement, and the careful distinction made between units involved in the festival is particularly evident in the role of the *toban-cho*. He is normally the head of the *wakamono-kai* running the festival, but is concurrently, the head of the entire *toban*. This is indicated in the ritual: he sits somewhat apart from the rest of the *toban*. He offers a *tamagushi* himself, bows and claps by himself. The individual is substitutable, filling an office or more as required. Positions in the ritual are not those of individuals but of aggregate and single roles. Their different natures, mutual relations, and separate activities and interests must be accounted for in some single analytic framework, in order to understand what is going on.

The substitutability of individuals in offices and aggregates is significant. For example, the *sai-cho* both symbolises and represents a figure who was the chief worshipper, and chief supporter of the festival in former times. The position is undertaken by a wealthy individual in the neighbourhood having responsibility for the *toban*. The ritual function, however, is performed by a child, usually a grandson of the nominal *sai-cho*. The child's relationship with the other participants in the ritual (who may be relatives or neighbours) is irrelevant. What is significant is the relationship of the *sai-cho* role to the other roles in the ritual.

The priests' group is internally undifferentiated. Priest-musicians are chosen from among the priests of shrines in the area of Yuzawa (Ashkenazi 1985). Some of them are *guji*, that is chief priests, in their own right. Participation in the Yuzawa ritual is dependent on certain minimal qualifications (e.g. a licence as a practising priest, and a shrine), and on the personal choice of the Atago-jinja *guji*. The priest has individual relations with the Atago-jinja *guji*: one of them is his son, others are colleagues who substitute for him occasionally, he performs *as a priest* at major rituals of others. But their relationship to other units in the ritual is *not* individual. They function as substitutable elements in an aggregate *vis-à-vis* the other units participating in the ritual. Moreover, the unit of priests in the ritual described has no continuing existence outside the ritual, though individual priests have individual relations with groups or individuals who participate, and the priests themselves, as well as others not present, do interact as individuals (cf. Ashkenazi 1985).

Two points need emphasising. First, the great degree of *substitutability* in the membership of priest-musicians. In three years of observing the ritual, the composition of this unit has never been the same. Now, this is true as well of all other units in the ritual, except for the *guji* and the *jigannushi,* but in the case of the *sai-cho* and the *toban,* while *individuals* are substituted freely, component elements are not. Thus the *toban* are *always* composed of representatives of the same corporate units, whereas the priests may come from different places and shrines as convenient.

A second related point is the relationship between different types of unit. The *guji* and the group of priests serves as an example. The performance and membership of the groups of priests is dependent upon, and in a sense subordinate to the chief priest (*guji*). The ritual must conform to the *guji*'s requirements, and membership is determined solely at his discretion. The fact that members participate voluntarily, limits the *guji*'s ability to dictate to the other priests. The relations between priests who come as 'guest performers' and the incumbents of shrines in the Yuzawa area can be explained in terms of the formal relations deriving from the different nature of the position of chief priest and of the unit of priests. In each shrine the incumbent plays the *guji* role for his own shrine whilst the others play the 'priest' role.

Corporate analysis as an analytic tool

A large number of questions can be raised from this bare-bones description. The symbolic, affective and descriptive levels are of no immediate concern in this paper. Here I am concerned with what may be learned from the description of the roles in the ritual as a social event. Over and above that, I am concerned with the issue of analysis: how such an event may be approached in a way that is most fruitful, that allows for comparison and for prediction.

Several analytical problems need to be addressed. First, an understanding of the internal operations of ritual units is complicated by the different types of units that are participating: individuals, enduring groups, ephemeral commissions. Each of these has different arrangements and internal rules. A second problem has to do with the relations between these different units, a problem compounded by the effect of these internal differences on the relations between the units. Finally, it must be determined to what degree the arrangements described here are representative for Japanese society as a whole. Paradoxically, in reality the problem faced in discussing Japanese society is the reverse: there is too often an assumption of greater homogeneity than actually exists. 'Similarity' is often presented as 'homogeneity' which obscures differences that may be critical for understanding Japanese society.

The analytical scheme I use here does not constitute the only valid analytical method, nor does it, nor should it, encompass all facets of a society. It has the advantage of enabling me to describe and compare organisational differences and their consequences in great detail. The tools used are consciously restricted to the group level of society. Its derivatives – the various rules of organisations – may be used to illuminate factors in other locales and at other levels of analysis. Obviously, such detailed analysis of one facet of complex social interactions suffers from the inability to address ideological, symbolical and other aspects of the interaction.

For the purpose of analysis it is useful to conceive of the various units in the ritual described as different kinds of corporations. Corporations are identifiable, organised social units with varying and definable degrees of complexity. The different degrees of complexity may be assumed to have implications for the social unit's internal functioning and external articulation with its environment.

The precise definition of a corporation or corporate group has been contested in anthropology for some time. The anthropological concept of corporate group derives from concepts by Maine (1931: 54) and Weber (1947: 145). As Dow (1973) points out, the use of the concept by various

Michael Ashkenazi

anthropologists (e.g. Fortes 1953; Befu and Plotnicov 1968; Goodenough 1971; Cochrane 1971) has been confused by the lack of distinction between the two original uses of the term. For Maine the concept was largely juridical in nature and emphasised the idea of a perpetual unit. For Weber the concept was essentially social and emphasised the idea of a communal unit. As a direct result, the concept of corporation has suffered from a lack of analytical rigour, and a great deal of confusion in its usage. At one extreme is Goodenough's (1971) use of the concept as little more than an etic label, at the other are rigid definitions such as M. G. Smith (1975) and Brown (1974) who provide detached, almost formulistic definitions. In the following discussion I rely heavily on Smith and Brown largely because their formulistic, almost structural approach fits the Japanese data very neatly.

To start from the most complex, *perfect* corporations have the following characteristics: 'identity, presumed perpetuity, closure and membership, autonomy within a given sphere, exclusive common affairs, set procedures, and organization' (M. G. Smith 1975: 94). This definition, though open to challenge (cf. Dow 1973), offers a means that is not bound to one specific culture, to examine social structures without prejudicing questions that might arise about the nature of such groups. Each of the items in the definition can be treated as a dimension, or category, against which data about existing groups can be examined. They constitute analytic variables which can be varied in a controlled fashion to test various hypotheses (cf. Brown 1974 for a detailed analysis of contrasting variables). Furthermore, we are able here to examine interrelationships between different groups, between groups nested hierarchically, and between groups and other types of identifiable corporate entities.

Generally speaking, corporations are at a minimum, presumptively perpetual social units having a unique *identity* that distinguishes them from other social units; an exclusive *membership* in which certain individuals are eligible or not, for given reasons; and rules of *closure* that separate members from non-members. Social units identified by the existence of these qualities are *corporate categories*. Any number of examples can be given of corporate categories in Japanese society. For example, De Vos and Wagatsuma (1966) and Brameld (1968) have both discussed the relation of *burakumin* to Japanese society, in the first case in terms of their caste-like characteristics, in the second in terms of communal interrelationships. The *burakumin* constitute a corporate category, one that exhibits within the traditional framework, nesting corporations of greater complexity (i.e. in *burakumin* hamlets) and which has, with the passing of time, begun evolving into a corporate group.

Four additional characteristics – the existence of *exclusive common affairs*, *autonomy* to turn these affairs, a set of recognised *procedures*, and some form of internal *organisation* to run the affairs – determine substantive differences between corporate units. The existence of all, or less than all, of these characteristics has different implications and requirements for the articulation of the given unit with others in the society.

It is also useful to distinguish between corporations *aggregate* in which the number of members of the corporation is greater than one, and corporation *sole*, or *offices*, in which there is only one member. Identification of corporations and their concomitants is essential for understanding the social rules in operation generally, as well as rules specific to any segment of a society.

Applying corporate analysis: ritual and festival organisation in other locales

The comparison of some of the roles played by the various component units in the ritual with those played elsewhere is instructive. It is possible to show using several examples (e.g. Akaike 1976; Davis 1977; Bestor 1985; Littleton 1986) that though the names and internal organisation of such units may differ across Japan, they fulfil similar roles in management and performance of festivals. They fulfil these roles by adopting very different procedures and processes. As noted above this has tended to obscure differences between different organisational forms in Japan in favour of overarching, general models.

The four instances of festival management come from various parts of Japan (Wakayama, Chichibu and Tokyo). They illustrate (and all of the authors have commented upon) a common principle of Japanese organisation: the interconnectedness and overlap between various groups and individuals who run the festivals. However, it is also worth pointing out structural similarities that go beyond differences in nomenclature, ritual practice, and locale.

The various units can be examined in terms of membership and recruitment, functioning, and relation with other units. I am concerned here with internal arrangements and organisation, scope of affairs, and autonomy.

Each of the examples cited above has three types of major corporate group. *Chonaikai* are civic associations, generally responsible for local government, whether informally as in Yuzawa and Miyamoto-cho (Bestor 1985: 127), or formally, as in Chichibu (Akaike 1976) Ao and Kuze (Davis 1977). *Festival associations* are corporations that manage and arrange a local festival and its ritual. *Shotenkai* are merchant associations that promote local business. Each of these types is autonomous, dealing with its affairs (within the limits of law and acceptable custom) on its own responsibility. Each of these three types differ in internal organisation. *Chonaikai* and festival associations include a number of identifiable nesting corporations: *fujinkai*, *wakamono-kai* and others. *Shotenkai* are apparently (at least based on the data here) relatively undifferentiated, with the possible exception of offices: elected head, treasurer and secretary.

This structural difference also reflects a difference in the objective of association and the basis of recruitment. *Shotenkai* are common interest associations with relatively simply goals: the promotion of business. Their membership is derived from individuals having business interests in the given community. The other two types have relatively heterogeneous aims (in the case of *chonaikai*), which must reflect, as Davis (1977: 27ff) notes, growing demands for participation by various categories in the community.

Chonaikai tend to have complex formal structures (cf. Akaike 1976: 132-9) in which various offices, their scope, and the degree of their autonomy are often clearly defined. This is not surprising. It is an implication of the fact that *chonaikai*, whatever their current legal status, must deal with, and therefore accommodate themselves to, the demands of the local civil bureaucracy even though they officially do not exist. In Yuzawa, for instance, *chonaikai* heads are careful to comply with the municipality's demands. Membership in *chonaikai* is on the basis of residence. Offices in *chonaikai* are usually filled by elderly residents of long standing. Corporations that are auxilliary to the *chonaikai* are arranged on very similar lines, but the recruitment qualifications are generally inherent qualities such as sex and age: women's associations (*fujinkai*) and elder associations (*rojinkai*) are examples.

The basis of recruitment to festival associations is more complex. This is not accidental. It reflects the real ambiguity of the shrine's status in a community, the dynamic nature of the changes that have overtaken Japanese religion over the past centuries (cf. Davis 1977b), and notably over the past fifty years (cf. Morioka 1975; Murakami 1980), the conflict of formal law and social and religious tradition, and other factors. The basis for recruitment is generally a complex of three factors. First is length of residence in the community (measured in generations), second is age, and third is interest and willingness to serve. In Yuzawa certainly, and in other places too (cf. Davis 1977a: 8–9, 16–17; Littleton 1986: 199–200) membership in festival association corporations is often voluntary. Unlike fulfilling *chonaikai* and possibly *shotenkai* duties, in which lack of participation is penalised in a number of ways, there are few explicit or implicit negative sanctions for failure to perform one's festival duties. A fourth qualifications is associated with upper-management echelons, these echelons where major policy decisions are made: this is prior service in lower-echelon group: 'When a vacancy in the ranks of the elders occurs, one of the older *sewanin* will usually be selected to fill it' (Littleton 1986: 199). It is also one of the main thrusts of Akaike's (1976) arguments: that success in lower echelons is a prerequisite for membership in upper echelons, and ultimately for a political career. The same in general is true of Yuzawa. 'Graduating' members of *wakamono-kai* (the main management group of the festival described above) are selected for membership in the Festival Preservation Association, whereupon they assume the functions of advisers and policy makers.

The complexity of festival assocations (by which is meant all the corporate units associated directly with the shrine and the running of its affairs) derives from the confluence of ritually required positions (e.g. *toban* in Ao – Davis 1977 – and *mikoshigakkari* in Daigakucho – Littleton 1986: 198–9), managerial requirements, legal stipulations that formally separate local administration from religious activity (cf. Akaike 1976) and power arrangements within any particular locale (Davis 1977: 21ff). The particular arrangements in any specific locale must be understood against the local conditions.

What is notable is that abstractable principles about the rules of membership are similar in all such groups, although the precise requirements and internal organisation of each group is different. This results presumably from local differences and historical constellations of events and individual actions. In Chichibu and Daigakucho 'promotion' is implicitly a function of age, in Yuzawa explicitly so: after the age of 42, men are expected to retire from the *wakamono-kai*.

In response to similar requirements, namely the need to run a festival, individuals *in the same society* come up with different organisational solutions. Since the analysis here is achronic, the historical circumstances of each community were no doubt quite different. But claiming historical origin and cultural continuity begs the question. Organisational forms are a response to current problems, and historical forms are modified by groups as needed. Moreover, a purely 'structural' explanation for these differences is weak as well. Yuzawa's neighbourhoods have similar socio-economic histories. Yet we find organisational differences within and between neighbourhoods. The organisational forms are chosen from a spectrum of culturally known structures, and modified according to local and individual preferences. Chichibu, Daigakucho and Yuzawa neighbourhoods all recognise the general cultural principle by which age affects position in community affairs. Yet each place, including the different Yuzawa neighbourhoods, applies that principle in different ways in response to individual and circumstantial pressure.

Implications of corporate analysis for the study of Japanese society: theoretical discussion

The ritual I have described above is affected, even within the same geographical area, by numerous factors. Its form, even when performed by some of the same people in different circumstances, exhibits significant variations. The general form remains recognisably the same, and yet the differences must be accounted for as well, particularly since they tend to be greater the farther afield one goes from any chosen point.

The general similarity of form of this ritual and others throughout Japan must not be allowed to obscure differences that might exist. The individuals and groups in each of the situations described face different circumstances and adopt different organisational forms for their needs. Though they all partake of 'Japanese culture' it does not need to mean that one single descriptive formula is appropriate for all of them.

I have described the festival management units in terms of their corporate nature because this particular analytical scheme frames this case quite well. In the first case, it reflects to a great degree the Japanese self-conception of themselves as a society of groups. By describing different types of such 'groups' in a careful manner, I have avoided the common pitfall of describing Japanese society as a 'group' society, a terminology which obscures very real differences. Moreover, as I have shown, differences in associative forms reflect on internal and external arrangements. The interaction of units with others are different and is affected by their nature. The relation of a 'group of groups' such as the *toban* with an ephemeral aggregate such as the priests is different materially from the *toban*'s relationship with an enduring, internally structured unit such as one of the *wakamono-kai*. In the one case there is little cognisance of the priests' existence as a unit beyond the ritual requirements. The priests do not, for instance, attend the final feast after the festival; nor are they invited to the self-criticism meetings – *hansei-kai* – that take place after the festival, though the *guji* is. In the other case individual *wakamono-kai* can and do make representations to the *toban* which materially affect its performance.

The descriptive power of critically examining the nature of social units enhances the ability to analyse observed events. The ritual primacy of the young boy (he offers an evergreen immediately after the *guji*) reflects a historical reality about the economics of the Yuzawa festival. This may be contrasted with the diminishing role of the former-owner representatives (the *jigannushi*). The young boy is always a grandchild of the nominal *sai-cho*. Among the *jigannushi* however, some of the former intendants have passed over their responsibilities to distant kin and even to neighbours. This reflects the actual and recognised diminution of the *jigannushi* role. *Jigannushi* is a local name for the type of shrine-owner association called *kabuza* which have been prevalent all over Japan. If we look further afield at the same phenomenon we can see that in many cases nation-wide, former owners of shrines and objects of worship (*shintai*) are passing their reponsibilities on to others, usually to neighbourhood associations. Specific cases can be examined against changes in the economic fortunes of families and members of these associations. Thus the Yuzawa case exemplifies in ritual form what amounts to a national trend, signifying a true cultural change.

Viewing Japanese society in terms of interconnected corporate units also helps avoid the assumption that Japanese society is homogenous throughout. As I have shown, overemphasis on single general models of Japanese society, such as Nakane (1970), leads to an obscuration of the differences implicit even in social forms that are labelled similar. That is, 'groups', even in the same organisational matrix (business firms, for example), are not necessarily the same phenomena. The consequences of these differences reflect on our ability to understand Japanese society whether as a whole or in parts.

Corporate analysis steers a course between viewing Japanese society as a 'group society' and between its internal complexities. The overemphasis on Japan as a 'group society', as Befu (1980) notes, is greatly misleading. However, in contrast to Befu, I am not proposing an alternative model or models, but rather an alternative way of examining the group phenomenon which is undeniably significant, not the least in that the Japanese themselves insist on seeing the group as a primary social form.

Corporate analysis, like any focused analytical tool, has stringent limitations. It is possible to demonstrate its utility in dealing with structured groups such as those discussed above. It is more difficult to analyse the limitations of an analytical system when it tries to address issues for which it is not fitted. In an earlier paper (Ashkenazi 1985) I discussed the ways in which shrine priests in Yuzawa maintain a coherent attitude *notwithstanding* not constituting a coherent group. Here I have avoided dealing with the internal arrangements made between the priests on an individual basis because these are not readily amenable to analysis in the terms used for enduring corporate bodies. It has yet to be shown how these two social levels, that of enduring, definable, corporate bodies, and that of ephemeral or ego-centred networks (Barnes 1972), non-groups (Boissevain 1968), or quasi-groups (Mayer 1977) can be interrelated analytically.

Corporate analysis represents an approach between grand theories of Japanese society (e.g. Nakane's) which may be empirically problematic and micro-analyses of specific events which rarely yield generalisable propositions. It represents a step towards what Merton (1967) has called 'mid-range theory'. Mid-range theories permit insights into the general workings of a society while remaining firmly anchored, and what is more important, based, on empirical data that relates to a specific 'locale': a type of event, organisation, group, or stratum in a society. On such a basis it is possible to evolve a paradigm that partly or wholly represents the society in question. Such a paradigm is not attempted here. It remains, however, to attempt to move corporate analysis to the position of being able to generate mid-range theory of human association.

Conclusions

The examples given here of a method for analysing festival management are equally valid to other comparable data in Japanese society, though not *all* data is so orderable. The analytic medium confines itself specifically to one level of generality; that of organised groups. In very broad and general terms Japanese society may be conceived of as a series of interconnected corporate units, each one exhibiting its own autonomy to some given degree. It is possible, in other spheres of life, to compare aspects of other corporations as I have done for ritual corporations.

I intentionally used the terms 'units' throughout so as not to prejudice the issue, and so as to be able to emphasise similarities and differences between different yet interacting phenomena. Broadly speaking, at one level human behaviour is conceptualised as a series of individual decisions (e.g. Barth 1981), with individual 'networks' (e.g. Boissevain 1968; Barnes 1972) tying people together in information and action networks which may become semi-permanent as 'quasi-groups' (e.g. Mayer 1977). At a more general level, the analysis is concerned with the arrangement of groups and permanent structures (Parsons 1951; Fortes 1969). At a further abstract level the unit of analysis is conceived of as a broader unit – a culture, a stratum, or general category – in which case structural variables are very general, and decision making and interaction can be seen solely as the sum aggregate of actions within the unit of analysis.

In the case of Japan, many of the analyses of *Japanese society* have tended to describe Japan in terms of the most abstractable level, while presenting data from specific loci. Examples are Nakane (1970) and Vogel (1965) whose descriptions of one aspect of business or social relationships are translated into general paradigms of Japanese society or major parts of it, obscuring differences within data and within Japanese society. In the same vein, Benedict (1946) – a long disputed but still powerful paradigm of Japanese society – obscures similarities between Japan and other societies by the emphasis of unique concepts current (but not necessarily omnipresent) in Japanese culture and thought. In other words, when dealing with Japan, the risk of confusing the levels of analysis has proved to be great.

Considering Japanese society in terms of a set of interrelated corporate units does not exhaust the analytical possibilities. Nor is it intended to. It does allow detailed comparisons of purportedly similar institutions in Japanese society and the similarities and differences between them. From the results it is possible to devise a theoretical explanation for the forms observed and for the different ways they interact with their environments. Flexible as such an analysis may be, it does not and cannot purport to present the only or the 'true' picture of Japanese society. It must be recognised that this form of analysis is intentionally confined to only one level of society. Other cultural factors such as the ideology which drives the ritual performance are not reflected in it unless they are expressed by the actions of corporation units.

Corporate analysis must be seen therefore as one important tool for understanding a society. Inasmuch as it addresses only one level of human life, it has restrictions. The Japanese case is particularly significant. The nature of Japanese society is such that there are numerous corporate units with similar goals, functions and internal arrangements throughout the society. These often differ in only one variable from others in the same social institution. Japanese society is, potentially at least, a laboratory in which it may be possible to go beyond mere description of differences. By comparing corporations of the same type which vary in a single aspect of their corporate nature it may be possible to generate statements about corporate analysis which will form the basis for a general dynamic social theory of interactions.

Note

1. The research on which this paper is based was supported by a Japan Foundation Dissertation Fellowship. I am grateful to the Foundation for its support.

References

Akaike, N. 1976. Festival and neighborhood association. *Japanese Journal of Religious Studies* 3 (2), 127–74.

Ashkenazi, M. 1985. Priests, carpenters, and household heads: ritual experts in Japan. *Ethnology* 24 (4), 297–306.

Ashkenazi, M. 1987. Religious conflict in a Japanese town, or is it? Paper presented at the Hebrew University Seminar on Conflict Resolution in Japan, Jerusalem, January 1987.

Barnes, J. A. 1972. *Social Networks*. New York: Addison-Wesley.

Barth, F. 1981. *Process and Form in Social Life*. London: Routledge & Kegan Paul.

Befu, H. 1980. A critique of the group model of Japanese society. *Social Analysis* 5 (6), 29–43.

Befu, H. and Plotnicov, L. 1968. Types of unilineal descent groups. In

Readings in Anthropology, ed. Morton Fried, Vol. 2, pp. 382–97. New York: Thomas Crowell.

Benedict, R. 1946. *The Chrysanthemum and the Sword*. Boston: Houghton Mifflin.

Bestor, T. 1985. Tradition and Japanese social organization: institutional development in a Tokyo neighborhood. *Ethnology* 24 (2), 121–36.

Boissevain, J. 1968. The place of non-groups in the social sciences. *Man* 3, 542–56.

Brameld, T. 1968. *Japan: Culture, Education and Change in Two Communities*. New York: Holt, Rinehart & Winston.

Brandt, V. 1974. Skiing cross-culturally. *Current Anthropology* 15 (1), 64–6.

Brown, D. 1974. Corporations and social classification. *Current Anthropology* 15 (1), 29–52.

Brown, D. 1984. More on corporations. *American Ethnologist* 11 (4), 813–15.

Cochrane, G. 1971. Use of the concept of the 'corporation': a choice between colloquialism or distortion. *American Anthropologist* 73 (5), 1145–50.

Davis, W. B. 1976. Parish guilds and political culture in village Japan. *Journal of Asian Studies* 35 (1), 25–36.

Davis, W. B. 1977a. The *miyaza* and the fishermen: ritual status in coastal villages of Wakayama prefecture. *Asian Folklore Studies* 36 (2), 1–29.

Davis, W. B. 1977b. *Toward Modernity: a Developmental Typology of Popular Religious Affiliation in Japan*. Ithaca, NY: Cornell East Asia Papers No. 12.

De Vos, G. and Wagatsuma, H. 1966. *Japan's Invisible Race*. Los Angeles and Berkeley: University of California Press.

Dore, R. 1958. *City Life in Japan*. London: Routledge & Kegan Paul.

Dore, R. 1978. *Shinohata*. New York: Pantheon Books.

Dow, J. 1973. On the muddled concept of corporation in anthropology. *American Anthropologist* 75 (3), 904–8.

Fortes, M. 1953. The structure of unilineal descent groups. *American Anthropologist* 55, 17–41.

Fortes, M. 1969. *Kinship and the Social Order*. London: Routledge & Kegan Paul.

Fukutake, T. 1962. *Man and Society in Japan*. Tokyo: University of Tokyo Press.

Fukutake, T. 1967. *Japanese Rural Society*. Ithaca, NY: Cornell University Press.

Goodenough, W. 1971. Corporations: reply to Cochrane. *American Anthropologist* 73 (5), 1150–2.

Havens, T. 1982. *Artist and Patron in Postwar Japan*. Princeton, NJ: Princeton University Press.

Irokawa, D. 1975. The survival struggle of the Japanese community. *The Japan Interpreter* 9 (4), 465–94.

Ishida, E. 1974. *Japanese Culture: a Study of Origins and Characteristics*. Honolulu: University Press of Hawaii.

Littleton, C. S. 1974. The organization and management of a Tokyo Shinto shrine festival. *Ethnology* 25 (3), 195–202.

Maine, H. 1931. *Ancient Law*. London: John Murray.

Mayer, A. 1977. The significance of quasi-groups in the study of complex societies. In *Friends, Followers, and Factions*, ed. S. Schmidt *et al.*, pp. 43–54. Berkeley: University of California Press.

Merton, R. 1967. *On Theoretical Sociology*. New York: The Free Press.

Morioka, K. 1975. The impact of suburbanization on Shinto belief and behavior. In *Religion in Changing Japanese Society*, ed. K. Morioka. Tokyo: University of Tokyo Press.

Murakami, S. 1980. *Japanese Religion in the Modern Century*. Tokyo: University of Tokyo.

Nakane, C. 1970. *Japanese Society*. Berkeley: University of California.

Parsons, T. 1951. *The Social System*. Chicago: The Free Press.

Rohlen, T. 1974. *For Harmony and Strength: Japanese White-Collar Organization in Anthropological Perspective*. Los Angeles and Berkeley: University of California Press.

Smith, H. D. 1973. The tyranny of Tokyo in modern Japanese culture. In *Studies in Japanese Culture*, ed. Japan PEN Club, pp. 367–71. Tokyo: Japan PEN Club.

Smith, M. G. 1974. *Corporations and Society*. Chicago: Aldine.

Vogel, E. 1965. *Japan's New Middle Class*. Berkeley: University of California Press.

Weber, M. 1947. *The Theory of Social and Economic Organization*. New York: Oxford University Press.

Wrapping up:
some general implications

The moiety system of anthropology and the study of Japan

Each essay in this collection tells its own story and draws its own conclusions. In this chapter it may prove useful to add another editorial voice in order to underline further some of the implications of each contribution as well as to point to the significance of the book as a whole.

The essays presented in this collection represent attempts at showing how the study of Japanese society, or aspects of this society, may contribute to anthropological theory and understanding. Borrowing from Hendry's piece, this task has been formulated as one of 'unwrapping': that is, a process by which each 'revelation' of Japan or a thing Japanese has been related to wider problems and questions prevalent in contemporary anthropological discourse. This kind of undertaking, however, raises a number of problems that have to do with the 'analytical status' of cases taken from a specific (geographical) 'area' of study within more general sociological or anthropological theories. To put this by way of the Japanese example, specific cases may be used in three ways in relation to social theory. First, a given piece may take as its prime focus a certain theoretical, or interpretative problem and use a case taken from the Japanese context in order to test or explore this problem. Second, a paper may take as its focus a Japanese case and mobilise certain conceptual or interpretative frameworks in order to highlight the special characteristics of the case. Third, a contribution may take as its centre of interest a certain theoretical or hermeneutical formulation *about Japan* and utilise an example taken from that society in order to examine this formulation. These are subtle distinctions, yet ones that bear directly upon the type of analyses we set out to do and upon the kinds of contribution we can make to wider intellectual currents in the humanities and the social sciences.

A claim about the theoretical or interpretative aims of this collection, however, should be seen against the background of a division that still marks our discipline. 'The moiety system of anthropology' is the metaphor Service (1985: chap. 19) has suggested in order to evoke both the differentiation *and* the relatedness between two intellectual 'camps' in anthropology: those who view anthropology as part of the natural sciences and those who see it as part of the humanities. This 'dual organisation' has been represented by a variety of oppositions such as generalisation v. relativism, the comparative method v. holism, social structure v. culture, determinism v. individualism, or the organismic analogy as against the language analogy (of society). Indeed, these kinds of oppositions can be traced back to the Kroeber–Lowie controversy in America and to the Radcliffe-Brown and Evans-Pritchard confrontation in England. As Holy (1987: 1) puts it, this is a contrast between two approaches to a prime objective of anthropology: the description of other cultures. This is a contrast, in other words, between description of particular societies as a means – via the comparative method – to generalisation, or description itself as the key task which need not lead to generalisation.

Despite pronouncements to the contrary (Rabinow and Sullivan 1987), the debates arising out of these differing approaches are still very much alive, as the recent exchange between Geertz (1984) and Spiro (1986) proves. Moreover, to add a note of candour to the argument, many of us who harbour doubts about 'who are we' intellectually (Service 1985: 287) are at times so uncertain or inconsistent as to follow or discard often irreconcilable models at different stages of our career. Why then present anthropology through a metaphor of two camps, a pair of moieties? Essentially, I would suggest that the use of such a metaphor may be, in Tambiah's (1966) words, 'good to think'. By this I do not wish to imply that the various dichotomies through which anthropologists have presented themselves conflate into one basic opposition around which we can 'pigeon-hole' any scholarly study. They do not. What I do suggest may allow us to better appreciate the kinds of aims, assumptions and methods of analysis which characterise different works. Along these lines in this concluding chapter I will deal with each of the essays presented here as it bears upon a particular moiety (and its 'problematique') and hence as it pertains to the relationship between the study of Japan and anthropology.

222

The 'hard moiety: comparison and generalisation

The 'harder' – at times termed 'positivistic' – part of anthropology has subscribed to a rather specifically scientific view of the theoretical relations between description, comparison and generalisation: description (following Holy 1987: 2) provides the facts while the comparative method is used in order to account for them. According to this view, description is seen as the means for formulating and testing hypotheses or generalisations which are valid not only for one specific society or culture, but also cross-culturally. Given this viewpoint, what is it about Japan or cases taken from the Japanese context that may make them useful or interesting for testing theories, generating hypotheses, or making comparative analyses?

Ashkenazi's contribution (Chap. 11) comes closest to dealing with these kinds of questions. His paper represents an attempt to show how Japanese society – or more precisely certain Japanese organisational forms – may be used in order to generate and test hypotheses derived from corporate theory. This methodological operation is carried out with the aim of reaching a number of generalisations about the function of corporate groups in this society. The method Ashkenazi chooses to work with is essentially comparative. By focusing on a number of roughly similar communal organisations (that is, by keeping constant as many variables as possible) he is able to explain the differences between them in terms of the operation of diverging local and individual preferences.

His contribution to theory is twofold. First, he underlines how certain characteristics of the Japanese case – for instance the existence of comparable social-structural arrangements in a variety of localities, or the basic similarity of religious beliefs throughout the society – make it amenable to a rigorous operational definition of variables and to their causal or functional correlation. Second, he shows how on the basis of this kind of hypothesis testing one can, as a number of scholars studying this society have argued (Sofue 1960: 312; Bennett 1970: 16), generalise to a wider range of organisational forms found in Japan. Ashkenazi shows us how a careful selection and comparison of the phenomena under study may make findings in regard to one or two segments appropriately representative of wider social sectors.

Yoshida's piece (Chap. 4) is an elegant exemplification of not only how a number of hypotheses derived from a theory developed elsewhere may be tested through the Japanese case, but how this testing may lead back to a modification or an alteration of the original theory. In using Japan as a site for a sort of 'quasi-experiment' (Campbell and Stanley 1963) he follows Beidelman's (1970: 510–11) older and Parkin's (1987) more recent arguments about the utility of intra-societal or intra-regional comparisons. This is because it is in this kind of comparative treatment that variables may be more clearly appreciated and controlled. The wider implication of Yoshida's analysis lies in his use of the crucial Okinawan case – within the general confines of the Japanese cultural region – in order to explore Mary Douglas's theory about the link between social structure and cosmology. His analysis shows that Douglas's sociology of knowledge – as expressed, for example, in the hypothesis about social contexts as predictors of the clarity of pollution beliefs – should be modified in order to take into account the relative 'independence' of ideas and beliefs. In other words, Yoshida furthers our understanding of how symbolic constructs are not just vague conceptualisations which merely reflect some kind of underlying social order, but are rather critical parts of the formation of this order (Yengoyan 1981: 325). In other words, he exemplifies through a concrete analysis what Sahlins (1976) has termed the 'autonomy' of culture and symbols.

Yoshida's essay, however, well highlights another point which is of significance for theory building and the study of Japan. This point is related to the question of how one can generalise, and to what one can generalise from a single case – that of Japan. What one must realise is that case studies are generalisable to theoretical propositions and *not* to populations or universes (Yin 1984: 21). This is a point sorely missed by many who devote themselves to the harder methodologies and who tend to view case studies as somehow weaker, less dependable, strategies for research. The Japanese case in Yoshida's analysis thus does not represent a 'sample'. His aim is to expand and generalise a theory (an analytic generalisation) and not ultimately to enumerate frequencies (a statistical generalisation).

It is along similar lines that Valentine's discussion (Chap. 3) of marginality should be seen. In the first place, his essay exemplifies how a study of the marginal, the deviant, or the liminal can reveal not only hitherto disregarded aspects of mainstream society, but how it can also promote an understanding of how the whole society – marginal *and* mainstream – works (Ben-Yehuda 1985: chap. 6). This seems to be an especially important point with regard to Japan, which has been populated for more than a generation of sociological thinking with such typical mainstream characters as the Organisation Man and his mate, the Professional Housewife (Plath 1983: 4). In this sense, just as Hane's (1982) book can be read as a 'complement' to the conventional portrayals of Japan's modernisation, so can Valentine's chapter be read as an alternative (counterpart) to present-day representations of this society.

On a more general level, Valentine shows how the specific case of Japan – or more precisely a number of its social attributes – allows one to explore a number of theoretical problems that have to do with marginality. In other words, the relatively highly developed ideas of purity and pollution and the emphasis on proper social forms alongside the accompanying exploration and use of ambiguity in religion and the arts which are found in Japanese society make it a fruitful case through which to study some of the following issues: the relations between the marginal and the mainstream, the limits of belonging to social groups, the 'symbolic' potential for inter-group mobility, or the types of strategies people use in order to cope with their marginal status. To reiterate, the study of a single case may limit the strength or range of general or comparative arguments (Kennedy 1979: 671). Yet such a study precludes neither a delineation of the relevant attributes of the case on the basis of which it may be compared to other instances, nor an exploration of the theoretical problems it raises.

Hendry's essay (Chap. 2) relates to anthropological and sociological theory in a different way. Her contribution does not lie in a systematic application of concepts nor in a careful testing of hypotheses. Rather, it should be seen as an imaginative suggestion that we explore the fruitfulness and utility of a stimulating analytical metaphor: the social processes of wrapping and unwrapping. Hendry begins by showing how ubiquitous the 'wrapping' principle is in Japanese society: in language, non-verbal behaviour, dress, food, gifts, or architecture for example. She goes on, however, to suggest that this principle may provide a way to interrelate the analyses and findings of such diverse theoretical frameworks as sociolinguistics (Brown and Levinson 1977), transactionalism (Kapferer 1976), dramaturgical approaches (Goffman 1974), or (following Moeran's comments in the introductory essay) studies of the creation of international images (Schiffrin 1986). Indeed, in one way or another, Hendry's insights permeate all of the papers presented in this volume as well as providing it with its title.

Methodologically, Kalland's paper (Chap. 10) represents a contribu-

225

tion to a relatively underdeveloped scholarly tradition within the anthropological study of Japan: the linking of anthropology and history (Bennett 1970: 15; cf. also Silverman 1979: 413). In this regard Kalland's analysis should be seen as one with such studies as Smith's (1960) on pre-industrial urbanism, Befu's (1965) on village autonomy, or Kelly's (1985a) on deference and demeanour. All of these works represent careful attemps to unite the more analytical formulations of problems found in anthropology with a sophisticated handling of Japanese historical data.

Of greater scholarly significance, however, is the connection that Kalland makes between his study and one of the most underdeveloped areas in the social scientific study of Japan: applied anthropology. Indeed, the conclusions of Norbeck and Parman (1970: 3) two decades ago still seem to stand: almost no research on social problems in Japan has been carried out by Western anthropologists. Yet unlike the majority of anthropologists around the world who do this kind of applied work (Britain 1978; Willner 1980; Goldschmidt 1986: 2), and who are usually oriented to the formulation of policies or to fostering official awareness of the values and social systems of the people they serve, Kalland's discussion provides something more. He is interested not only in the application of theory to specific practical cases, but also in what impact a study in applied anthropology can have for anthropological theory. In brief, Kalland suggests a basic reconceptualisation in Western theories of maritime anthropology. By carefully placing the Japanese case *vis-à-vis* the Western one, he shows how these theories (which have been derived from a wider Western conception of an 'open sea') have tended to disregard not only indigenous concepts of fishing rights, but also the potential for managing marine resources through a concept of limited resources (the 'closed sea').

At this juncture it would do well to echo a remark Moeran made in Chapter 1. Kalland's theoretical contribution may be more fully recognised through the suggestion that his paper be read alongside the works of such people as Lock (1980, 1987) on medicine or Reynolds (1980) on psycho-therapy (although these latter works do not represent applied anthropology in the strict sense of the term). Kalland's chapter, like these other works, suggests the need for a more holistic approach to human ecology: in his case in order to understand how both Western and indigenous Japanese concepts may contribute together to the workings of sea tenure and management systems. All these kinds of works – which are based on the practicalities of medicine, psycho-therapy and fishing respectively – encourage us to rethink our general theoretical models.

The 'soft moeity': towards adequate description and representation

The 'softer' interpretative anthropology has been driven by a basic realisation that at times 'the social sciences require different methods of inquiry from those used in natural science investigations due to the subjective quality of social phenomena' (Holy 1987: 5). If the aim of more 'positivistically' inclined anthropologists is to arrive – through the use of the comparative method – at cross-culturally valid generalisations, the problem facing interpretatively inclined scholars is how to 'adequately describe' the phenomena studied. The emphasis within this tradition has thus come to be placed on 'producing accounts of specific culture which do not alter the cultural reality studied through the imposition of criteria external to it' (Holy 1987: 8).

Tanaka's essay (Chap. 5) falls squarely within this interpretative tradition. By linking a sociolinguistic analysis of advertisements to some basic theoretical contentions about power and subordination, she shows how the language used by advertisers forms part of the process by which certain groups of Japanese women are manipulated. The wider implications of her analysis lie not only in her exemplification of how hidden assumptions about unequal relations seep into communication and thereby contribute to the reproduction of these very relations. On a deeper level she demonstrates how this process holds even when one 'goes international'. Tanaka does this through a delicate analysis of how foreign (especially English) words are taken out of their original contexts to become part of the Japanese discourse defining social relations. In this course these words are transformed to fit the 'cultural logic' of Japanese discourse. Moreover, this kind of analysis seems all the more important today when many Japanese are emphasising a need for the 'internationalisation' of society (Befu 1981; Goodman Chap. 9). Tanaka's discussion would thus caution any over simple promotion of such aims.

The paper by Martinez (Chap. 6) is a sustained attempt to deal with what Cohen (1984: 379) in a comprehensive review has characterised as a major omission in the literature on tourism: the nature and dynamics of the tourist–local relationship. The discussion of how Kuzaki turned into a tourist-centre underlines three points of theoretical significance. First, it

227

questions the quite common scholarly portrayal of the locals as passive 'dupes' of commercialism: that is, as being passively manipulated by organisations outside of the locality and with no recourse even to developing their own uses of what these organisations provide. By contrast, Martinez describes Kuzaki's inhabitants as actors highly cognisant of the threats and opportunities posed by the development of their village as a leisure resort, and as very active in the creation of what MacCannell (1973) has termed 'staged authenticity' in which they 'play the natives'.

The second point is related to Valentine's suggestions (Chap. 3) about the utility of studying the marginal. Martinez shows how the analysis of a marginal group – and the Kuzakians are in more than one sense at the periphery of Japanese society – may illuminate the special cultural dynamics of what Kelly (1985b) has characterised as Japan's 'new middle class'. What her analysis shows is how Kuzaki's touristic image – that special mix of exoticism and tradition, of eroticism and nostalgia – feeds upon *and* recreates the processes by which this new class has come to define itself. Finally, Martinez well cautions us as to the seriousness with which this class is undertaking the search for 'non-serious' leisure activities. As Plath (1969: 128) has put it 'the search is not some simple craving for personal or social paroxysm, though that may be part of it. It is a search for forms of play that an adult can take seriously.'

Underlying the analyses of Tanaka and Martinez lies another question which has to do with anthropological understanding in general and an understanding of Japanese society in particular. Joseph M. Kitagawa (1987: 294), the historian of religion, has formulated this issue:

> Today there is a feeling in quarters in Japan that it is almost impossible for foreign scholars to understand Japanese culture and religions. Here the question lies in what kinds and levels of understanding are involved . . . Japanese culture, like other great cultures, has an enduring individuality with its own history, language, art, religious tradition . . . thus, in a sense only those who live within Japanese culture and society can fully understand the mystique of Japan, although not every Japanese attains such a lofty goal. On the other hand, a disciplined foreign scholar can experience the structure and attain a certain kind and level of understanding.

Given that one agrees with Kitagawa's conclusions – and I think that most anthropologists would – the problem of the anthropological understanding of Japan does not end with an individual's potential for comprehension or familiarity. The issue, being a *social* one, becomes one of how an individual's understanding is grounded in and conveyed to colleagues, be they area specialists or otherwise. This realisation is far from being a methodologically trivial one, for it raises the problem of textual representation. In other words, it raises the problem of how we construct ethnographic texts that adequately communicate, portray, or impart the experience of a specific culture to other scholars. The chapters by Ben-Ari, Goodman and Moeran all deal with this issue.

Ben-Ari (Chap. 8) devotes his analysis to the literary and aesthetic possibilities for ethnographic presentation that can be found in such non-Western societies as Japan. He shows that the use of indigenous Japanese literary genres in the construction of ethnographies may have a certain special potential. Their use may allow the evocation of experiences, or the discussion of certain ambiguous issues, in ways that are usually limited either by conventional norms of ethnographic portrayal or even by some of the post-modern literary forms, be they of the dialogic (Tedlock 1983) or essay (Tyler 1986) varieties.

Goodman's analysis (Chap. 9) exemplifies and extends some of the implications of what Marcus and Fischer (1986) have termed the 'crisis of representation' which anthropology now faces. As they (1986: 8) aptly put it, the key feature of this crisis 'is the loosening of the hold over fragmented communities of either specific totalizing visions or a general paradigmatic style of organizing research'. This 'crisis of representation' has thus emerged out of the uncertainties and doubts many of us hold about what are the adequate means for describing reality. Goodman's telling account lets us share in his uncertainties and doubts by describing how he 'moved through' – and was, of course, 'moved by' – a number of theoretical positions in regard to the phenomena of returnee schoolchildren. What he goes on to illuminate, however, is not only the essential partiality of each position and its limitations in accounting for this social phenomenon. More importantly, Goodman goes on to raise a set of difficulties that the recent preoccupation with textuality has hardly faced: the ethical implications of anthropology's 'crisis of representation'. Goodman thus echoes Kalland's emphasis on the importance of applied anthropology, but from a totally different perspective. Such questions as 'whom do we serve' (Besag 1983) are placed through his essay under a new light. As Goodman stresses, these have not just become questions about the various authorities – without *and* within academia – that we serve. On a deeper level these are problems that have to do with the 'fit' between different types of anthropological knowledge and various authoritative positions. In other words, these are questions about how to relate an anthropologist's changing perspectives on the world with the more stable interests and rules of conduct of different institutions.

Moeran's Chapter 7 can be read on two levels, each of which includes a number of implications for anthropology. On one level this piece is a personal account of Moeran's experience in the art world of Japanese ceramics. As such an account, however, it does not represent a retrogression into private musings or intimate thoughts. Rather, Moeran's personal learning process in the field (Yengoyan 1981: 325) is used in order to illuminate and to go beyond conventional views of artistic production. The analysis of the social processes which accompanied the preparations for and execution of a ceramics exhibition contributes to an understanding of the different 'values' – aesthetic, commercial and social – which underlie decisions about the essentially arbitrary worth of artistic objects.

On another level – and Moeran has made this point explicitly in Chapter 1 – his account can be read as an allegory of the anthropological world. As such an allegory, Moeran's piece would seem to invite us to dwell on the kinds of social and political processes which underlie the creation of anthropological knowledge. In other words, Moeran would seem to be encouraging anthropologists to begin to dwell not only on the actual construction of texts. Or, as Sangren (1988: 407) puts it, the 'anthropological analysis of the authority of ethnography must specify the conditions of ethnography's production and reproduction in society, especially academic institutions, not just texts'.

What essentially I am arguing for is the need to add to our recently heightened awareness of the problems of textual authority, a greater mindfulness of the problems of *social* authority within anthropology. This is because the discourse with our research subjects is ultimately subordinated to the discourse (hidden assumptions, language, or intellectual agendas for instance) of the discipline. Since so few of us become 'popularisers' – like the sociologists Vogel (1979) or White (1986) – it is primarily on the basis of our superiors' and peers' reactions that our ideas (and through them ourselves) are evaluated and allowed into the public arenas of disciplinary debate. Against the background of the explosive growth in academia of Japanese Studies in the last decade or so, might it be that the anthropological study of Japan act as a test case for the analysis of the competition and co-operation which underlie the production and propagation of certain views of Japanese society?

For all of this, however, because such issues bear upon our careers (and the stakes we have in them), it would seem difficult for such a sociology of anthropological knowledge to be carried out by 'regular' members of our discipline. Perhaps it will be written in any of a number of alternative ways: through parables (Flannery 1982), novels (Bowen 1964), historical studies (Silverman 1981), or personal reminiscences by eminent members of our profession (Leach 1984). Or, let me suggest a peculiarly Japanese genre of unmasking authority: would we not benefit from the work of a number of *manzai*-artists (comic diologists). Could groups of these comedians, each of which may represent its own moiety, expose at one and the same time both the 'naturalness' and the arbitrariness of our profession's dual organisation.

References

Befu, H. 1965. Village autonomy and articulation with the state. *Journal of Asian Studies* 25 (1), 19–32.

Befu, H. 1981. Internationalisation of Japan and *Nihon Bunkaron*. In *The Challenge of Japan's Internationalization: Organization and Culture*, ed. H. Wagatsuma and G. De Vos, pp. 232–66. Tokyo: Kodansha.

Beidelman, T. O. 1970. Some sociological implications of culture. In *Theoretical Sociology: Perspectives and Developments*, ed. J. C. McKinney and E. Tiriyakian, pp. 499–527. New York: Appleton.

Bennett, J. W. 1970. Some observations on Western anthroplogical research on Japan. *Rice University Studies* 56 (4), 11–28.

Ben-Yehuda, N. 1985. *Deviance and Moral Boundaries*. Chicago: University of Chicago Press.

Besag, F. 1983. Whom do we serve? A short discussion on freedom, justice and power in educational research. *Anthropology and Education Quarterly* 14 (1), 81–4.

Bowen, E. S. 1964. *Return to Laughter*. New York: Anchor.

Britain, G. M. 1978. The place of anthropology in program evaluation. *Anthropological Quarterly* 51, 119–28.

Brown, P. and Levinson, S. C. 1977. Universals in language usage: politeness phenomena. In *Questions and Politeness*, ed. E. Goody, pp. 56–289. Cambridge: Cambridge University Press.

Campbell, D. T. and Stanley, J. C. 1963. *Experimental and Quasi-Experimental Designs for Research*. Chicago: Rand McNally.

Cohen, E. 1984. The sociology of tourism: approaches, issues, and findings. *Annual Review of Sociology* 10, 373–92.

Flannery, K. V. 1982. The golden Marshalltown: a parable for the archaeology of the 1980s. *American Anthropologist* 84, 265–78.

Geertz, C. 1984. Anti anti-relativism. *American Anthropologist* 86 (2), 263–78.

Goffman, E. 1974. *Frame Analysis*. Harmondsworth: Penguin.

Goldschmidt, W. 1986. *Anthropology and Public Policy: a Dialogue*. Washington, DC: Special Publication of the American Anthropological Association Number 21.

Hane, M. 1982. *Peasants, Rebels, and Outcastes: the Underside of Modern Japan*. New York: Pantheon.

Holy, L. 1987. Introduction: Description, generalization and comparison: two paradigms. In *Comparative Anthropology*, ed. L. Holy, pp. 1–21. Oxford: Blackwell.

Kapferer, B. (ed.) 1976. *Transaction and Meaning*. Philadelphia: ISHI.

Kelly, W. W. 1985a. *Deference and Defiance in Nineteenth-Century Japan*. Princeton, NJ: Princeton University Press.

Kelly, W. W. 1985b. Rationalization and nostalgia: cultural dynamics of new middle-class Japan. *American Ethnologist* 13 (4), 603–18.

Kennedy, M. M. 1979. Generalizing from single case studies. *Evaluation Quarterly* 3 (4), 661–78.

Kitagawa, J. M. 1987. *On Understanding Japanese Religion*. Princeton, NJ: Princeton University Press.

Leach, E. R. 1984. Glimpses of the unmentionable in the history of British social anthropology. *Annual Review of Anthropology* 13, 1–23.

Lock, M. M. 1980. *East Asian Medicine in Urban Japan: Varieties of Medical Experience*. Los Angeles and Berkeley: University of California Press.

Lock, M. M. 1987. Introduction: Health and medical care as cultural and social phenomena. In *Health, Illness and Medical Care in Japan: Cultural and Social Dimensions*, ed. E. Norbeck and M. Lock, pp. 1–23. Honolulu: University of Hawaii Press.

MacCannell, D. 1973. Staged authenticity: arrangements of social space in a tourist setting. *American Journal of Sociology* 79 (3), 589–603.

Marcus, G. E. and Fischer, M. M. J. 1986. *Anthropology as Cultural Critique: an Experimental Moment in the Human Sciences*. Chicago: University of Chicago Press.

Norbeck, E. and Parman, S. 1970. Introduction. *Rice University Studies*

56 (4), 1–8.

Parkin, D. 1987. Comparison as the search for continuity. In *Comparative Anthropology*, ed. L. Holy, pp. 52–69. Oxford: Blackwell.

Plath, D. W. 1969. *The After Hours*. Berkeley: University of California Press.

Plath, D. W. 1983. Life is just a job resume? In *Work and Lifecourse in Japan*, ed. D. W. Plath, pp. 1–13. Albany: State University of New York Press.

Rabinow, P. and Sullivan, W. M. 1987. The interpretive turn: a second look. In *Interpretive Social Science: a Second Look*, idem. (eds). pp. 1–30. Berkeley: University of California Press.

Reynolds, D. K. 1980. *The Quiet Therapies: Japanese Pathways to Personal Growth*. Honolulu: University of Hawaii Press.

Sahlins, M. 1976. *Culture and Practical Reason*. Chicago: University of Chicago Press.

Sangren, S. P. 1988. Rhetoric and the authority of ethnography: 'postmodernism' and the social reproduction of texts. *Current Anthropology* **29** (3), 405–35.

Schiffrin, H. Z. 1986. The response and reaction of east Asia to its scholarly study by the west. *Comparative Civilizations Review* **13/14**, 253–65.

Service, E. R. 1985. *A Century of Controversy: Ethnological Issues from 1860 to 1960*. Orlando, Fla: Academic Press.

Silverman, S. 1979. The uses of history as anthropology: the *Palio* of Siena. *American Ethnologist* **6** (3), 413–36.

Silverman, S. 1981. *Totems and Teachers: Perspectives on the History of Anthropology*. New York: Columbia University Press.

Smith, R. J. 1960. Pre-industrial Japan: a consideration of multiple traditions in a feudal society. *Economic Development and Cultural Change* **9** (1), 241–57.

Sofue, T. 1960. Japanese studies by American anthropologists: review and evaluation. *American Anthropologist* **62**, 306–17.

Spiro, M. E. 1986. Cultural relativism and the future of anthropology. *Cultural Anthropology* **1** (3), 259–86.

Tambiah, S. J. 1966. Animals are good to think and good to prohibit. *Ethnology* **8** (4), 423–59.

Tedlock, D. 1983. *The Spoken Word and the World of Interpretation*. Philadelphia: University of Philadelphia Press.

Tyler, S. A. 1986. Post-modern ethnography: from document of the occult to occult document. In *Writing Culture: The Poetics and Politics of Ethnography*, ed. J. Clifford and G. E. Marcus, pp. 122–40. Los Angeles and Berkeley: University of California Press.

Vogel, E. F. 1979. *Japan as Number One: Lessons for America.* Tokyo: Tuttle.

White, M. M. 1986. *The Japanese Educational Challenge.* New York: The Free Press.

Willner, D. 1980. For whom the bell tolls: anthropologists advising on public policy. *American Anthropologist* 82 (1), 79–94.

Yengoyan, A. A. 1981. Cultural forms and a theory of constraints. In *The Imagination of Reality: Essays on Southeast Asian Coherence Systems*, ed. A. L. Becker and A. A. Yengoyan, pp. 325–30. Norwood, NJ: Ablex.

Yin, R. K. 1984. *Case Study Research: Design and Methods.* Beverley Hills: Sage.

Index

Index